HONOR THE PROMISE

Books by Robert F. Drinan

Religion, the Courts and Public Policy, 1963
Democracy, Dissent & Disorder, 1969
Vietnam and Armageddon, 1970
The Right to Be Educated (editor), 1968
Honor the Promise—America's Commitment to Israel, 1977

HONOR THE PROMISE

America's Commitment to Israel

ROBERT F. DRINAN

1977
Doubleday & Company, Inc. • Garden City, New York

ISBN: 0-385-08699-7
Library of Congress Catalog Card Number: 73-9022
Text Copyright © 1977 by Robert F. Drinan
Foreword Copyright © 1977 by Elie Wiesel
ALL RIGHTS RESERVED
PRINTED IN THE UNITED STATES OF AMERICA
FIRST EDITION

CONTENTS

A WORD OF GRATITUDE

When the eminent historian Jules Isaac was an old man and broken by suffering, he visited his friend John XXIII in order to discuss the role that the "teaching of contempt" had played in the holocaust. Their conversations at the Vatican lasted three days. They spoke of theology and pedagogy, literature and liturgy. As they were parting, the Jewish historian asked his host: "Can I return home a little more hopeful than before?" The leader of the world-wide Catholic community smiled and answered: "You have a right to much more than a little hope."

It is this that Robert F. Drinan seems to be telling us again in this impassioned and fascinating book: "The Jews have a right at least to that much."

The book is both an indictment and a speech for the defense: a relentless indictment of hatred and a moving defense of its victims. It is a contribution to the Jewish-Christian dialogue and, thanks to the author, that dialogue will continue at a more than superficial level.

The author's qualifications are beyond criticism: he is a Catholic priest; he rejects the fanaticism found in his own milieu; he believes in the primacy of ethical principles even in politics; and in his eyes action and faith are not necessarily at odds.

This fervent Christian defends the people of Israel, and his book lets us see why, for behind all the positions he takes we can glimpse the shadows, the countless shadows that haunt our communal memory.

In 1945 Robert Drinan saw from reading the newspapers that evil had broken through its dikes. A congressional delegation returned from a quick visit to liberated Buchenwald and told of their stupefaction and horror at what they had seen. It was clear that man is indeed capable of transcending himself—and becoming inhuman.

Disturbed and fascinated, the young Drinan began to read and kept on reading more and more of the memoirs and documents, the essays and studies that dealt with the nocturnal realm in which men were trying to kill God by slaughtering their fellows. Was this the logical climax of history or only a false trail? The Nazi system was the consequence of a movement of ideas and followed a strict logic; it did not arise in a void but had its roots deep in a tradition that prophesied it, prepared for it, and brought it to maturity. That tradition was inseparable from the past of Christian, civilized Europe. Drinan tells us that once he had learned of the concentration camps, he "never thought of the holocaust without pondering the question whether there was something fundamentally anti-Semitic in the Catholic and Protestant versions of Christianity."

With an intellectual courage that will surely bring upon him the wrath of fanatics of every stripe, especially those of his own Church, he says: "For thirty years the vast majority of Christians have sought to evade or avoid that question. But if Christians want to be honest with themselves they simply have to come to some conclusions about the enormity of that anti-Semitism which permitted, if not promoted, the death of about one third of the entire Jewish people."

For a believing Christian there can be no question more distressing than this: How is it that Christianity, which originated in a call to love and peace, has inflicted so much suffering? How is it possible that once Christianity attained power, it used that power to dominate and conquer amid fire and slaughter? How can we explain the fact that while those who died in the accursed world of Treblinka and Auschwitz were not all Jews, those who killed them were all Christians? How is the silence of Pius XII to be justified? Can there be any defense of the Church's passivity when the Jews of occupied Europe were being massacred? Can there be any justification for the fact that Hitler was never officially condemned?

As he studies anti-Semitism, the author realizes that its history is identical with the history of official Christianity. Justin and Cyril, Gregory and Jerome, John Chrysostom above all, and even Augustine: what they say of the Jews will be elaborated and exaggerated later on. We read Chrysostom's statement that "the odious assassination of Christ means that there is no expiation possible, no indulgence, no pardon"—and we think of Belsen. In the memory of peoples everything is of a piece.

"It is overwhelmingly humiliating," says Robert F. Drinan, "for a Christian to recognize that in the age of Aquinas and Dante, in the time of a Francis of Assisi, during the period that the Cathedral of Notre Dame in Paris was constructed, Christians were simultaneously terrorizing Jews in such fearsome ways that the sons of Abraham quite literally became the pariahs of Europe." If this was the case in that period—and it was—what can we say of the Nazi era? Hatred, too, has a power and follows an inevitable course; hatred, too, is transmitted from one people to another, one generation to another, and those who preached love did nothing to disarm that hatred. Quite the contrary: Vile laws and decrees followed in endless succession, pogroms and ritual murders, yellow stars and ghettos, inquisitions and expulsions, and few were those who dared raise their voices in behalf of the victims, in the name of divine love and human brotherhood.

Drinan spares no one. His indictment embraces all the groups, all the ideologies, all the systems that produced Auschwitz or allowed it to happen. He is hard on Catholics but he is equally hard on Protestants. And on the philosophers, on Voltaire and

Fichte and Goethe—yes, even Goethe. And on Luther who said that the Jews must be expelled and their property confiscated. "It seems fair to conclude," Drinan writes, "that Catholics and Protestants disagreed vehemently and fought violently over every single aspect of the Christian faith which both united and divided them. One of the very few issues on which Catholics and Protestants did not contend . . . was the place of the Jew in society." What was the Jew's place? Outside. Apart. Always branded, always in danger, always threatened. On one side, the Jew; on the other, the rest of mankind. On one side, the Jew; on the other, salvation.

There were, of course, exceptions down the centuries—and there were exceptions during the holocaust: priests who defied the Gestapo, pastors who risked their lives to save Jews. Unfortunately, they were but a handful.

When the people of God needed Christian friends during the years of terror and death, they found almost none.

And yet, even in the eyes of Christians, the Jewish people are the people of the promise, says Robert Drinan. It is a promise which God and men must keep. That is why he takes the admirable approach he does: pleading for Israel, fighting for the oppressed Jews, siding with the persecuted everywhere.

The author's detailed report on Israel and American commitments to Israel is eloquent, his discussion brilliant. Documents, figures, facts: they are all here. Strategy, economics, demography: Drinan shows the mechanics that have produced past wars—and future wars that must be avoided. Will he persuade the enemies of Israel? Let us hope he will influence at least the neutral and the lukewarm.

The important thing is that his voice should be heard, especially now as the moment for weighty decisions is approaching in the Near East. We shall be seeing the unleashing of passions that always occurs when events raise the question of the destiny of the Jews. Thanks to the present book, the debate will be located in the context of history so as to transcend history.

Since I am neither theologian nor political scientist, I must justify these few pages of mine: I have written them as a Jew, in order to express my gratitude.

I belong to a people who remember their allies even more than their enemies. No other national or religious community cherishes so much love for its friends and benefactors.

Robert F. Drinan, friend and defender of Israel—and this in the noblest and fullest sense—will occupy a special place in Jewish history. Because we find him present wherever Jews are most alone, because his name is signed to every petition in behalf of the persecuted, because we can always count on him to raise his voice for the victims who are forgotten, cheated, or betrayed, we read his testimony with admiration—and gratitude.

ELIE WIESEL

HONOR THE PROMISE

1

CHRISTIANS AND
AMERICA'S PROMISE TO ISRAEL

I remember the day in 1945 when I learned of the final un-
deniability of the massacre of six million Jews by the Nazis. Ever
since that day when I read about a group of American Congress-
men in Germany expressing their horror at what they personally
found at Buchenwald, I have never thought of the holocaust without pondering the question of whether there was something fundamentally anti-Semitic in Catholic and Protestant versions of
Christianity.

For thirty years the vast majority of Christians have sought to
evade or avoid that question. But if Christians want to be honest
with themselves they simply have to come to some conclusion
about the enormity of that anti-Semitism which permitted, if not
promoted, the death of about one third of the entire Jewish people. In addition, Christians must confront the question of the
meaning of the state of Israel and what Christians should do for
that country in reparation or restitution for the genocide of Jews
carried out in a nation whose population was overwhelmingly
Christian.

Those few Catholics who understand even a little about the tragedies and upheavals that have come to the Jewish people in the past generation take some comfort in the fact that in 1965 the Second Vatican Council, for the first time in Catholic history, issued a pronouncement which decried anti-Semitism and clarified the dignity and uniqueness of the Jewish religion. But this proclamation, however laudable, almost fades into insignificance when compared with the mounting series of incredible and horrible tragedies to Jews which have occurred in the world since Auschwitz. These ghastly events include a vast forced emigration to Israel of hundreds of thousands of Jews from all of the Arab lands, a planned destruction of Israel by the nations surrounding it, an intensification of the persecution of three million Soviet Jews, and a campaign of vilification by the General Assembly of the United Nations, where seventy-two nations proclaimed that Zionism is a form of racism and racial discrimination.

To some extent, all of these profound and perplexing problems have become and will continue to be a political question for the Congress of the United States. Almost alone among the nations of the earth, the United States has remained loyal to its original unwritten pledge of loyalty to Israel. Without treaty or written agreement, the United States has steadfastly and uninterruptedly asserted its resolve to guarantee the self-determination of Israel as a country conceived by the United Nations and dedicated to the ingathering of the Jewish exiles from all of the nations of the earth. In a sense the commitment which the Congress has toward Israel is a concession that Jews cannot live safely or freely in Christian or non-Christian countries in the modern world. Almost no one ever puts it that way, but unconsciously not a few Christians must feel that the only way to eradicate that anti-Semitism which has brought shame to virtually every period of Christian history is to permit the separation of Jews from Christians in a nation where Jews will not be tormented daily by a Christian majority which by instinct, prejudice, or a misconceived religious belief feels justified in discriminating against and even persecuting a tiny minority of persons who are Jews.

Most Christians would shrink from any conclusion which seems to rest on the premise that anti-Semitism is endemic and irremovable from Christianity. In view of the fact that Christ and all of his early followers were Jewish, the assertion that Christianity is anti-Semitic appears to be erroneous and absurd on its face. It is perhaps for that reason that Christians have seldom been enthusiastic about the dream of Theodor Herzl for a homeland for the world's Jews in Palestine. Christians might well feel that subscribing to such a concept would be an admission on their part that Jews cannot be certain of receiving freedom and equality in lands where the vast majority of people are Christians. The same reluctance and ambivalence which are found on this point among Christians can be discovered among Americans when they have to face the question of aiding Israel. Americans, like Christians, wonder why the three million Jews in Israel went there or stay there. For Christians the very concept of a homogeneous theocratic Christian society is an anachronism in the modern world which they would never think of re-establishing. Both Catholics and Protestants would feel that any thought of separating themselves from other types of Christians or non-Christians would be a concession that their faith is intolerant of others and cannot coexist in peace with persons of differing theological views.

There is, however, a profound bond between the Christians of America and the Jews of Israel. This bond goes back to the fact that the original pilgrims who came to America from Europe did so because they were persecuted for religious or political reasons in their fatherland. Because of the similarity of the origin of immigration to Israel, Christians in America have a profound, if unconscious, affinity for the hundreds of thousands of Jews who have gone to Israel since the holocaust. At the same time the phenomenon of Israel is very difficult for contemporary Christians to understand because Christians today generally do not view themselves as a counterculture or as a group which any modern government could deem to be subversive of that nation's public morality.

The promises which the United States has silently made to Israel did not formally arise from pronouncements of Christian religious groups within the United States. These religious bodies, as we shall see, were frequently averse to or at least apathetic to the existence of Israel. The promises which the United States has made to Israel have arisen from the conscience and the convictions of the great majority of Americans speaking or acting through their elected public officials.

It seems clearer each day that the promises and commitments which the United States has made to Israel will in the next few months and years be challenged in ways that America has never before experienced. The country and the Congress will seek to resolve these challenges on the basis of political principles alone. Public officials will state that America's relationship with Israel should be determined solely on the basis of what is good for the United States. This principle will have continued validity, but it should be noted that the "best interest" of the United States is a concept which includes the moral ideals on which America and international law are based. To some extent, Christian attitudes toward Judaism will play an unconscious or indirect role in the formulation of the policies which America will adopt or continue with respect to the safety and survival of Israel. Among the Christian concepts almost certain to be at issue will be the perception which Christians have of Judaism since the holocaust and since the establishment of Israel. Christians may well be forced by events to affirm or deny that negative pre-holocaust concept of Judaism held by not a few Christian denominations. These groups looked upon Judaism as a surviving religion whose vitality and significance had been sharply eroded by the divinely decreed inception of the Christian Era. Christians may be required in the relatively near future to recognize or reject, as a result of the holocaust and the establishment of Israel, an entirely new form of Judaism.

Among the issues which the Congress and the country must confront in the relatively near future are the following:

1. If the Arab neighbors of Israel continue to be armed with Russian military equipment, Israel will be required to continue a military establishment whose cost is simply beyond what the three million citizens of Israel can afford. It is, after all, logical that a small nation like Israel can hardly be expected to pay from its own resources for armaments to defend itself against several na-

tions which over the past generation have received at least $20 billion worth of armaments from the U.S.S.R. Astonishingly, the United States up until 1973 had given Israel only $430 million in economic and military assistance. This compares with a sum almost seven times larger which the United States during the same period gave to the Arab nations surrounding Israel. It seems predictable that, beginning in 1977, Israel will be required to ask from the United States some $2 billion worth of armaments each year. The sum of $2.2 billion in grants and loans was allocated by the Congress to Israel in 1974. A continuation of such military assistance by the United States may be the only way in which Israel can protect its citizens from potential land and air attacks from its enemies.

The enactment of a request for some $2 billion in military or economic assistance to Israel will in all probability test virtually every assumption on which U.S. foreign policy has rested with respect to Israel. In the pages that follow, those assumptions and all of the assumptions behind those assumptions will be examined— in the light of the historic, philosophical and, to some extent, theological approach which the United States has traditionally taken toward Israel.

2. It is not impossible that the United States may eventually be called upon to separate itself in some way from the United Nations if a majority of the countries in that international body should suspend or expel Israel from membership. If the United States were required to choose between continued membership in the United Nations and continued alliance of friendship with Israel, once again every assumption underlying the friendship between America and Israel would be up for re-examination. In that re-examination, it would seem that the biblical and theological attitudes which Christians in America have toward Judaism and Zionism could not really be excluded from a consideration of the political question of what policy would be best for America as a nation.

3. In late 1974 the Trade Reform Act containing the Jackson-Vanik Amendment was passed. For almost the first time in American history the United States Congress placed in a major interna-

tional agreement a stipulation that the U.S.S.R. could not obtain advantageous trade or tariff relationships with the United States unless or until it allowed free emigration from that nation. This amendment, authored by Senator Henry Jackson and Congressman Charles Vanik, eventually won overwhelming approval by both houses of Congress. The hostility of the Kremlin to the amendment endured through 1975 with the result that the objectives of the Trade Reform Act to which the Jackson-Vanik Amendment was appended are apparently not being implemented. Eventually it may be that the Congress and the country must choose between the desirability of increasing international trade with Russia and a guarantee that Russia will permit Soviet Jews and others to emigrate. In early 1976 a total of about 120,000 Soviet Jews had been able over the past five years to emigrate from Russia to Israel. Although it is uncertain whether Soviet leaders can accommodate themselves to the purposes of the Jackson-Vanik Amendment, it may be that the people of America will once again have to re-examine their fundamental moral and religious perceptions of Judaism and Zionism if other major industrialized nations rather than the United States continue to increase their profitable commercial transactions with Russia.

4. For many years prior to the quadrupling of the price of oil by the Arab nations in late 1973, these countries had maintained a list of some 1,500 American corporations on an Arab boycott list. Since trade with the Arab oil-producing nations was relatively insignificant, the boycott list was almost without meaning. When, however, these nations began in 1975 to spend up to $15 billion in the United States, American corporations were torn between entering into a new and profitable market or rejecting this avenue in order to be able to do business with Israel. Some legal resolution of this problem may be possible but, once again, national policy with respect to America's moral commitment to Israel will be at issue.

5. In 1976 the United States sold about $12 billion worth of armaments to other nations. About one half of that incredible sum was sold to nations in the Persian Gulf. Israel obviously is opposed to such sales, since these weapons, bought from the United

States by Iran and by Arab nations in the Middle East, can obviously be turned against Israel. State Department officials have asserted that the United States Government has given permission to allow this vast armada to grow in the Middle East because the presence of arms in nations opposed to each other will "stabilize" that area of the world. The argument is also made that if the United States does not sell arms to these nations they can easily buy them elsewhere.

Almost inevitably, Americans must sooner rather than later make a decision as to whether it can permit massive amounts of arms to be collected by those nations which have been the enemies of Israel since its establishment in 1948.

The foregoing five emerging issues are only the most visible and most obvious dilemmas America will face as it seeks to evolve the fulfillment of the promises it has made to Israel. The nature of those promises must be explored fully, but first the attitudes of American Christians toward Jews and Zionism must be studied at some length.

2

CAN CHRISTIANITY AND JUDAISM COEXIST IN PEACE?

Until very recently Christians have tended to obliterate from their history books those dreadful chapters in which anti-Jewish events transpired. Jews, on the other hand, have almost memorized the dates and circumstances of the worst anti-Semitic outbursts in the history of the Christian Church.

On the basis of what has happened to Jews in Christian countries, one could hardly be optimistic about the way in which people in nations traditionally Christian will react to the Jews gathered together as a nation in Israel. The antipathy or at least the apathy of so many Christians toward Israel as a nation manifests the profound theological, racial, or pathological dimensions of that anti-Semitism which has been the sin, the evil, or the disease of the Christian West almost from its very beginnings.

If Christians are inclined to reject the proposition that Christianity is by nature anti-Semitic, they can point to a virulent type of anti-Jewish feeling among the Greeks and the Romans. The famed orator Cicero expressed his contempt for the Jews—a tradition perpetuated in the writings of Horace, Ovid, Quintilian, and

Martial. The quintessence of pagan anti-Semitism is reflected in the prose of Tacitus, the celebrated historian. The charges brought by Tacitus against the Jews are so scurrilous that one is almost ashamed to reproduce them. He wrote that the Jews descended from a group of lepers who were deported from Egypt. Jewish institutions, he said, were "sinister, shameful, and have survived only because of their perversity." To Jews, he added, "nothing is illicit." The first instruction "they are given is to . . . abjure their fatherland, forget their parents, brothers and children."

Historians appear to be unanimous in believing that the anti-Semitism of pagan Greece and Rome was a result of Jewish separatism and not really theological. Nonetheless, certain Christians, seeking to validate their contention that the Jews by divine plan will always be persecuted, point to the examples of anti-Semitic literature and conduct in pre-Christian times to prove their contention. In 1945, for example, a French priest, Monsignor Charles Journet, wrote as follows:

> Yahweh himself, in choosing the Jews as a unique messianic and theophoric people, would . . . design them for the hostility of the world and pagan people, long before the Incarnation, long before the deicide. In Egypt in the fifteenth century and in Persia in the fifth before Christ, the pogrom is already there.

As the Christian Era developed, those who wanted to rationalize anti-Semitism by postulating that divine providence had cast the Jews in the role of a race that will always suffer sought to use the New Testament and Christian doctrine to support their position. The undeniable fact, however, is that there is nothing in Scripture or Christian teaching that can justify any assertion that the Jews are destined to undergo suffering because of any claimed infidelity to the revelations of the God of Abraham. St. Paul sought to at least outline a complete Christian theology with respect to Jews. In Chapter 9 of Paul's letter to the Romans he states, as translated in The Jerusalem Bible, "my sorrow is so great, my mental anguish so endless," that, he continues: "I would willingly be condemned and be cut off from Christ if it could help my brothers of Israel, my own flesh and blood."

Paul asserts categorically that "it is unthinkable that God should have repudiated his own people, the people whose destiny he himself appointed" (Romans 11:2). He concedes "a partial insensibility which has come to Israel" (11:26) but concludes that the people of Israel "are still beloved for their fathers' sakes" (11:29).

Paul closes his sections on the relationship between Christians and Jews in Chapters 9–11 of his Epistle to the Romans by exclaiming, "I stand amazed at the unfathomable complexity of God's wisdoms and God's knowledge. How could man ever understand his reasons for action, or explain his methods of working?"

The anguish which Paul felt for his fellow Jews—the "pain that never leaves me"—is the daily torture of the Christian who looks back at the scandals brought to his religion by the carnage and massacres carried out against the Jews in the name of some theological tenets not discoverable in the New Testament or in Christian teaching. Those tenets spurious to Christianity found their origin in the fathers of the Church. St. Justin appears to have been the first to enunciate the conception that Jewish misfortunes were the result of divine punishment for the death of Christ. This profoundly un-Christian idea appears in the first two or three centuries of the Christian Era to be typical of the Christian polemics against the theology of Judaism. The error of St. Justin's belief that the Jews are a people who can never hope to escape from their misfortunes, which are willed by God, became the central heresy of the anti-Semitism of the next thousand years.

Countless forces converged after the Edict of Milan in the year 313 to alter the relationship between Christianity and Judaism. The triumph and establishment of Christianity helped to induce Judaism to retire into the world of the Talmud. The pressures against the synagogue mounted as countless middle-class pagans entered the Christian Church, bringing with them all of the anti-Semitic viewpoints they had imbibed from antiquity. The barbarians from the north, almost at the gate, impelled the Romans, now officially Christian, to close ranks against all dissidents from the official religion.

All of these converging forces constituted a matrix for the flowering of the anti-Pauline theology which would authorize and indeed compel the punishment of Jews as something required by Christian teaching. St. Cyril of Jerusalem and St. Gregory of Nyssa slightly antedate the sweeping indictments and condemnation of Jews manifest in the writings of St. Jerome. But it was St. John Chrysostom who by the viciousness of his anti-Semitic theology inflicted the greatest injury on the Jews both of his own generation and for generations to come. To Chrysostom, the "odious assassination of Christ means that there is no expiation possible, no indulgence, no pardon." The Jews would remain forever without a temple or a nation. The dispersion of the Jews was, furthermore, the work of God and not of any temporal ruler.

It is a gross understatement to aver that any Christian must be shocked and scandalized at the diatribes of Chrysostom. In rereading his vituperations, one has the fanciful hope that perhaps someone might discover that they are a forgery like the *Protocols of the Elders of Zion.*

It has always been a disappointment to me that St. Augustine, the author of the magnificent *Confessions,* was never clear or coherent in his reassertion of St. Paul's rejection of any teaching which even by implication could be deemed to be anti-Semitic. But Augustine evolved an amorphous theory of the Jews as a "witness-people"—a role that is providential in that they are simultaneously witnesses of evil and of Christian truth. For centuries after Augustine, minds less subtle than his own would use his witness-people theory as justification for aggravating the miseries of the Jews as a way of assisting God in the supposed divine plan for the Jews.

It is appalling for a modern Christian to be forced to accept the fact that so many brilliant Christian apologists in the patristic age of the Church enunciated so many un-Christian, untrue, and unjustified slanders against the Jews. One seeks to exculpate these writers, at least in part, by putting their predicament into perspective. They were required to defend their faith in Christ as the messiah, and for this purpose they felt compelled to refute and reject Judaism. But whatever extenuating circumstances might be developed for the most learned defenders of Christianity in the first four hundred years of its existence, there can be nothing but condemnation for their ominous elaboration of the theme that a divine curse or punishment was decreed by God upon the Jews for their role in the crucifixion of Christ. That un-Christian allegation, fully elaborated in the fourth century, was seen at that time to be supported by the deteriorating social and political situation in which the Jews found themselves. Then, as now, people overlooked the fact that the Jewish dispersion did not come with the destruction of the temple in Jerusalem in the year 70 A.D. but had begun many centuries before Christ. In addition, Christians in the fourth and in the twentieth centuries apparently do not want to know that a community of Jews, sometimes substantial, has always remained in Jerusalem and Palestine.

Chrysostom and many others in the early centuries of Christianity pointed to the destruction of the temple in Jerusalem as a direct intervention of God to punish the Jews and to fulfill New Testament texts. Neither assumption nor assertion has any basis in sound exegesis.

Although the handful of modern-day Christian historians who have written about anti-Semitism in patristic literature do not seem to mention the influence of Pelagianism, it seems to me that the pervasiveness of this heresy might well have entered into the viewpoints adopted by the Church fathers. Pelagius, influenced by Stoic philosophy, taught that Christians could merit divine grace by the exercise of natural virtue. This approach had the broadest appeal for Christians then as it does now, since it appears almost contrary to basic human nature for a Christian to recognize that he can do absolutely nothing, directly or indirectly, to merit a vocation to be a Christian or the grace to remain one. Even the great theologian St. Augustine was for a period of his life at least a semi-Pelagian. After many decades of controversy the Christian Church made it clear beyond doubt that the beginning and continuation of one's faith in Christ is a pure gift of God, which cannot be obtained or merited by any human initiative however heroic. Following inexorably from the condemnation of Pelagianism is the fundamental truth that neither pagans nor Jews could of their own power or virtue merit in any way whatsoever even a desire for faith or for baptism.

Implicit in every statement inimical to the Jews made by early Christian apologists was the assumption that somehow Jews individually or collectively were reprobates because they had voluntarily rejected belief in Christ as the messiah. Such an assumption is, of course, totally contrary to the fundamental Christian conviction that God calls whom He will to belief and to baptism. The utter falsity and perniciousness of Pelagianism was not, however, accepted until after the death of St. Augustine in the year 430.

St. Paul clearly understood that the Jews could not be faulted for not accepting Christ. Paul was sometimes impatient and even imperious with his fellow Jews, but he recognized that he, unlike his former coreligionists, received the unowed and unmerited divine visitation on the road to Damascus.

In addition, St. Paul's approach to the Jewish people seems totally at variance with that of the Church fathers, culminating in Chrysostom. St. Paul asks in his letter to the Romans (11:1): "This leads naturally to the question, 'has God then totally repudiated his people?' Certainly not!" In addition, St. Paul clearly understood that the sin of those Jews who participated in the crucifixion of Christ was forgiven. He, unlike the vehemently anti-Judaic fathers of the early Church, realized the implications of the words of Christ on the cross, "Forgive them, Father, for they know not what they do."

The promulgation of the Justinian Code in the first half of the sixth century was the first open and blatant attempt by a Christian society to alter the practices of Judaism. In view of the fact that Justinian considered himself to be Emperor by divine right, he contended that he could do to Judaism what he had done for the Church. The Justinian Code invaded Jewish theology, altered synagogue services, stripped Judaism of its previously explicit legal authorization and, consciously or not, opened up a new frontier of persecution for the Jews. The oppressions of Justinian's Code worked, however, to arouse the Jews to protect their sacred traditions. Incredible wars between Jews and Christians were initiated in not a few places throughout the Roman Empire. These scenes of violence were a foretaste of the dismal centuries to follow in which forced baptisms and the removal of baptized children from their unbaptized Jewish parents were some of the practices that gave rise and credibility to the feeling that Jews were treated more justly under the crescent than under the cross.

Although no clear downward trend in Christian-Jewish relations can be sketched out between the years 400 and 1200, it can be argued that what Jules Isaac has called the "teaching of contempt," as epitomized in Chrysostom, had finally penetrated the Christian mind of Europe by 1096, the year of the First Crusade. Father Edward Flannery, in his excellent book *The Anguish of the Jews*, states that "1096 marks the beginning of the harassment of the Jews that, in duration and intensity, was unique in Jewish history." In unbelievable outbursts of hatred, disguised as acts of pious zeal, mobs in France and Germany offered Jewish communities the option of baptism or death. In the first six months of the year 1096, it is calculated, one fourth to one third of the Jewish population of Germany and northern Europe was massacred.

Other atrocities continued in the decades leading up to the golden ages of Christian learning and culture. It is overwhelmingly humiliating for a Christian to recognize that in the age of Aquinas and Dante, in the time of St. Francis of Assisi, during the period that the Cathedral of Notre Dame in Paris was constructed, Christians were simultaneously terrorizing Jews in such fearsome ways that the sons of Abraham quite literally became the pariahs of Europe. In 1215 the Fourth Lateran Council, in a most extraordinary decree, prescribed a distinctive dress for Jews. The reason given was the prevention of intermarriage between Christians and non-Christians. The "badge of shame" appears to have become the ultimate reason why after 1215 many Jews lost their self-respect and adopted that form of obsequiousness which characterized some groups of Jews during the period from the Middle Ages until their emancipation.

The virtual absence in America of any of the legal forms of servitude imposed on Jews on the Continent is due to many factors, one of which is the different pattern of Christian-Jewish relations that obtained in England. Jews came to England from France at the invitation of William the Conqueror in the late eleventh century. Their economic and cultural fortunes prospered in England, but circumstances conspired to bring about in the year 1290 the first nationwide expulsion of Jews. In October of that year 16,000 Jews left England for France and Belgium. The odious badge decreed by the Lateran Council was enforced against the Jews of England as was the prohibition against the commingling of Christians and Jews. Incredible calumnies were circulated about the Jews, the remnants of which echo in Chaucer's "Prioress' Tale" and in Shakespeare's Shylock and in Dickens' Fagin. Nonetheless, there were no Jews in England from 1290 until Cromwell invited them back. As a result, there are no traces in early English law, brought to America by the colonists, of the barbarous anti-Jewish practices developed on the Continent during the Middle Ages.

Although Catholics might have hoped that the Protestant reformers would correct the perverse errors of a thousand years of Catholic practice with respect to the Jews, the melancholy fact is that Luther and his coreligionists perpetuated the worst of the anti-Jewish errors of the Church they sought to reform.

As a Catholic looks back on the Reformation, he searches in vain for some indication that the reformers recognized the spuriousness of the anti-Semitic teachings and practices of the Catholic Church over fifteen hundred years. But despite the reformers' heavy emphasis on the Old Testament, there is virtually no indication in the works of Zwingli in Switzerland or Calvin in France or Knox in Scotland that these founding fathers of Protestantism recognized the centuries-old deviation from Pauline truths in Catholic teaching concerning Judaism.

For at least a few years there was hope that Luther might battle anti-Semitism in the Catholic Church. Abram Sachar, in his classic *A History of the Jews*, writes that Luther "sent a thrill of hope through Jewish hearts" by publishing in 1523 a pamphlet in which he defended Jews in these words:

> They [the Catholics] have dealt with the Jews as if they were dogs rather than human beings . . . if the apostles, who also were Jews, had dealt with us Gentiles as we Gentiles deal with the Jews, there would never have been a Christian among the Gentiles. . . .

Luther went on to state that "we are but Gentiles, while the Jews are of the lineage of Christ. We are aliens and inlaws; they are blood relatives, cousins and brothers of our Lord." But Luther's motivation was not hidden; he added that "we . . . are to treat the Jews in a brotherly manner in order that we might convert some of them. . . ."

Just twenty years after this unprecedented call for charity and compassion toward the Jews, Luther made it clear that neither the Reformation nor the Counter-Reformation offered the Jews of Christendom any alleviation of the curse of theological anti-Semitism. In 1543, Luther excoriated the Jews in language that equaled or surpassed anything in Christian writing before or after that year. He stated that Jews were parasites on Christian society, that they were guilty of poisoning the wells of Christians, murdering innocent children, and exploiting everyone by usury. Luther urged the destruction of synagogues, the expulsion of Jews by Christian princes, and the confiscation of all of their wealth. In Luther's last sermon shortly before his death, he urged the expulsion of Jews from all of Germany.

In retrospect it seems almost impossible that the reformers who defied the power of organized Christendom in the search for what they conceived to be truth should not have discovered in the New Testament a clear understanding of the early Christians that the covenant of Jewish tradition should exist peacefully with Christian revelation. The survival of the Jews after fifteen hundred years of the harshest Christian treatment would seem to have constituted evidence that God had not extinguished the covenant He made with Abraham with the inception of Christianity. In addition, the reformers could clearly see that Judaism was no longer a threat to Christianity. In Luther's day Europe was fully Christianized except for an area of the Iberian Peninsula. The reformers' emphasis on the Old Testament and their principles of private interpretation of the Bible should have led them to a feeling of revulsion against Torquemada and all of the hideous events which under his leadership led to the expulsion of the Jews from Spain in 1492.

In his book *Jews, God and History*, Max I. Dimont theorizes that Jews assumed a great importance to both Catholics and Protestants in the stormy years immediately after the Reformation. Dimont states that the "Jews' learning, idealism, and ethical conduct were seen by millions of Christians who did not believe all the slurs against the Jews." As a result, Dimont continues, "both Catholics and Protestants felt it would be a persuasive argument for millions of waverers between Catholicism and Protestantism if Jews would join their side." Consequently, the centuries-old Christian obsession with converting the Jews became more intense and fanatical than ever before. Hostility to Judaism was thus raised by both Catholics and Protestants to the level of a new touchstone of Christian orthodoxy.

In the decades after the Reformation, Christians in both Catholic and Protestant countries continued incorrigibly their efforts to convert the Jews. Ghettos were established in all Christian nations under circumstances which more and more brought about the dehumanization and the denigration of the Jew. It almost seemed as if Christians wanted to blot out the thirty-five-hundred-year-old cultural heritage of the Jews along with knowledge that the Jews were the only ethnic group in all of the civilized world to have universal education.

As one looks back on the period between the Council of Trent in 1545 and the beginning of the French Revolution in 1789, it seems fair to conclude that Catholics and Protestants disagreed vehemently and fought violently over almost every single aspect of the Christian faith which both united and divided them. One of the very few issues on which Catholics and Protestants did not contend during those two hundred and fifty years was the place of the Jew in society. Increasingly, Protestant nations, as they became more mercantile and capitalistic, needed Jews who were financiers. Catholic and feudal countries, on the other hand, did not want Jews for theological reasons nor did they need them for financial purposes. It seems unbelievable that during the two hundred and fifty years prior to the French Revolution, virtually no savant in all of Europe protested against the prison in which European society had confined the Jew. Even Voltaire, who made war on almost every existing abuse, inveighed against the Jews. Likewise the brilliant German poet Goethe spoke of Jews as inferior and degraded beings. The philosopher Fichte, before he became the rector of the University of Berlin, rejected political emancipation for the Jews unless society should first "cut off all of their heads in one night and set new ones on their shoulders, which should contain not a single Jewish idea." Interestingly, Fichte stated that "the only means of protecting ourselves against them is to conquer their promised land and send them thither."

This curious reference to the idea which much later would be transformed into the Zionist movement suggests the question which recurs over and over again to any person who ponders the agony of Jewish persecution over almost two thousand years of Christian civilization. That question is: Why did not Jewish leaders conceive and execute the migration to their "promised land" long before the twentieth century? Obviously the question simply does not have any clear answers. One could theorize that Jews instinctively knew that Christianity simply did not hold as one of its basic doctrines that the Jews were a deicide people. Or one could speculate that the creation of Jewish ghettos in almost every city constituted protection enough for Jews anxious to preserve and perpetuate their cultural and religious heritage. The isolation of the ghetto was intensified in the fifteenth century by the development everywhere in eastern Europe of the Yiddish language—a derivative of German intermingled with Hebrew and other languages.

But if a Christian seems to imply criticism of Jews for not conceiving the idea of returning to Jerusalem before they did so in 1897, such a Christian may be conceding either that his religion is inherently anti-Jewish or that Christians are so lax in living up to their religion that they are unable or unwilling to give that Christian love which they should to Jews who are their neighbors. Even today, when the idea of Zionism has flowered spectacularly into a nation of almost three million Jews, most Christians would in my judgment still refuse to concede that the establishment of Israel was the only possible way by which the Jews of the world could escape the ineradicable bias against Judaism contained in Christianity or in the incorrigibly anti-Semitic attitudes of Christians.

Christians who believe that nothing in Christian teaching or nothing unreformable in Christian practice leads inexorably to widespread anti-Semitism could maintain that Jews who migrate to Israel are doing so to erect a nation appropriate to their religious and cultural preferences and not because in all other nations they are liable to persecution for religious, political, or cultural reasons.

On the basis of the hideous suppression and persecution of Jews in the Christian Era until roughly the year 1800, it would be difficult for a Christian to maintain that Jews who withdrew from a Christian-oriented society in favor of citizenship in a Jewish state would be acting out of mere convenience or cultural preference. Christians probably would have to concede this point but would argue that, in the era of the enlightenment and Jewish emancipation in Europe beginning roughly after 1800, the case for withdrawal into a predominantly Jewish society evaporated. But the Christians who would accept this position have no answers for the unexplainable, unfathomable, and unimaginable event which occurred a hundred and forty years after the presumed emancipation of the European Jew—the holocaust. It is to the events that led up to that awful conflagration that we now turn our attention.

3

AN EMANCIPATION WHICH LED
TO A HOLOCAUST

In 1871 the 700,000 Jews of France, by a plebiscite of the sixty districts of Paris, became citizens with equal rights. For the first time in more than a thousand years Jews were citizens of the nation in which they lived. This event was at least symbolically the beginning of an era of emancipation for Jews. They no longer must look to baptism as their means of entry into European civilization. Many of the cautious and conservative Jewish leaders were not, however, enthusiastic about the emancipation since they felt it would almost inevitably lead to assimilation.

After 1796 the history of Europe became to some extent the story of Napoleon Bonaparte. In an act which suggests a love-hate relationship with Jews, Napoleon summoned 112 of the leading Jews of France, Italy, and Germany to meet him in Paris in 1806. In a melodramatic move to galvanize to his support the Jews residing in countries hostile to him, Napoleon proposed and carried out the spectacular idea of re-establishing the ancient Sanhedrin of Jewish temple days. The Sanhedrin faded away immediately after Napoleon had used it for his own purposes. But the European unity of the Jewish people had perhaps become a concept that could endure.

Jewish historians who wrote before the holocaust almost invariably looked upon the nineteenth century in Europe as the golden age for Jews and Jewish culture. The century was not, of course, one of complete emancipation, since Pope Pius VII reestablished the Jewish ghetto along the Tiber and re-instituted a form of the Inquisition. In Frankfurt, Germany, the Jewish ghetto reappeared shortly after French control had disappeared. After Waterloo the repression of Jews in Austria was resumed. The world that was remade by the Treaty of Vienna diminished substantially but did not extinguish completely the intoxication which European Jews experienced by reason of the freedom which followed the French Revolution.

The revolutions of 1848 brought both new catastrophes and new freedoms to the Jews of Europe. The economic revolutions of capitalism, accompanied by emerging forms of socialism and communism, brought both opportunities and temptations to the Jewish middle class.

Even in Russia, where roughly half of all the world's Jews lived in 1800, freedom of a sort came for at least a brief time to a part of the world where Jews had been oppressed more outrageously than anywhere else. In 1801, Alexander I extended to Jews and others at least paper rights to attend Russian schools and universities, settle in Moscow, and enter the professions. At the Congress of Vienna, however, Alexander I became frightened at his own ideas and shortly thereafter re-established the iniquitous Pale of Settlement, a region comprised of certain towns where Jews were compelled to live.

In 1855, Alexander II liberated Jews for a brief period, but when he was assassinated in 1881 there was a reaction. The disasters that befell Russian Jews in the last decades of the nineteenth century led to the emigration to the United States of hundreds of thousands of them. But the millions of Jews who could not escape to America or elsewhere lived in a world—both before and after the Communist Revolution—in which they were imprisoned, deported, dehumanized, and degraded. Not until 1971 were any meaningful number of Soviet Jews finally able to emigrate from a land from which rabbis, synagogues, seminaries, and Yiddish literature had been abolished.

If historians writing before the holocaust looked upon the nineteenth century as the second spring of Jewish culture, historians after the holocaust almost overlooked the flowering of Jewish living in the nineteenth century because of their passion to discover the seeds and origins of that anti-Jewish violence which brought about the slaughter of six million Jews in the years 1939 to 1945. Historians have found clues in the nineteenth century that betray the gathering storm of the madness that would grow into a philosophy of mass murder. The racism that led to the holocaust derived ultimately from that form of well-intentioned nationalism whose parents included Edmund Burke and Thomas Jefferson. But somehow the concept of "blood" was added by extremist writers to the notion of nationalism, and from this confusion the race theorists began to talk of Nordic supremacy. Race and blood were welded into a pseudo-scientific philosophy from which the ultimate Aryan-race and superman theories were formulated.

It seems impossible to deny that the religious or theological anti-Jewish feeling of the early Christian Era and the Middle Ages entered into the development of the racist anti-Semitism that emerged in the political order in the late nineteenth century. A Christian simply has to ask himself whether or not the racism that led to Auschwitz could have materialized if it had not had some eighteen hundred years of vehemently anti-Judaic feeling upon which to build. The unscientific and indeed superstitious ideas undergirding the anti-Semitic mystique of the Third Reich could scarcely have sufficed to bring about the death of two and a half million Jews at Auschwitz.

The century that ended in 1918 was for the Jews the best of times and the worst of times. Jews in western and central Europe during that century constituted less than one half of one per cent of the total population. The Jews who had just emerged from the ghetto became avant-garde intellectuals, scientists of world renown, and winners of more Nobel prizes in science than any other national group. But even profound envy of Jewish accomplishments or intense resentment at whatever prominence or power they possessed simply cannot explain the crematoria of Auschwitz. Neither Christians nor social historians manifest much unanimity concerning the ultimate origins of the logic of extermination that led to the holocaust. Some commentators offer the "scapegoat" theory, while others advance a concept of irreversible anti-Semitism. Hannah Arendt, in *The Origins of Totalitarianism*, rejects both of these theories as inadequate:

> The scapegoat explanation therefore remains one of the principal attempts to escape the seriousness of anti-Semitism and the significance of the fact that the Jews were driven into the storm center of events. Equally widespread is the opposite doctrine of "eternal anti-Semitism," in which Jew-hatred is a normal and natural reaction to which history gives only more or less opportunity.

Jules Isaac, on the other hand, in *The Teaching of Contempt*, emphasizes the religious sources of anti-Semitism, pointing out that the centuries in which the Christian Church taught contempt for Jews inexorably brought about an atmosphere in which the Nazis were able to indulge in genocide.

Some Christians like to point out that the Third Reich was just as much an enemy of Christianity as it was of Judaism. Consequently, citing Hitler's assault against the Church, some Christians would seek to disassociate Christianity from the evolution of Nazi attitudes and practices. For Christians who reason this way, Auschwitz would not be a crisis for the Church; but it is difficult to deny that Auschwitz, an obscure village in Poland, geographically and symbolically located in the heart of Christian Europe, simply has to remind Christians at all times of the profound disorders of a Christian civilization that allowed the Nazi philosophy to grow in its very midst.

Some Christians and understandably not a few Jews would trace a direct line from the ravings of Chrysostom to the insanity of Buchenwald.

The resolution of the German Evangelical Church in 1950 acknowledged the responsibility of Christians for the fate of the Jews under Hitler. The resolution confessed that "We by failure and silence are guilty before the God of mercy, of the crime that has been committed against the Jews by men of our people."

The extent and the appropriate imputability to Christians of the holocaust were, of course, among the fundamental underlying issues in the long debate that led to the compromise 1965 Vatican schema, the declaration on the relation of the Church to non-Christian religions. That declaration unfortunately, as we shall see later, does not really resolve the question of the complicity which traditional anti-Semitic Catholic practices logically must have with anti-Semitism.

The vicious theological slanders against Jews may have abated somewhat in the last decades of the nineteenth century, but pogroms and persecutions continued. In Germany, France, Austria-Hungary, and elsewhere the Catholic clergy and their congregants waged war against the Jews in the name of protesting the deepening secularization of all human life—especially in the area of education. Liberals everywhere sought to emancipate education from Church control and to end the alliance between Church and State. Since the Jewish community felt that Church-related education continued to teach slanders about Judaism, they had little choice except to associate themselves with the Church-State separationists who in many instances were active anti-clericals. Catholic and, to some extent, Protestant groups more and more identified Jewish participation in the anti-clerical movement as a manifestation of the alleged anti-Christian sentiments of Judaism.

The classic struggle over the Church's place in the education of the young occurred in Germany when Bismarck sought to liberate education from the control of the Church. Church leaders, strengthened and unified by the First Vatican Council, fought the 1871 laws of Bismarck and, after six years of the *Kulturkampf*, succeeded in repealing a great deal of the anti-Catholic legislation. But along the way Catholic hatred against the Jews had been intensified. At Christmastime in 1872, Pope Pius IX, the reactionary pontiff who years before had issued the Syllabus of Errors, made a pronouncement denouncing the Jews as enemies of Christ and a pernicious influence in society. Pronouncements of this kind helped to bring about in Germany an era of Jew-baiting which was completely unforeseeable and unpredictable to those who had hailed the era of Jewish emancipation as a time when anti-Semitism would wither away.

The emergence of the Christian Socialist Party in Germany during this period did not result in any lessening of anti-Semitic feeling. The common canard was everywhere: the Jews were either too rich or too radical or both. In the 1890s it was clear in Germany that the political emancipation of the Jews failed to bring about their identification with the German people. An exodus to America of the best and the brightest began and continued until the beginning of the First World War.

In Austria-Hungary the clergy and the aristocrats engaged in a multifaceted assault on the Jews. The Christian Socialists denounced Jewish control of the land. In Vienna the anti-Semites controlled the municipal government from 1895 to 1914.

In countless other ways the Jews of Austria and Hungary learned the emptiness of mere legal equality. They had associated themselves with liberal and even radical political parties in order to fight against reactionaries and bigots. But even the legal protection of the nation's constitution did not protect the Jews from the orgy of hate that was stirred up by the revival of the incredible blood accusations which, according to everyone's understanding of what political emancipation would bring, should have been banished as the worst of superstitions. Even France, the most liberal and progressive of all European nations at that time, was not immune in the late 1800s from that virulent anti-Semitism which in everyone's expectations was to have been anesthetized and even annihilated by the political emancipation of the Jews. The establishment of the Third French Republic in 1871 produced a vehement protest from Catholic and clerical leaders whose influence was sharply curtailed. Catholic spokesmen, joined by the royalists, jointly exploited every source of potential anti-Semitic propaganda. The culmination of decades of anti-Semitic activities came in 1894 with the famous Dreyfus case. A Jewish captain in the French army, Alfred Dreyfus, accused of selling military secrets to German officials, was court-martialed and condemned to solitary confinement for life. The long series of well-known events which eventually led to the vindication of Dreyfus in 1906 unleashed on

France and the world tidal waves of inflammatory anti-Semitic slanders which even today exacerbate animosities against the Jews.

The anti-Semitism that afflicted the emancipated Jew undoubtedly contributed to an unprecedented unity among all the Jews of Europe. But this was small comfort indeed in view of the fact that the Jewish community, in contemplating the opening of the twentieth century, had to conclude that the political emancipation attained in the nineteenth century had not protected them from the savage animosities of the masses in European nations whose basic legal and social institutions trace their origin to Christianity. On the other hand, the Jewish community had to recognize that their unemancipated religious brethren in the East had been afflicted by great pogroms that commenced on Easter in 1881 and continued sporadically until 1906. During that period Russian Jews initiated a vast emigration that became the greatest exodus in all of Jewish history. By the year 1900 a million Jews had left Greater Russia, and after that this number almost doubled.

As the twentieth century approached, the emancipated Jew of western Europe could or should have known that pogroms and persecutions would continue unless somehow a new and deeper rapprochement could be brought about between Christians, infected by nationalism, and Jews, whose fundamental faith made them unassimilable. But Jews, like Christians, were unable or unwilling to accept the conclusion that nineteen centuries of coexistence in western Europe only prove that such coexistence cannot bring peace and dignity to the Jew.

There is virtually no trace in Christian writings in the late nineteenth or early twentieth centuries lamenting the demise of all of the hopes that so many people had for Christian-Jewish amity in the era of the political emancipation of the Jewish people. Christians seem to have altered or modified the prejudices which they had accepted almost by osmosis from their Christian forefathers. No one seemed to point out that antagonism between Jews and Christians should have been unbelievable. The common heritage of Judaism and Christianity included at least five major sources of identification—both religions pray to one God, both derive their faith from the Bible, both believe in the necessity of a messiah, both were evolved in the land of Israel, and both had Jews for prophets, priests, and legislators.

In addition, Judaism has never taken any official position with regard to Christianity. A pious Jew who somehow had never heard of Christianity could observe every precept of his faith despite his total ignorance of the Christian religion. A Christian, on the other hand, can hardly understand the essentials of his religion until he comprehends and accepts much of the Old Testament. Reinhold Niebuhr, the distinguished Protestant theologian, put it well when he stated that no one can be a good Christian until he is first a good Jew.

Why then did the twentieth century open with so few Christians concerned that their fellow believers in the God of Abraham, Isaac, and Jacob had not found peace or dignity in any age of the Christian Era—including that period in which adherence to Judaism had been given formal legal recognition and emancipation?

That question bothers many more Christians today than it did in 1900. One wonders whether Christians today are more and more anxious for discussion and common action with Jews because Christians, increasingly desperate at the pervasiveness of the modern secular state, are reaching out for potential religious allies against the encirclement of religion by nations and international societies which have the material betterment of mankind as their sole objective.

There is reason to hope, however, that Christians today, recognizing the disasters that have overcome their Jewish brothers in twenty centuries of Christian culture, realize that they have a profound moral obligation to both alter the Christian conception of Judaism and civilize the attitudes which all too many Christians, either individually or collectively, assume with regard to the negative or hostile practices which Christians have indulged in through the centuries.

It seems fair to state that Christians in 1900 could and should have either controlled the widespread anti-Semitism in Europe or, alternatively, recognized the emerging aspirations of the Zionist movement. Although it is easy and perhaps fruitless to pinpoint accountability retroactively, it must be said that some group in the year 1900 had the solemn moral obligation to transform the Christian nations into places where Jews could live and practice their religion or, if this was not possible, to assist the exodus of Jews to a place where, freed from anti-Christian harassment, they could reside in tranquillity. After all, the Christians around the year 1900 were in a position to understand that, as far as can be discovered, some seven million Jews had been killed in the first nineteen hundred years of Christian civilization. But unfortunately, almost no Christian voices were raised to demand that the societies in which they lived eradicate their traditional anti-Semitism and provide not for the assimilation of the Jew but for a society in which he could retain the wholeness of his faith while being a complete partner in the society in which he lived.

It is not entirely fanciful to compare the situation of the Christian in the late 1970s with the Christian around the year 1900. Both of them have experienced at first hand the purges, pogroms, and persecutions which have come to Jews in the nineteenth and twentieth centuries. The Christian in the year 1900 knew that even the Jew in an emancipated political situation would have to endure shocking sufferings. The Jew in the late 1970s has seen the holocaust consume the lives of six million Jews and now sees the frightening perils which threaten the three million Jews in Israel.

The Christian in 1900 said virtually nothing either to deplore the oppressions of the previous fifty years or to encourage the emerging Zionist hope of establishing a Jewish state in Palestine. The Christian in the late 1970s appears to be equally silent; he has seldom been stunned by the magnitude of the holocaust nor has he been anxious to do everything necessary to preserve the security and safety of Israel.

American Christians, moreover, seldom if ever recognize that they among all of the Christians of the earth have a unique role to play in formulating the attitude which the family of nations will adopt with respect to Israel. The United States is virtually the only major power which remains affirmatively loyal to its moral commitments to assist Israel in securing defensible borders against its surrounding enemies. As a result, the Christians of America have a unique and compelling role to play in developing and radiating that positive approach to Judaism and to Zionism which is compelled by the Bible, mandated by Christian principles, and dictated by the political exigencies of contemporary Israel.

American Christians, therefore, should be very well informed about the historical and theological ideas underlying the work of Theodor Herzl, the founder of modern Zionism. It is to this towering figure, one of the most important in all of Jewish history, that we now turn our attention.

4

ZIONISM:
THE ONLY ESCAPE FROM
CHRISTIAN ANTI-SEMITISM

The age-old attachment which the Jewish people have always had to the land of their fathers makes it surprising not that about one fourth of the Jewish people now reside in a re-established Israel but that this movement did not come about centuries before it actually happened. One of the many reasons why some nineteen hundred years passed before a significant ingathering of the exiles occurred was the feeling in Jewish tradition that God had promised the Jews an end to their captivity in His own good time and that, therefore, it would be improper, even blasphemous, to try to force the hand of God by action. But the idea of a restored Jewish life in the Holy Land was and is deeply imbedded in Jewish liturgy. The Passover festival concludes with the words "next year in Jerusalem." The same hope is echoed every year at the conclusion of the ceremonies on the High Holy Days.

Although the Jews had always claimed to be a nation, older than any of the others, it was not until the age of nationalism that small groups of them, disillusioned by their afflictions, began to think seriously of the fulfillment of those ancient prophecies which Jews had not forgotten, even if they had not implemented them, since the destruction of their political state by the Roman legions. At least a few Jews theorized that they would always suffer discrimination in non-Jewish nations unless they themselves had some actual geographical nation with which they and those with whom they associated could be identified.

It is paradoxical that the first organized movement among Jews to re-establish their nation did not come about until a century after the French Revolution had destroyed the ghettos and had in effect guaranteed legal equality for all peoples in Europe. More than ever before in Jewish history, publicists were arguing that Judaism is exclusively a religion and not a race or a nation, actual or potential. But this narrow interpretation of Judaism, always held by a tiny minority of Jews such as the members of the contemporary American Council on Judaism, had little cogency or credibility in an era in which many of the Jews of Europe felt that they could be neither good citizens of the country where they resided nor good Jews.

It was into this atmosphere that Theodor Herzl impelled himself. Born in Budapest in 1860, with an education in his early years totally divorced from Judaism, Herzl became the impassioned rhetorician of Zionism—influenced perhaps by his experiences as a journalist at the Dreyfus trial. His pamphlet, *The Jewish State*, published in 1896, touched the nerve endings of Jews and Christians and precipitated an enormous volume of discussion. Herzl's idea was simply "to establish for the Jewish people a publicly and legally assured home in Palestine." Herzl was not a Jewish theologian nor was he solely a pragmatist proposing the only possible solution to the Jewish predicament. But the zeal with which he pursued his messianic pilgrimage was infused with a compelling humanitarianism combined with traces of Jewish mysticism. Nonetheless, both Reform and Orthodox Jews reacted unfavorably. Reform Jews, who had abolished references to Zion from their prayer books, maintained that the mission of modern Judaism is to be a light unto the Gentiles and to spread justice by precept and example throughout the universe. Orthodox Jews pointed out that Herzl and the leaders of the Zionist movement were recommending a purely secular state in the Holy Land and that, in addition, Herzl and his associates were not observing, religious Jews and therefore Israel in their hands could hardly be deemed to be safe.

Herzl did, however, win a substantial following among humble, oppressed Jews everywhere. But they could hardly be carried away with the dream of Herzl when they realized that it called for the formation of a nation in a forlorn land controlled by a Turkish government.

The literature on the origins of Zionism has scarcely any mention of Christian interest or involvement in this then revolutionary concept. About the only reference to contact made by Herzl with Christians is the interview which the founder of Zionism had with Pope Pius X in 1903. Herzl is the only source for what transpired at that meeting, but there is no reason to doubt the authenticity of his report. As summarized in the book entitled *Herzl* by Amos Elon, published in 1975, we learn that Herzl first met with the Papal Secretary of State, Cardinal Merry del Val. After Herzl requested of the Cardinal "the good will of the Holy See," the prelate responded as follows:

"I do not quite see why we should take an initiative in this matter. As long as the Jews deny the divinity of Christ we cannot declare ourselves in their favor. Not that we wish them ill. On the contrary. But how could we agree to the repossession by the Jews of the Holy Land without abandoning our highest principles?"

Two days later Herzl put the same request to Pope Pius X, who, according to Herzl, replied:

"We cannot approve of the Zionist movement. We cannot prevent the Hebrews from going to Jerusalem, but we could never sanction it. The Hebrews have not recognized our Lord, therefore we cannot recognize the Hebrew people."

Herzl assured the pontiff that he and his associates intended to provide in every way for an extraterritorial status for the holy places in and around Jerusalem. He reminded Pius X that "the Jews are in terrible straits. I do not know if Your Holiness is familiar with the full extent of their sad situation. We need a land for the persecuted." According to Herzl's account, the Holy Fa-

ther did not express approval of his plan and concluded with these
words:

"We pray for the Jews. May their minds be enlightened . . .
and so if you come to Palestine and settle your people there, we
shall keep churches and priests ready to baptize all of them."

Sometime after this interview Cardinal Merry del Val told one
of Herzl's aides, "If the Jews believe they might greatly ease their
lot by being admitted to the land of their ancestors, then we will
regard that as a humanitarian measure. We shall never forget that
without Judaism we would have been nothing."

The first reaction of the Holy See to the very concept of the
state of Israel reveals a negative and unfavorable attitude which
has unfortunately persisted in the viewpoints of many if not most
Catholics since the time of Herzl. Catholics have generally not
opposed the creation of Israel, but they have been on the sidelines
watching as if the unfolding drama of the world's first Jewish nation in two thousand years is an event almost irrelevant for Christians. For centuries the majority of Christians have declared Judaism to be static, lifeless, and vestigial. Catholics may not have a
death wish for Judaism, but they have no understanding of the
Jewish religion that would create a desire within them that Judaism should continue and flourish. As a result, the tradition which
Catholics receive from the atmosphere around them suggests that
they evaluate an event such as the establishment of the state of Israel through the one inflexible formula of whether this will or will
not contribute to the conversion of the Jews. Since this question is
entirely irrelevant to the objectives and the motivations of Jews
who share the dream of Herzl, the Christian is remanded to a
state of mind with neither enthusiasm nor enmity toward a Jewish
state in the Near East.

The negative view of Israel revealed by the Holy Father to
Herzl had not improved by the day of Israel's birth on May 14,
1948. On that occasion, *L'Osservatore Romano*, the semi-official
daily of the Vatican, declared editorially that "Modern Israel is
not the heir to Biblical Israel. The Holy Land and its sacred sites
belong only to Christianity: the true Israel."

If Catholic attitudes toward the dream of the rebirth of a
Zionist state have been negative, it is understandable but very

tragic. Catholics simply are not in a position to understand the centrality of the state of Israel for modern Judaism. Often the Catholic spokesmen who are the best informed and the most sympathetic to contemporary Judaism write about that religion with the greatest empathy but refer to modern Israel almost as an afterthought. It is self-evident to even the least informed that the holocaust and the establishment of Israel are the two overpowering events through which and in which the modern Jew views everything else about his religious background. A Jewish reader might well be disappointed when he sees, for example, in a most sympathetic treatment of Judaism today by Father Gerard S. Sloyan, the following words:

> He [the Catholic] must learn Jewish Judaism, not Catholic Judaism; he must know something about a Simchas Torah, the ordinary Friday night service, the modern dietary observances; he must give outward signs—heartfelt signs—that Jewishness is a thoroughly acceptable human condition and that the Jewish religion is a way to serve God in reverence and love; he must even try to comprehend the United Jewish Appeal and the case for the state of Israel.

If the most ardent supporter of Judaism and its total integrity suggests an understanding of the "case for the state of Israel" as an afterthought, what can be expected in the sentiments toward Israel of the average Catholic?

The isolation of Europe's Christians from the real life of Jews living within their midst was exemplified once more by their almost total ignorance of the eight-year drive by Herzl for Zionism —while simultaneously in the Jewish communities of eastern Europe Herzl was creating a conflagration of emotions, at least among less educated and more pious Jews. Even today those Christians who view the tomb of Herzl in a majestic spot in Jerusalem, where his body was reburied in 1949, have almost no knowledge of Herzl's dream, which brought about the first world conference on Zionism in 1897 in Basel.

A review of Herzl's eight years of hectic activity on behalf of Zionism suggests the question of whether or not the result would be different if the birth and growth of Zionism had been predominantly motivated by theological or biblical convictions. If Jews from several European nations had announced that for purely religious or even mystical reasons they desired to return to the land from which centuries ago their forefathers had been expelled, would European princes and parliaments have felt more kindly toward the proposed exodus than they actually did? Herzl used both philosophical and pragmatic reasons to motivate Jews in the Diaspora to return to the "land of milk and honey." Zionists themselves were deeply divided as to the nature of their principal motivations. The story of Herzl's visit to the Jewish community in Vilna in Lithuania and his subsequent proposal at the Sixth Zionist Congress that Jews accept Britain's offer of Uganda as their homeland manifests the ambivalence of Herzl himself with respect to the really controlling reasons underlying the Zionist dream. Before the sixth world conference on Zionism Herzl visited the Jewish community in Vilna. This Lithuanian city was in the heart of the Jewish pale of settlement where millions of Jews had been confined in incredibly restricted areas. Vilna—a community that Napoleon, passing through, had called "the Jerusalem of Lithuania"—exemplified the melancholy and violence among the Jewish masses of eastern Europe. It was a hotbed of revolutionary activity and a headquarters for left-wing Zionist activities. Herzl visited this city at the high point of the frenzied reaction to the pogroms in Kishinev. A tumultuous reception was extended to Herzl. He saw almost for the first time in his life the degradation and desperation of Jewish communities, which, feeling that they, too, were marked for extinction, were not prepared to wait much longer for either a revolution of violence or an exodus to a new land.

Shattered by the sight of the Jews huddled together in the ghettos of Vilna, Herzl decided to announce and recommend at the forthcoming Zionist congress the offer which he had just received from the British government for the establishment of a Jewish colony in Uganda in East Africa. A few days later he proposed to the 592 delegates in Basel that, in order to give immediate relief to the Jews of Vilna and dozens of other Jewish ghettos in eastern Europe, the Zionist congress accept the offer of Uganda as a provisional site with the ultimate aim still to be the Holy Land of their fathers. After tumultuous applause, Herzl uttered these words:

"Many of us believe that things could not become worse, but things have become worse. Like a flood tide, misery has swept Jewry. . . . Kishinev is every place where Jews are physically or morally afflicted, dishonored, impoverished because they are Jews. Let us save those that can still be saved."

Most of the delegates who spoke in favor of accepting the offer of Uganda came from Western Europe or, like Cyrus Sulzberger, from New York. But many of the Jews from eastern Europe, despite the shame and suffering of their own people, stated in effect that they did not want the age-old history of Israel to end in an African jungle. One young Russian student, Chaim Weizmann, who thirteen years later would obtain the Balfour Declaration from the British government, opined that the British people could be induced to give a better offer to the world's Jews.

The formation of a committee to visit Uganda and report back was accepted by the delegates in a vote of 295 to 178 with 99 abstaining. A Western delegate named Martin Buber voted against.

Those who were opposed to even considering Uganda, along with the 99 who were ambivalent or undecided, threatened secession from the Zionist congress, some of them stating mournfully that Zion had been abandoned forever. After viewing the frenzied division among delegates presumably united by profound religious and philosophical principles, a working journalist, Leon Trotsky, predicted the quick demise of the Zionist movement.

The possibility of the Zionists settling in Uganda was severely chilled by a hostile reaction from the British settlers in that East African protectorate. The newspaper of Uganda's handful of British citizens protested the introduction of East European Jews into that nation, stating that they did not want the country to become "Jewganda." The opposition of Englishmen in Uganda became so vehement that Herzl himself dropped any thought of the projected migration to East Africa.

The controversy over Uganda as a refuge for oppressed Jews illustrates the melancholy fact that the fears and paranoia which

Europeans have acquired through the centuries with respect to Jews will almost always manifest itself in some attempt, however bizarre, to prevent or to protest the presence of any community of Jews. No fully rational explanation can be articulated for such a phenomenon. Europeans could presumably concur with the statement of Bismarck, who said that he was born with an anti-Jewish bias. It would seem that the antipathy toward Judaism and Jews which has characterized every generation of European civilization has now descended so deeply into the unconscious and subconscious psyche of modern man that we should beware of the danger of overrating the rational components of this prejudice at the expense of the psychotic.

If anti-Semitism in Europe had been at least predominantly rational, the citizens of that continent should have logically accepted with relief the proposition made by Jews and not by Christians that the Jews should resettle in a land in which Europeans had no political interest. One would think that political types in the day of Herzl could have theorized that the emigration of European Jews into an area of the empire of the Ottoman Turks could be useful to Europe in the containment of a fundamentally anti-Western empire.

The vast majority of non-Jewish European citizens were probably totally unaware of the revolutions proposed by Herzl and his almost rhapsodic followers. The response, as usual, of Christian-related nations and their religious leaders was silence. Apparently there was no feeling for the need of forgiveness for sins against the Jews nor was any thought given to the desirability of Herzl's proposal to remove once and for all the opportunity for anti-Semitism in Europe.

Ironically, Herzl's Jewish state even promoted a new form of anti-Judaism in those Arab areas of the world that had up to that time appeared to be historically immune to hatred of the Jews. The tragic irony of Herzl's Zionism was its role in begetting at least indirectly a new type of Palestinian-Arab nationalism. Ultimately, something akin to Arab Zionism came into being, echoing that of Herzl in that the Arabs felt driven by the myth of a lost homeland and the anguish of dispersion. The tempestuous passions generated among Arabs grew through the years with every new success that came to Zionism.

Herzl and his companions chose the term "Zion" because it appears 152 times in the Old Testament, always referring to Jerusalem, the royal city and the city of the temple. Zion meant Jerusalem and the place where the Lord had David installed as king. The congress at Basel accepted the term "Zion" because over the previous three thousand years it had grown to mean the whole of Israel. Zion was central to Judaism because since the demise of Jerusalem every Jew, while praying anywhere in the world, turns his face toward Jerusalem.

Despite the storms that beset the entire world concerning the nature and meaning of Zionism, its mystery and its majesty seem clear to those who visit the tomb of Herzl in Jerusalem, to which his body was taken from Vienna in 1949. As one looks to the right from Herzl's grave, there is the Memorial Center on the western slope of Mount Herzl which honors the memory of the six million slaughtered Jews of Europe whom Herzl might well have saved if he had not died at the age of forty-four. The north slope of Mount Herzl is covered by a huge military cemetery, a remembrance of the four wars Israel has fought since 1948 to establish the ideals of Zionism in the land of Zion. Directly in front of Herzl's tomb is the new campus of Hebrew University, and to the left lies the vast imposing building of the Knesset, Israel's parliament. Farther to the east lie the Mountains of Moab, where Moses, according to tradition, saw the promised land but, like Herzl, could not enter.

Pope John XXIII might well have been thinking of this scene and of the afflictions and agonies of Jews and Zionists everywhere when he wrote the following in 1963:

We are conscious today that many, many centuries of blindness have cloaked our eyes so that we can no longer see the beauty of Thy chosen people nor recognize in their faces the features of our privileged brethren.

We realize that the mark of Cain stands upon our foreheads. Across the centuries our brother Abel has lain in the blood which we drew, or shed tears we caused by forgetting Thy love.

Forgive us for the curse we falsely attached to their name as Jews. Forgive us for crucifying Thee a second time in their flesh. For we know not what we did. . . .

5

THE TRANSCENDENTAL ANTI-SEMITISM OF HITLER'S THIRD REICH

Christians familiar with anti-Semitism before the rise of Adolf Hitler cringe at the quantum leap in hatred of Jews that is revealed in *Mein Kampf*. A Christian seeks to disassociate his religion from the ravings of the fanatic Fuehrer. After all, Hitler wrote in 1919 that "Jewry is without question a race and not a religious fellowship." He continuously described Jews not in any language that classical Christian anti-Semitism had used but in terms of filth and disease. Hitler, furthermore, appears to have virtually overlooked the Christian period and sets forth his vision of human existence as a conflict between the Aryans and the Jews.

But the understandable and persistent desire of contemporary Christians to disavow any responsibility for the heinous form of anti-Semitism created by Hitler cannot deny or explain away the fact that Hitler's depiction of the Jews as the carriers of filth and disease had its implicit origins in the Middle Ages when Jews were accused of poisoning the wells and spreading the plague.

On the other hand, it does not appear to be just to say that the grotesque excesses of anti-Semitism that were put into practice in the Third Reich can be attributed exclusively or even principally to Christianity. After all, the Christian churches had been ousted as the moral leaders of Europe several generations before Hitler came to power. Neither Catholic nor Protestant leaders, with or without the concurrence of their congregations, could deter the horrendous injustices brought about by unbridled industrialism. Nor did the churches have any overarching influence in curbing the exploitation of underdeveloped nations by the European colonial powers. Assuming, therefore, that the Christian churches would not necessarily have been in a position to deter the rise of Hitler's *ersatz* religion of anti-Semitism, the question nonetheless recurs as to whether or not the churches could have done more to prevent the rise of that anti-Semitism which was incorporated into the platform of the Nazi Party as early as 1920. That document called for denial of citizenship and public office to Jews, the expulsion of all Jews who had come to Germany since 1914, the exclusion of Jews from the press, and the designation of all German Jews as "foreigners." In Italy for many decades Catholics had been forbidden to join political parties which refused to recognize the rights of the Holy See. There is no indication that any suggestion was made to Catholics that they could not join the Nazi Party because of the injustices against Jews proposed in the platform of that political party.

The anti-Semitic bias was of course everywhere in Germany before and especially after the First World War. Lucy S. Dawidowicz, in her 1975 definitive book, *The War Against the Jews, 1933-1945,* states that in the years 1907 to 1910 in Vienna "Anti-Semitic politics flourished, anti-Semitic organizations proliferated, anti-Semitic writing and propaganda poured forth in an unending stream." That was the atmosphere the young Adolf Hitler absorbed when he lived in Vienna during those years. It may be, therefore, that any answer to the haunting question about what Christians did to blunt the escalation of anti-Semitism in the 1930s in Germany should appropriately be directed not to the Christians of that decade but to all of the Christians in previous decades who had acquiesced in the propagation of ideas about the Jews which were contrary both to the Scriptures and to basic natural justice. The heresies and the hatreds which Christians had permitted for some nineteen hundred years could hardly be excised or even cauterized during the dozen years of the Nazi nightmare.

Hitler's extravagant assaults on the Jews were, however, different in a significant way from anything that had preceded them. Hitler's anti-Semitism was transcendental, all-purpose, and final. In the view which he made the policy of the Third Reich, neither baptism nor the renunciation of Judaism could alter the status of the Jew. As early as 1919, Hitler had written that "rational anti-Semitism" must have as "its final objective" the unswerving "removal of the Jews altogether."

Christians should certainly have known that the proposed extermination of the Jews, however veiled, was contrary to the very essence of Christianity.

Christians should also have been able to discern the perniciousness of Hitler's association of the Jews with Russian Bolshevism. If such an allegation had any credibility, the conclusion that Hitler drew from it lacked any shred of plausibility. Hitler added: "In Russian Bolshevism we must see the attempt undertaken by the Jews in the twentieth century to achieve world domination."

Christians will almost certainly continue to resist any unilinear argument that the ideas and events which led to the holocaust are traceable to Christian teaching or practices. But after all of the distinctions are made and the inferences drawn, one still has to accept the fact that both Luther and Hitler were obsessed with fantasies about the Jews. Luther wrote that "next to the devil life has no enemy more cruel, more venomous and violent than a true Jew." Hitler echoed these sentiments in *Mein Kampf* in words not rejected by the religious leaders of Germany: "I believe that I am today acting in accordance with the will of the Almighty Creator: by defending myself against the Jew I am fighting for the work of the Lord." These statements, issued four hundred years apart by the theological father and the political dictator of Germany, made it possible and perhaps inevitable for millions of Germans to accept and believe in the lies set forth in the *Protocols of the Elders of Zion* which was translated into German in 1920. This fantasy purports to be a plan for a conspiracy of Jews and Freemasons to ruin Christendom and found a world state ruled by Jews and Freemasons.

All of these factors worked together to produce in Germany in 1932 a nation intoxicated with hate, obsessed by paranoia, searching for a national unity that would restore dignity at last to the German people, and prepared through some insanity to believe that the elimination of the alleged Jewish conspiracy would bring about the consummation of all of the aspirations of the German people.

Drastic steps against the Jews were taken within a matter of days after Adolf Hitler became Chancellor of Germany in 1933. But the development and execution of the "Final Solution" under Adolf Eichmann and his fellow executioners came many years later. Consequently, the nagging question remains and recurs: could not the other nations of the earth have done much more than they did to prevent the murder of six million Jews? There is, of course, the question of how much knowledge the outside world was permitted to obtain; Hitler's agents sent out deliberately obfuscating and untrue reports about the evils being planned and fulfilled against non-Aryans in Germany. The number of Jews in Germany, furthermore, diminished very sharply in the first four years after Hitler came to power. This exodus presumably gave rise to the feeling in world opinion that the most vulnerable Jews had been able to flee before the Austrian house painter could carry out his barbarous intentions. Nonetheless, one must still wonder whether some apathy toward the fate of Jews or even some covert anti-Semitism prevented more nations from adopting affirmative action to make places available for any Jew who desired to flee from the foreseeable and foreboding wrath that was to come.

The United States has traditionally welcomed political refugees whose lives or safety were endangered in their country of origin. During the years after Castro came to power in Cuba, for example, the United States accepted at least 400,000 Cubans simply on their undocumented statements that they would be in danger if they remained under Castro's Communism. The welcome given to Cubans harks back to the Displaced Persons Act passed by

Congress immediately after World War II. In the thirty years from 1946 to 1976, the United States accepted at least 1.2 million persons as permanent residents on the basis of their being political refugees.

One must wonder whether the United States in the late 1930s lived up completely to its proud tradition of giving haven to the "huddled masses." The generosity of the United States after World War II was extended by statute to those individuals who were political escapees from Communist countries; but Congress understood that the vast majority of these people would be Christians. It is not clear that the Congress or the country extended the same generosity to the victims of the Nazi regime who were known to be Jewish.

The same doubt exists with respect to the congressional resolution of 1922 that approved the idea of a homeland for the Jews in Palestine. A question can be posed about the total sincerity of this resolution in view of the fact that in 1921 the Congress had enacted a new immigration law which, because it discriminated invidiously against persons living in eastern and southern Europe, made it much more likely that non-Jews rather than Jews would be able to emigrate to the United States.

Almost no group, Christian or otherwise, can boast of its role in preventing, postponing, or alleviating the holocaust. The usual way most Christians treat it is to ignore it. When pressed or challenged, Catholics can point to an encyclical by Pope Pius XI in 1937 entitled "With Burning Sorrow"; this document was delivered secretly to the German hierarchy by then Father Francis Spellman. Again, when challenged, Catholics can assert that Pope Pius XII was not as silent or unconcerned as he was portrayed in the famous play *The Deputy*.

Both Catholics and Protestants have at least a few heroes who stood up against the Nazi onslaughts. Catholics can be proud of Cardinal Faulhaber of Munich while Protestants can rightfully proclaim Pastor Niemöller and theologian Dietrich Bonhoeffer. But Christian passivity in the face of the enormity of the holocaust can be explained only by that strange, unfathomable, and humiliating unconcern with, or unconscious rejection of, Jewish suffering which has characterized the Christian centuries.

It may be that the concern of Christians in America for the slaughtered Jews can be measured against the level of involvement which Americans have for the victims of other tragedies, such as those inflicted by the United States in Nagasaki and Hiroshima. Even then comparison is misleading, however, because the vast majority of Americans have never come to the conclusion that the use of nuclear weapons by their own nation was immoral in these two instances. If most Americans so believed, it might be possible to compare the depth of their compassion for these Japanese victims with the intensity of their feeling for the Jews killed by the Third Reich—killings which hopefully all Americans would deem to be unjustified.

THE CATHOLIC RECORD IN GERMANY ON
ANTI-SEMITISM DURING THE THIRD REICH

The evidence on Catholic resistance to and rejection of the cruel anti-Jewish policies of Hitler is not entirely one-way. But the silence of Catholic leaders on the slaughter of Jews is hardly edifying or commendable.

On July 20, 1933, the Nazi government concluded a concordat with the Vatican which guaranteed the freedom of the Catholic religion and of its schools. The agreement, signed by the then papal Secretary of State, Monsignor Pacelli, later Pope Pius XII, was violated by the Nazi government almost immediately after it had been ratified. Nonetheless, the concordat almost certainly gave the Hitler government some very valuable prestige at a moment when the first extreme actions on the part of the new regime in Germany had elicited world-wide repudiation.

Although Catholic resistance to Nazi excesses grew during the 1930s, no Catholic authority or author appears to have repudiated the wisdom of the concordat. Gordon C. Zahn, in his volume *German Catholics and Hitler's Wars*, raises the question of why the Catholic Church in Germany did not "make a total break with the Nazi regime." Dr. Zahn, an articulate Catholic pacifist, agrees with the opinion of Pope Pius XII, who in 1945 stated that the concordat had spared the Church in Germany a far greater measure of hardship and persecution than that actually suffered by it during the Nazi years. Zahn goes on to raise this fundamental question:

"Is it enough for the leadership of any national segment of the Catholic Church to limit its concern to its own institutional interests or the personal welfare of its own membership?"

He concludes that in Nazi Germany "the areas of open Catholic resistance were almost exclusively those directly affecting" the institutional interests of the Church. These included the secularization of religious schools, the closing of convents, the suppression of Catholic organizations, and the pressures upon those who aspired to civil service to renounce their membership in the Church. Dr. Zahn concludes sadly that "only the heroic resistance to the infamous euthanasia program and the more direct Nazi assaults upon traditional family values went beyond these self-centered interests to a more general level of moral concern."

He documents this conclusion by reviewing all of the relevant annual statements of the German Catholic hierarchy made in Fulda from 1933 until the demise of Hitler. In virtually all of these documents the Catholic hierarchy reaffirmed its judgment that the German Catholic population had a moral obligation to obey the legitimate authority of the National Socialist rulers. After the war began in 1939, there was hardly a mention of any possibility of sincere conscientious objection on the part of a German Catholic to what Hitler was doing.

Episcopal statements in Germany during this period, along with other documents revealing the Catholic mentality at that time, demonstrate that, aside from several condemnations of racism, there was little sustained objection to or protest about the crescendo in anti-Semitic actions by the Nazis.

Guenther Lewy, in his book *The Catholic Church and Nazi Germany* (1964), concluded that the Catholic Church in Germany "shared the widely prevailing sense of nationalism and patriotism." This author adds that the "bishops, many of the lower clergy and their parishioners concurred in certain Nazi aims."

Professor Lewy describes the passivity of the German episcopate as in marked contrast to the often heroic conduct of the French, Belgian, and Dutch bishops, all of whom sought to use their high position to condemn the barbarous treatment of the Jews by the invading Nazis. The situation was, of course, different since the conduct of the Catholic leaders in the invaded nations was almost universally regarded as signs of patriotism and resistance.

Dr. Lewy summed up his study of the attitudes of the German bishops and the Holy See toward anti-Semitism in these words: "But once the Nazis were established in power, the pontiff, like the German episcopate, seemed to have limited his concern to Catholic non-Aryans." Lewy notes that the Holy See repeatedly took issue with the Nazis' glorification of race but that "the Jewish question specifically was never discussed." Even in Pope Pius' encyclical "With Burning Sorrow" of March 1937, the myths of race and blood were rejected as contrary to real Christian truth, but the document neither mentioned nor criticized anti-Semitism as such.

It is very easy to be harsh and one-sided in concluding that German Catholic leaders did not do all they could to impede the advance of anti-Semitism and the opening of the first death camp for Jews on December 8, 1941. One is almost tempted to weight the evidence in this direction so that there will be a solemn warning to all Christians never again to temporize or compromise with a ruler or an organization that preaches anti-Semitism. But even the minimal effort to be fair to those persons involved requires that we seek to evaluate whether or not they really believed that the Nazis were exterminating Jews—as subsequently became known; whether in addition they thought that their protests might have some value or, on the contrary, whether they thought their protestations might bring about even greater evils for both Christians and Jews.

But even when all the extenuating circumstances are set forth, the mind comes back to the conviction that the silence of the Catholic bishops in Germany was reprehensible. A contrary policy would surely have brought about the imprisonment of thousands more priests and nuns than actually were confined during the

Nazi period. It seems safe to conclude that countless Christian leaders in Germany were deterred from speaking out because of the amorphous and ambiguous theological premises which they had inherited from their training. Even the brilliant Catholic author and theologian, Karl Adam, defended the preservation of the German people's pure blood as a justified act of self-defense; he theorized that the physiological basis of all thinking and feeling was blood and that, as a result, German culture and history would be decisively shaped by the preservation of that blood. If a great mind like that of Karl Adam can be deceived by a gross lie about Aryan blood, one can imagine the falsehoods which would be accepted at lower levels of the Church!

The worst possible interpretation of all the facts can probably be seen in the conclusion made by Guenther Lewy, who wrote as follows:

> When thousands of German anti-Nazis were tortured to death in Hitler's concentration camps, when the Polish intelligentsia were slaughtered, when hundreds of Russians died . . . and when six million human beings were murdered for being "non-Aryan," Catholic Church officials in Germany bolstered the regime perpetuating these crimes. The Pope in Rome, the spiritual head and supreme moral teacher of the Roman Catholic Church, remained silent. In the face of these greatest of moral depravities which mankind has been forced to witness in recent centuries, the moral teachings of a church, dedicated to love and charity, could be heard in no other form but vague generalities.

The same indictment is reflected in the question the young girl in Max Frisch's *Andorra* asks of the priest: "Where were you, Father Benedict, when they took away our brother like a beast to the slaughter, like a beast to the slaughter, where were you?"

COULD THE HOLY SEE HAVE BEEN MORE EFFECTIVE
AGAINST HITLER'S ANTI-SEMITISM?

The entire Western world might well have been liberated from its anti-Semitism if everyone had subscribed in 1945 to Pastor Niemöller's avowal made in that year:

> Nobody wants to take the responsibility for the guilt. Nobody admits to guilt but instead points to his neighbor. Yet the guilt exists, there is no doubt about it. Even if there were no other guilt than that of six million clay urns, the ashes of burnt Jews from all over Europe. And this guilt weighs heavily on the German people and on the German name and on all Christendom. These things happened in our world and in our name. . . . I regard myself as guilty as any SS man.

As the Christian looks back at the horrors of Buchenwald, Dachau, Maidanek, Belsen, and Treblinka, he wonders whether there was in fact any Christian resistance to the madness of Hitler. Of what relevance is it that some three thousand priests died in these death camps? Is there any place to hide from the accusation that the Christians of Germany and the nations which it conquered betrayed the Jews by silence and by neglect? Perhaps some consolation can be obtained by reflecting on the accepted view that the intellectual and cultural classes did far less to save the Jews than did church groups. A rare tribute to the Catholic Church was enunciated in 1940 by Albert Einstein in these words: "Only the Catholic Church protested against the Hitlerian onslaught on liberty. Up until then I had not been interested in the church, but today I feel a great admiration and a great attachment to the church which alone has had the courage to struggle for spiritual truth and moral liberty."

Critics seeking to understand why Christian resistance to Hitler's genocide of the Jews failed so badly have understandably turned their attention to Popes Pius XI and Pius XII. The evidence for and against these pontiffs is summarized in a 1967 volume by Pinchas E. Lapide entitled *The Last Three Popes and the Jews*. The volume gives the unmistakable impression that Pope Pius XI, who died in 1939, and Pius XII did more to protect the Jews from the wrath of Hitler than is commonly assumed. At the same time, the author makes clear in a 40-page section those things which Pius XII did *not* do. It would seem that the emergence of a consensus on any culpability to be attributed to these two Popes and particularly to Pius XII will be difficult because of the vehement rejection by the Catholic community of the blunt charge by the Protestant playwright Rolf Hochhuth in *The Deputy*. The harsh criticism in Catholic circles of this dramatic charge of the sin of silence against Pope Pius XII derives from the enormous and unshakable veneration for the person of the Holy Father which Catholics cherish.

It is uncertain whether Catholic or world opinion with regard to the actions of Pius XI and Pius XII will ever advance beyond that state of doubt and ambiguity which now characterizes them. As more evidence is discovered and additional information becomes available, Catholics will probably feel like the famous French Catholic author, François Mauriac:

> We French Catholics, whose honor was certainly saved by the heroism and charity shown hundreds of Jews by so many bishops, priests, nuns and monks, but who never have the consolation of hearing Galilean Simon Peter's successor clearly condemn the crucifixion of these innumerable brethren of the Lord in plain terms, not diplomatic allusions . . .

Those who would have liked the Holy See to speak in such unambiguous terms are fearful that the world will believe what Father Riccardo says in the fourth act of *The Deputy*: "A vicar of Christ who has the deportation of Jews under his eyes, and who keeps silent for reasons of state . . . such a pope is a criminal."

It may seem self-serving for a Catholic to demonstrate that Pope Pius XII did more to resist anti-Semitism than any previous Pope of any age. The genocide of six million Jews seems to contradict such a possibility. In addition, it seems hard to theorize that, but for Pope Pius XII's intercessions and interventions, the slaughter would have been worse. Nonetheless, there is cogent evidence that Pius XII did all within his power and the power of the Holy See. In his Christmas messages, for example, of 1939 through 1944, Pius XII condemned racism in unmistakable terms.

His Christmas message of 1942 pleaded for the lives of "the hundreds of thousands, who, through no fault of their own, only because of their nationality or descent, are condemned to death." The words "nationality or descent" so clearly referred to Jews that the message was withdrawn from publication by the Nazis. Similar evidence is manifest elsewhere in many places. But the shadow of the holocaust is so mind-numbing that the genuine and persistent heroism on the part of the Holy See during the nightmare of Nazism may rest in obscurity for the foreseeable future.

In November 1975, American author Robert Katz was found guilty of defamation by an Italian tribunal for his 1973 film *Massacre in Rome*, which alleged culpable Vatican inaction in the face of forthcoming atrocities by the Nazis at the height of the war. Katz, in his film, postulated that Pius XII overlooked the atrocities of the Nazis because he saw the Germans as a lesser enemy than the Communists.

In 1976, Pope Paul VI issued Volume IX of his multivolume history of the wartime activities of the Vatican. Volume IX reveals and documents scores of Vatican attempts in 1943 to help Jews in Rumania, Bulgaria, Poland, Yugoslavia, and Italy.

A total of six books have to date explored the question of whether Pope Pius XII could have done more to save six million European Jews from extermination. A 1975 volume on this question, *The Race for Rome* by Daniel Kurzman, contended that the Pope feared that he himself might be kidnaped by the Nazis and the Vatican destroyed if he spoke out publicly against Hitler's atrocities. Volume IX of the Vatican's own history of the war tends to confirm the rumors of such a kidnap plan in 1943.

More facts are emerging all the time about the activities of Pius XII in the difficult and desperate years when the holocaust was taking place. Perhaps the following evaluation by Professor Guenther Lewy is about as balanced as one can expect:

> Given the indifference of the German population towards the fate of the Jews, and the highly ambivalent attitude of the German hierarchy towards Nazi anti-Semitism, a forceful stand by the Supreme Pontiff on the Jewish question might well have led to a large-scale desertion from the church. . . .

The pope knew that the German Catholics were not prepared to suffer martyrdom for their church; still less were they willing to incur the wrath of their Nazi rulers for the sake of the Jews, whom their own bishops had castigated as a harmful influence in German life. In the final analysis, then, the Vatican's silence only reflected the deep feeling of the Catholic masses of Europe.

Whatever one might conclude about the Holy See's attitude toward the holocaust, it is unfortunately impossible to conclude that the Holy See gave very much encouragement to the next struggle of the world's Jews—the establishment of Israel.

6

CHRISTIAN REACTIONS TO THE EMERGENCE OF ISRAEL AS A NATION

One would think that Christian leaders, having seen the persistence of anti-Semitism among the followers of Christ and particularly having witnessed the holocaust, would lend some affirmative acquiescence to the idea of a homeland to which the twelve million surviving Jews in the world, if they so desired, might emigrate. In theological terms, one could imagine that moralists would theorize that the separation of Jews in a separate nation would relieve Christians of a constant proximate occasion of sin.

It is perhaps another manifestation of the perversity and subconscious irrationality of anti-Semitism that the Christian leaders of the world, both Catholic and Protestant, when confronted with the live option of giving at least tacit support to Jewish groups in Europe desiring to travel to Israel, extended not acceptance but open rejection of the idea.

AMERICAN PROTESTANT VIEWS OF ZIONISM

Although American Protestants have been profoundly influenced by the Old Testament and understand thoroughly the

biblical concept of Zion, they have never been able or willing to
accept the concept of Zionism as set forth by contemporary Judaism. In the non-denominational weekly, the *Christian Century*, an
overt and persistent campaign against all versions of Zionism continued from the time of the Balfour Declaration in November
1917 through the establishment of Israel in 1948. Although the
Christian Century speaks more for the main-line churches than
for the evangelicals, there appears to have been little substantial
dissent from its basic contention in 1917, following the Balfour
Declaration, that "it is the conviction of most modern biblical
scholars that the Old Testament contains no anticipation of the
restoration of Israel to its ancient homeland which can apply to
the Jewish people and the present age."

Twelve years later the *Christian Century* applauded the report
of a British commission which recommended stopping sales of
land to the Jews and curtailing Jewish emigration to Palestine.
The magazine considered this report to be the death of the Balfour Declaration, stating that it was a "mischievous and ambiguous promise." Toward the end of 1929 the *Christian Century* editorialized as follows:

> As long as the Jews were the victims of persecution and
> outrage in any of the lands of their occupation, it was inevita-
> ble that they should dream of a homeland where they might
> be at peace and work out their cultural and religious ideals.
> But the new world of today is open to them with growing
> freedom and opportunity. The Jew is respected and honored
> in all of the regions where he has exhibited his powers in the
> fields of industry, commerce, politics, art and literature. Does
> he really desire to emigrate to a small, poverty-stricken and
> unresourceful land like Palestine?

The beginnings of Nazi persecution disturbed the certainty of
the editors of the *Christian Century*. In May 1933 an editorial admitted:

> The Christian mind has never allowed itself to feel the
> same human concern for Jewish sufferings that it has felt for

the cruelties visited upon Armenians, the Boers, the people of India, American slaves, or the Congo blacks under Leopold imperialism. Christian indifference to Jewish suffering has for centuries been rationalized by the tenable belief that such sufferings were the judgment of God upon the Jewish people for the rejection of Jesus.

The editorial went on to distinguish between Jews as Jews and Jews as nationalists. It exonerated "Jews as Jews" from the crime of the crucifixion but somehow inculpated Jews as nationalists— especially modern Jewish nationalists. It may be that the hostile attitude of the *Christian Century* against all forms of Jewish nationalism derived from that magazine's own concept of what it would conceive to be authentic Americanism. In that framework, Roman Catholics and indeed all non-Protestants appeared to be something less than completely American.

The *Christian Century's* opposition to the Balfour Declaration logically led to its rejection in 1937 of the report of the British Royal Commission, which recommended partition. The magazine's editors recognized the existence of "the needs and rights of the Jews . . ."; but they evaded the issue by stating that "there is no solution that is entirely right."

It is an indication of the indifference of American Christians to the plight of the Jews that until the end of the 1930s no major organized religious group took issue publicly with the attitudes of the *Christian Century*. It seems fair to conclude that the overwhelming majority of Christian officials in the United States were interested in advancing the objectives of Christian missionaries in the Arab world and of protecting the de facto control which Christians had over the holy places in Greater Jerusalem. These were the two ostensible reasons why Christians would hardly think of encouraging or even allowing a Jewish state to be established in the Holy Land.

To Jews everywhere in the world, and particularly to those with Zionist aspirations, the voice of American Protestantism as reflected in the *Christian Century* must have seemed very harsh in 1939 when, reacting to the British government's White Paper of May 17, 1939, the magazine approved of the policy recommended in that document of drastically limiting Jewish emigration to Israel for a five-year period. The White Paper, in addition, recommended subjecting Jewish emigration after the five-year period to Arab consent. The *Century* wrote:

> What today looks to many Zionists like black defeat will, in the light of history, turn out to be glorious victory. . . . The ambition to make Palestine a Jewish state must be dropped, but there is no reason why under the new British proposal it cannot still become a cultural and spiritual center for world Jewry. . . . If Jewish devotion can . . . make of Zionism a demonstration of a universal value in Judaism, social as well religious, the great blow which has fallen on Jewish hopes with the publication of the British White Paper may turn out to be a blessing in disguise.

In Jewish eyes this editorial is, of course, that familiar bifurcation of Judaism into a piety and a nationalism—with the latter to be removed almost as if it were an offender unwanted by everybody.

If the *Christian Century* remained adamantly opposed to the idea of a Jewish state in the Middle East, one might have hoped that logically they would recommend a more liberal American immigration policy for refugee Jews. Even this did not, however, win the approbation of the magazine. On March 22, 1938, the United States Government invited thirty-three nations to establish an international committee to facilitate the reception of political refugees from Austria and Germany. The federal government did not, however, recommend the altering of any immigration laws. The *Christian Century* editorialized that the United States could absorb "100,000 or so of Jewish emigrants . . . without difficulty." But the editor concluded that the "evils" of such a proposal would be "as great as those which it is designed to cure." The Protestant weekly recommended against any letting down of the immigration barriers because of the economic condition of the country with its large unemployed population. Furthermore, opined the magazine, the entry of "an appreciable number of Jews" into the United States could cause anti-Semitism. How such a phenomenon might arise was not clear, but the journal concluded that "it would be a tragic disservice to the Jews in America to increase their number by substantial immigration."

The rejection by the *Christian Century* of any proposed modification of America's immigration laws was made clear in these words:

> There is no ethical principle that requires either an individual person or a nation to expose itself to a condition sure to involve a moral overstrain. . . . Our immigration laws . . . should be maintained and even further strengthened. Christian and other highminded citizens have no need to feel apologetic for the limitations upon immigration into this country.

During the war years the pages of the *Federal Council Bulletin*, the official monthly publication of the Federal Council of Churches of Christ (the forerunner of the National Council of Churches), reflected sympathy for the victims of Nazism and anti-Semitism. But it was not until December 1942, after the Nazis' "Final Solution" policies had become undeniable, that the Federal Council of Churches concluded "that something like a policy of deliberate extermination of the Jews in Europe is being carried out." No mention of Palestine as a possible place of refuge for Jews appears anywhere in the *Federal Council Bulletin* during the war years. Recommendations were made that nations provide for emigration opportunities, but specifics were generally lacking.

There were in America at least a few individuals and denominations at variance with the positions of the *Christian Century*. The fundamentalist church denominations had always been vaguely committed in a theological way to the return of the Jews to the Holy Land as a prelude to the Second Coming. Liberal Protestant leaders and many Unitarians, noting the absence of any realistic alternative for Jewish refugees, advocated an open-door policy in Palestine.

The isolationist and restrictive outlook of the *Christian Century* and the Protestant establishment was challenged first and above all by Reinhold Niebuhr, professor of social ethics at Union Theological Seminary. In the *Nation* magazine in February 1942,

Dr. Niebuhr endorsed the right of the Jews to survive as a people and urged, like Louis Brandeis before him, that American Jews should be considered to have a "nationality" like all other ethnic groups. Niebuhr pointed out that even the most generous immigration laws of Western democracies did not permit the entry of the dispossessed Jews of Europe. At the same time he warned Zionists to stop proclaiming that their demands in Israel entailed no injustice to the Arab population. He wrote: "It is absurd to expect any people to regard the restriction of their sovereignty over a traditional possession as 'just' no matter how many other benefits accrue from that abridgment."

In 1944 and 1945, as the plight of the Jewish refugees became more tragic, other Christian voices joined that of Niebuhr. According to Hertzel Fishman in his excellent book *American Protestantism and a Jewish State* (1973), the "first full-fledged pro-Zionist article in *Christianity and Crisis* was by Dr. Henry Atkinson, Chairman of the Christian Council on Palestine; for the first time an American Christian argued not merely for a homeland in Palestine for the Jew but as an 'answer to the Christian problem' of anti-Semitism." But such profound sentiments concerned few Christians indeed in America in the last days of the Second World War. Most Christian Americans were manifestly not concerned with the question of what to do with the 250,000 Jews who were in displaced persons camps at the end of the war. Reinhold Niebuhr editorialized in *Christianity and Crisis* on April 3, 1944, as follows:

> Christians who do not believe that the "White Paper" restriction on immigration to Palestine should be abrogated, as advocated by a pending Senatorial resolution, ought to feel obligated to state a workable alternative. The homeless Jews must find a home, and Christians owe their Jewish brother something more than verbal sympathy. . . .

During all of the many months when Reinhold Niebuhr and his associates were waging an organized campaign to influence American public opinion in favor of the Zionist position, many other American Protestant leaders were doing everything in their power to guarantee an anti-Zionist U. S. Government policy. The powerful forces behind such an anti-Zionist policy became fully organized in February 1948 as the Committee for Justice and Peace in the Holy Land. The principal objective of this organization was to induce the United Nations to reconsider its November 29, 1947, partition resolution. Among the executive members of this group were some of the most distinguished Protestant clergymen in America; they included Dr. Henry Sloane Coffin, Dr. Harry Emerson Fosdick, Paul Hutchinson, the editor of the *Christian Century*, and other less well known churchmen from virtually all denominations. The Committee for Justice and Peace in the Holy Land visited with then Secretary of State George Marshall and with the then head of the U.S. delegation to the United Nations, Warren Austin. The committee disbanded in February 1950 after lobbying systematically as a Protestant-oriented group against a Jewish state. Hertzel Fishman theorizes that if this lobby had been organized several years earlier "its chances for success might have been greater." This Protestant group spoke on behalf of the 126,500 Christians then in the Holy Land. Its legitimate concern for them caused the committee to enunciate strong anti-Zionist statements, the tone and content of which still influence American Christians.

The vehemence of some Protestant spokesmen was unbelievable. Dr. Henry Sloane Coffin stated that "the plea for the necessity of a Jewish national state is no more cogent than would be a similar plea for an Armenian national state." Dr. Henry Van Dusen, president of the Union Theological Seminary, declined to counsel Christians to be enthusiastic about Israel because by doing so Christians would be making common cause with American political parties which were not concerned with the humanitarian considerations of persecuted Jews but with the "shrewd calculation of the voting strength" of American Jews. Dr. Van Dusen also felt that the partition of Palestine might spawn conflict in the Near East and that "American lives would be demanded." Van Dusen's bottom line was that the Jewish state in Palestine should be called off because if American lives were ever needed to protect it the "final outcome might be fuel for the always smoldering fires of anti-Semitism"!

American Protestant anti-Zionist forces did not prevent the establishment of Israel, but they succeeded in projecting a largely negative and sometimes even sinister attitude toward the Jewish state. The American Friends of the Middle East (AFME), founded in 1951, institutionalized in a predominantly but not exclusively Protestant group a feeling against the very existence of Israel.

American Protestants joined with some Catholics in raising serious questions about the internationalization of Jerusalem. The partition resolution adopted by the U. N. General Assembly on November 29, 1949, called for an international regime for Jerusalem in these words:

> The City of Jerusalem shall be established as a corporate corpus separatum under a special international regime and shall be administered by the United Nations. The Trusteeship Council shall be designated to discharge the responsibilities of the administering authority on behalf of the United Nations.

In a short time after the adoption of this resolution it became clear that it could not be implemented. The Secretary General of the United Nations, Trygve Lie, reported to the Third Session of the General Assembly: "The Arab authorities were unwilling to cooperate under existing conditions with any Jerusalem Commissioner appointed by the United Nations, while Jewish authorities had declared their readiness to cooperate with him."

The question of the proposed internationalization of Jerusalem was made more complicated by the pervasive presence there of Catholic custodians, generally Franciscan monks. European Protestant spokesmen tended to accept the reality of Jerusalem's political division rather than to insist upon internationalization of the city by both Jordan and Israel. The continued pressure by the Vatican and by influential American Protestants on behalf of the internationalization of Jerusalem embarrassed Israel at the United Nations and around the world. Although it was very clear by 1950 that no form of internationalization of Jerusalem was feasible, the

National Council of Churches of Christ, on September 17, 1953, reminded the U.S. delegation to the United Nations that the NCC was still in favor of internationalization. This group, which represents virtually all Protestant religious bodies in America, declared that "the great majority of the people of our churches would like to see this recommendation put into effect." The NCC knew at that time that the United Nations itself had abandoned the issue at the end of 1952. The question of the internationalization of Jerusalem did not appear on the United Nations agenda for the next fifteen years. And all of the dire predictions as to the disasters that would occur if Jerusalem were not internationalized failed to materialize.

One of the few Christian advocates of Israel, who differed from the generally anti-Israel attitude that dominated Protestant thinking around the time of the birth of Israel, was the brilliant Professor A. Roy Eckardt, a former student of Dr. Henry Sloane Coffin, and now one of the most prolific and profound writers about contemporary Judaism and Zionism.

AMERICAN CATHOLIC REACTIONS TO PROPOSED PLANS FOR A JEWISH HOMELAND

Although there does not seem to have been any widespread enthusiasm or militancy in the Catholic community on behalf of the establishment of the state of Israel, some constructive thinking was enunciated in *America* magazine, the national Catholic weekly edited by American Jesuits. On the other hand, not a few negative Catholic viewpoints were expressed elsewhere in the months before and after the founding of Israel.

America magazine on January 5, 1946, wrote very constructively of the then contemporary Anglo-American Commission on Palestine. It expressed the hope that the commission would recognize that "the rights of the Jews already in Palestine or who emigrate there need protection" and that they "want an active voice in governing Palestine." The journal of opinion opted with some diffidence for a "bi-national state in which the interests of both groups are guaranteed and both have a share in the government of the country towards the development of which both groups have contributed."

At the same time, *America* pointed out very forcefully that the United States and other nations had a strong moral obligation to admit more refugees. The magazine noted that during the eleven years from 1933 to 1944 only 365,955 Europeans—most of them refugees—had come to American shores. That represented only 16.8 per cent of the total number admissible under existing quotas. As a result, the magazine hailed the December 22, 1945, decision of President Truman to facilitate immigration within the quotas.

On October 25, 1947, *America* commended Zionist groups for being realistic in accepting partition, despite their long-standing hopes for something more. The magazine pointed out that the "great obstacle to successful partition is Arab intransigence." The Catholic weekly noted that there was something unrealistic about the Arabs' recital of historic claims.

America thought little of the proposed international administration of the Holy Land, in view of the fact that "previous world experience with such international administrations . . . leaves doubt as to the feasibility of such an arrangement."

This editorial, which was more of an acceptance of Israel than a note of triumph at its existence, was probably the nearest thing to enthusiasm for the founding of Israel to be found in the Catholic press or Catholic public opinion during the several months before Israel finally became a nation in 1948.

Commonweal, a liberal weekly magazine edited from a Catholic point of view, admitted on May 17, 1946, that "we have never been able to make up our minds on the subject of Jewish immigration into Palestine." The magazine recognized "the desperate need of Europe's remaining Jews for a homeland in which they can be reasonably confident of living unmolested." It conceded that the "Jewish colonies in the Holy Land have in fact proved a great economic asset to their Arab neighbors." Despite all of this, *Commonweal* confessed that it felt "suspicious of Zionist nationalism" and unable to make up its mind—"especially since we believe that the first duty of our own country is itself to provide a haven of refuge to the harborless."

On October 10, 1947, *Commonweal* in a signed article by C. G. Paulding expressed the gravest reservations about the proposed partition of Palestine. Paulding noted that the Jews had accepted the proposed "map and the text" while the Arabs had rejected the plan and had promised that they would drench "the land of our beloved country with the last drop of our blood in the lawful defense of all and every inch of it." Paulding feared continuous conflict if the partition were adopted. He felt certain that it would be very difficult for the Arabs in Palestine to accept the existence of an independent Jewish state and, should any open conflict arise, "the Jews are lost." With incredible insensitivity to the aspirations of the Jewish people at that time but apparently with total sincerity, Paulding recommended that "we had better ask the British to change their minds and stay in Palestine, and leave the Jews without a state."

On February 27, 1948, *Commonweal* returned to the question of Palestine, noting that the Arabs had declared that they would regard "any attempt by any power . . . to establish a Jewish state in Arab territory as an act of aggression which will be resisted in self-defense by force." The magazine was troubled that events were developing which would deliver the Jews into a land surrounded by hostile Arabs. It noted:

It is largely by our fault that the Jews feel they must have a separate place, that they cannot be, as so many of them earnestly desire, simply good Americans, or Austrians, or Frenchmen or Poles, good citizens of the country in which they, like the rest of us and their ancestors, like ours, were born and raised, and to which they, like us, felt they belonged until we Christians taught them to feel otherwise. . . .

There is grave danger that in taking the Jews out of the European concentration camps . . . and clearing an internationally guaranteed space for them, that space may become an international concentration camp, to which every country, looking for a political scapegoat, will upon occasion drive its Jews.

Commonweal's only response to its hypothesis was: "Yet, what is now the alternative?" The magazine limply concluded that America should probably stand by its vote in favor of the U.N. five-man Palestinian Committee.

On November 5, 1948, *Commonweal* exalted the sentiments of the Holy Father, who in an encyclical that deplored any destruction or damage to the holy places in Jerusalem had asked for an "international character for Jerusalem and its vicinity. . . ." The magazine, stressing the spiritual role of the pontiff, went out of its way to state that the Pope was "not concerned with the sovereignty of Israel, nor of any other state." It went on to understate or misstate the meaning of Jerusalem to Jews by declaring that, "for most of the Jews, Jerusalem is symbolic, not sacramental."

The editors of *Commonweal* today would almost certainly concede that their treatment of the emergence of Israel was episodic, disjointed, and inadvertently almost insulting to the Zionists of that era. Even the editors appeared to know practically nothing about the vision and dream of Theodor Herzl. Those who expressed their viewpoints in *Commonweal* during the dramatic months that witnessed the birth of a Jewish state reluctantly confessed that they did not disapprove of this development because they themselves did not have a better scenario to offer.

Other elements in the Catholic press were less favorably disposed toward the establishment of Israel. In April 1948 the *Sign* magazine, a popular family monthly, stated that "American backing for the Zionist cause comes chiefly from politicians and from kindly hearted people with a laudable sympathy for the sufferings of their Jewish people but a meager knowledge of history and geography." The politicians, the *Sign* editorial alleged, were trying to outdo one another in advocating Zionism in order to capture the "Jewish vote." The editorial did go on to warn the Arabs, however, that they should realize that "over half a million people who have come peacefully to the shores of Palestine, who have bought land, cultivated and irrigated it so that the deserts bloom, who have enriched the country with new industries and raised the general standard of living cannot be deprived of all rights and pushed back into the sea." The editorial concluded by suggesting vaguely that the United Nations should protect the rights of Jews and Arabs in Palestine but "also of the millions of Christians who look to Palestine as the birthplace of their religion, a land made sacred by the life and death of Jesus Christ."

The *Catholic World* was even more hostile to Israel. In an editorial comment in July 1948 the late Paulist editor Fr. James Gillis stated that America "declared the birth of Israel before it was well out of the womb." Once again the alleged political influence of the "Jewish vote" was deemed to be the cause of action taken by the United States at the U.N. The editorial referred to the "hysteria in the atmosphere of Madison Square Garden filled with 19,000 Zionists or Zionist sympathizers and some 75,000 more listening on the outside." The anger of Father Gillis —an anger which he protested did not make him anti-Jewish— derived apparently from his feeling that the Christians who had been subjugated by Russia in the satellite nations of eastern Europe should also have asylum or a refugee status. He warned the Jews in these words: "Will the Zionists themselves be as generous about finding a homeland for all other wanderers as they were about finding a home for themselves?"

Although Christians during the period when Israel was being established still looked upon Judaism only in relation to Christianity, it is perhaps consoling, nonetheless, that there was infinitely more sympathy for the Jewish and Zionist position in 1947 than there had been for such a position in possibly any previous period of the Christian Era. There was a feeling, however underdeveloped, that Christians must completely rethink virtually every concept which they had about Judaism. Christians also seemed to have some intuition that as a result of the holocaust and the founding of Israel the relationship between Christians and Jews could not and would not ever be the same again.

7

RESISTANCE BY
THE UNITED STATES GOVERNMENT
TO THE ESTABLISHMENT OF
THE STATE OF ISRAEL

The legal bonds which unite America and Israel are of long standing and deeply held. At the same time, paradoxically, they must be described as tenuous, somewhat ambiguous, and entered into with reluctance and caution. It is very important for the future of this relationship that its exact traditional, statutory, and diplomatic origins be fully understood.

When one views the unbroken friendship between the United States and Israel from 1948 to the present time one is astonished to learn of the enormous resistance offered by the highest officials of the American government in the years immediately prior to the establishment of the state of Israel.

In one of the first international agreements related to Palestine, the United States signed on December 3, 1924, a British-American convention which stated the following in Article VII:

Nothing contained in the present convention shall be affected by any modification which may be made in the terms of the mandate as recited above, unless such modification shall have been assented to by the United States.

One can argue logically that Great Britain violated this agreement by its reversal of previous policies in the White Paper of May 7, 1939. The interests of the United States and of Jews in America were adversely affected by this decree of Great Britain banning them from acquiring land in 94.8 per cent of western Palestine. Fifteen of the twenty-two members of the House Committee on Foreign Affairs, seven days after the publication of the White Paper, voted that it was a "clear repudiation" of the British-American convention on Palestine as well as the Balfour Declaration and the mandate of the League of Nations. The State Department, however, after months of delay, asserted in a lengthy statement that Article VII of the 1924 treaty did not "empower the government of the United States to prevent the modification of the terms of any of the mandates." What the State Department refused to recognize was the devastating effect of the White Paper which closed the gates of Palestine to Jewish victims of the Nazi persecution.

Shortly before the issuance of the British White Paper, President Roosevelt told a Jewish delegation who visited him that he had instructed the U.S. ambassador in England to demand that the British government's plan be postponed. Around that same time President Roosevelt, in a significant letter to Justice Brandeis, discussed a project by which several hundred thousand Arabs would be transferred from Palestine to Iraq in order to provide room in Palestine for the thousands of Jewish refugees in Europe.

Despite these protestations the Roosevelt Administration did little publicly or effectively about the White Paper which would limit all Jewish immigration into Palestine without Arab consent after March 31, 1944. Bartley C. Crum, a member in 1945 of the Anglo-American Commission of Inquiry on Palestine, described the conduct of the Roosevelt Administration in these words in his book, *Behind the Silken Curtain*:

Since September 15, 1938, each time a promise was made to American Jewry regarding Palestine, the State Department promptly sent messages to the Arab rulers discounting it and reassuring them in effect, that, regardless of what was promised publicly to the Jews, nothing would be done to change the situation in Palestine. . . .

On December 20, 1943, a resolution was unanimously endorsed by the Senate Foreign Relations Committee which would establish a special agency to aid in the rescue of European Jews. This resolution did not clear the House Committee on Foreign Affairs —owing to pressure from the State Department. Rabbi Stephen S. Wise testified before the House Committee that the Senate resolution was not adequate since it did not mention Palestine specifically as the country to which refugees should be taken.

On January 22, 1944, President Roosevelt by Executive Order established the War Refugee Board. This unit, created fifty-three months after the outbreak of the war and only fifteen months before the final collapse of Nazi Germany, accomplished little. The World Jewish Congress stated in a report that, if the board "had been set up some three years earlier, it might have spared humanity much agony and saved many, many lives."

In 1944 both the Republican and Democratic parties included comprehensive Zionist planks in their platforms. The Republicans unanimously adopted on June 27, 1944, the following language:

In order to give refuge to millions of distressed Jewish men, women and children driven from their homes by tyranny, we call for the opening of Palestine to their unrestricted immigration and land ownership, so that in accordance with the full intent and purpose of the Balfour Declaration of 1917 and the resolution of a Republican Congress in 1922, Palestine may be constituted as a free and democratic commonwealth. . . .

The Democratic plank adopted in July 1944 reiterated the commitment to unrestricted Jewish emigration to Palestine and the establishment there of a "free and democratic Jewish commonwealth."

Militants among American Zionists sent the following open letter to President Roosevelt on November 2, 1944:

> You promise us that action in favor of a Jewish commonwealth will be taken "as soon as practicable." What does this mean? For months, every vestige of a threat to the security of the Middle East has vanished, so that the much abused argument of "military expediency" can no longer even be advanced. Your own Secretary of State has recently acknowledged this fact. Every excuse for delay has gone. Why then is it not practical *now* to open the gates of Palestine to the Jews? . . .

The activist Zionists also asked this pointed question of President Roosevelt:

> You promised to help "if re-elected." Why? The candidate of an opposition party can make promises contingent only upon election. A President in office does not have to wait for election in order to carry out his promises. . . . Why, then, if you truly consider a Jewish Palestine a just and necessary aim, do you make your action on its behalf contingent upon re-election?

The Congress in October 1944 was far less reluctant than the Administration to commit itself to Israel. Of 535 members of the Seventy-eighth Congress, 411 endorsed the Zionist call for immediate American action to sanction a Jewish commonwealth in Palestine. In addition, 86 per cent of the Senate and 75 per cent of the House affirmed the Jewish right to settle Palestine, unimpeded by British restrictions imposed by the White Paper of 1939.

This resolution had little effect, however, because earlier in 1944 the House Committee on Foreign Affairs by a vote of 11 to 3 had capitulated to the wishes of the Secretary of War and had postponed indefinitely any further consideration of a resolution recommending that the doors of Palestine be opened for free entry of Jews. Later in 1944, on November 29, the House Foreign

Affairs Committee reported favorably on the resolution, but the Administration blocked concurrent action in the Senate.

A last attempt to secure the passage of a pro-Zionist resolution was made in a new Congress and under a new President. On October 26, 1945, a resolution calling for unrestricted immigration into Palestine was introduced in the House and Senate. It was a devastating disappointment to Zionists everywhere when, on November 29, 1945, President Truman declared at a press conference that he no longer favored the pro-Zionist resolution. White House opposition was not, however, able to prevent the passage of a resolution. A concurrent resolution, which does not require the President's signature, passed the House and Senate in late 1945. But it was clear then and thereafter that a resolution of Congress had very limited value if the executive branch did not act vigorously to create a Jewish national home open for the free entry of Jews from all of the nations of the earth.

Early in 1945 disappointment with and resentment against President Roosevelt's record on the Palestine question had become bipartisan and widespread. Roosevelt was clearly and specifically in defiance of the platform of the Democratic national convention. On March 18, 1945, Congressman Emanuel Celler, addressing a Zionist group in New York, spoke angrily of Roosevelt as follows:

"What of his mighty promise to reopen the doors of Palestine . . . a promise that garnered many votes? . . . They [the Jews] tipped the scales in favor of Roosevelt. They now look to Roosevelt with bewilderment. Why his silence? They cannot understand his retreat from fulfillment of his mighty promise."

The famed Rabbi Abba Hillel Silver stated in December 1946: "Throughout the Roosevelt Administration, the United States Government was determined to take no action whatsoever and to make no representation whatsoever to the British government either to open the doors of Palestine to Jewish immigration, or to live up to the other obligations which it had assumed under the mandate."

If President Roosevelt was deceptive and duplicitous with regard to the establishment of a Jewish state, President Truman actually went back on statements made by President Roosevelt and commitments given by the Democratic Party. In November 1945,

Truman announced the formation of a joint commission of inquiry into the Palestinian problem. This committee was looked
upon by knowledgeable people as an abdication by the United
States Government to the British policy on Palestine. The committee eventually recommended that 100,000 Jewish immigrants
be permitted to enter the Jewish area only of Palestine and that
the United States be asked to undertake the sole responsibility for
their transportation to Palestine.

After the inadequacy of this plan became very clear President
Truman proposed an extremely modest program by which special
legislation could authorize the entry into the United States of a
very limited number of displaced persons including Jews. This
proposal, made in 1946, was the first time that such a project had
ever been mentioned during the twelve years of the Nazi regime.
From 1933 to 1944, when hundreds of thousands of Europeans
had been made homeless, the American quota had been so administered that only 16.8 per cent of the authorized number of immigrants had actually come to the United States! Immigrants from
1936 to June 30, 1945, had averaged only 28,425 each year; the legally established annual quota was 153,879. In the fiscal year 1942,
only 10 per cent of the immigration quota was used; in 1943, 5 per
cent; in 1944, 6 per cent; and in 1945, 7 per cent.

During the awful months from May 1945 through September
1946, when hundreds of thousands of Jewish refugees were desperately looking for some place to go, only 5,718 Jews and displaced persons were admitted to the United States.

On December 22, 1945, President Truman declared that "This
period of unspeakable human distress is not the time for us to
close or narrow our gates." But he almost nullified this generous
statement with the proviso that he did not intend to ask Congress
to change the existing pattern of immigration and that "unused
quotas . . . do not accumulate through the years." The results
were meager; by April 1947 only 12,400 European immigrants, including some 8,000 Jews, had been admitted to the United States.

The attitude of Presidents Roosevelt and Truman stands in dramatic contrast to the evacuation in 1975 to the United States of
some 130,000 South Vietnamese citizens. President Ford, antici-
pating the inevitable downfall of the Saigon regime, exercised to

the full the inherent power of the President and the Attorney General to declare citizens of another nation to be political refugees and consequently eligible for a parole status to enter the United States. The Congress with minimal controversy ratified the actions of President Ford; actually the Congress had little choice since the South Vietnamese citizens who would allegedly be in danger of their lives if they remained in South Vietnam were irreversibly on their way to the United States when the Congress had to decide their destiny.

There appears to have been no serious thought within either the Roosevelt or the Truman Administration of exercising the power of declaring certain European Jews as political refugees eligible to enter the United States. In 1947 former U. S. Secretary of the Treasury Henry Morgenthau, Jr., confirmed that as early as August 1942 the United States Government had firm knowledge from many sources that Jews were being killed wholesale. Morgenthau wrote in November 1947 that "officials dodged their grim responsibility, procrastinated when concrete rescue schemes were placed before them, and even suppressed information about the atrocities in order to prevent an outraged public opinion from forcing their hand."

One can speculate or infer that it was anti-Semitism or an attitude very close to it that prevented the United States Government from acting to save the hundreds of thousands of European Jews whose captivity and slaughter were or should have been known about by American officials. America's failure to contribute even in a modest way to the solution of the refugee problem immediately after the war undoubtedly undermined the moral position of America on the Palestine issue. Obviously the United States appeared in a bad posture when it argued against Great Britain that 100,000 Jews should be permitted to emigrate to Palestine when simultaneously the United States Government would not relax its own immigration laws for the benefit of some of these homeless people. Ernest Bevin, speaking at a British Labor Party meeting on June 12, 1946, portrayed the American posture in a blunt and even boorish way with these words: "Regarding the agitation in the United States, and particularly in New York, for 100,000 to be put into Palestine, I hope it will not be misunderstood in America if I say, with the purest of motives, that that was because they do not want too many of them in New York."

The misgivings and contradictions in President Truman's attitudes with respect to Palestine apparently subsided as the plight of European Jews in the postwar world became more ghastly. In October 1946, President Truman spoke as follows:

"Furthermore, should a workable solution for Palestine be devised, I will be willing to recommend to the Congress a plan for economic assistance for the development of that country. In the light of the terrible ordeal which the Jewish people of Europe endured during the recent war and the crisis now existing, I cannot believe that a program of immediate action along the lines suggested above could not be worked out with the cooperation of all people concerned. . . ."

This first pledge of economic assistance to Israel by any American President provoked the angriest reactions in the Arab nations. Those countries were also distressed that President Truman on October 4 publicly announced for the first time his acceptance of a partition of Palestine along the lines suggested by the Jewish agency. President Truman proposed a "solution of the Palestinian problem by means of the creation of a viable Jewish state in control of its own immigration and economic policies in an adequate area of Palestine instead of in the whole of Palestine." That declaration was the beginning of the agonizingly slow evolvement of a U.S. policy which eventually led to the decision in November 1947 of the U. N. General Assembly which recommended the partition of Palestine by the required two-thirds majority vote, 33 to 13, with 10 abstentions.

8

PALESTINE BEFORE
THE UNITED NATIONS

The long and tortuous series of events between the end of World War II and the final establishment of Israel in May 1948 are described in an excellent book by Joseph B. Schechtman, *The United States and the Jewish State Movement* (1966). One can read many motives into the events that prompted the United States to be so ambivalent about acting affirmatively in the task of giving statehood to Israel. Mr. Schechtman chronicles every bit of evidence on how the question of Palestine eventually got to the United Nations and how it was resolved there. But the powerful oil interests of the Middle East were undoubtedly working on English public officials as well as on persons high in the American government. In addition, there was undoubtedly a pro-Arab attitude at the policy-making level of the State Department. There is no available evidence that Christian clergymen in England worked openly and vigorously against the establishment of Israel as did certain prominent Protestant clergymen in the United States. But the mere silence of the churches in all probability added to the reluctance and resistance of the American government to assist in the establishment of the Zionist dream.

It is distressing to discover that virtually no Christian writer during the years immediately prior to the establishment of Israel or in the years since that time has decried the silence of Christians during the period when the Jews sought after two thousand years to re-establish a homeland and a nation for themselves. Christian leaders had powerful and cherished connections with Christians in Arab lands. But is the desire to protect or advance Christianity in the Arab lands sufficient to justify the silence or quiet the opposition which Christian leaders offered to the establishment of Israel? Such an attitude on the part of Christian leaders in European nations and America can be explained only if these individuals felt that the survival of Judaism was not a matter of any concern. Christians could come to such an attitude if their theology told them that the Jewish religion had been superseded by Christianity and that its unique role in foreshadowing the Incarnation had long since been terminated. Many Christians without doubt hold such an erroneous position with regard to Judaism. They may not describe their attitude as contempt for Judaism, but the apathy and indifference to an institution which one deems to be an anachronism can very easily rise to the level of contempt.

This indifference to Judaism entered in all probability into the thinking of American public officials, who for three years after World War II were unable or unwilling to fight for a way which would allow the pitiable Jewish refugees to go to Palestine. In early 1946 it became clear that England was not about to relinquish a Palestinian mandate. In three decades of British rule Palestine had developed into an important link in the complex chain of direct and indirect controls that added up to the British imperial defense system in the Middle East.

On August 1, 1946, Winston Churchill added his booming voice to the increasing demand that England get out of Palestine. He recommended that England "lay our mandate at the feet of the United Nations organization and thereafter evacuate the country." This position was contrary to that of the United States Government and particularly to the policy makers in the State Department.

After endless delays and equivocation on the part of American officials, the United Nations finally appointed the Special Committee on Palestine. The committee signed its final report at Geneva on August 31, 1947. The majority report recommended in effect the early establishment of a sovereign Jewish state along with another Arab state within Palestine. The American attitude continued for some time to be ambiguous. Secreatary of State George Marshall was enigmatic. The State Department continued as usual to argue that a U.S. stand in favor of partition would alienate the five Arab member states of the United Nations as well as the new Moslem state of Pakistan—and thus throw the Arabs into the clutches of the Russians.

The stalemate was broken when the U.S.S.R., for reasons of its own, endorsed the Zionist-backed partition scheme. After that, events appeared to tumble, with or without United States approval, toward the dramatic day on November 29, 1947, when the General Assembly adopted the report of its Committee on Palestine and by a two-thirds vote recommended partition.

The joy of Zionists was intense, but the long and tragic series of Jewish-Arab wars began on the day after the U.N. partition decision. By January 18, 1948, a total of 720 Arabs and Jews had been killed and another 1,552 had been wounded.

The ghastly events in the Middle East prompted the Truman Administration to seek somehow to go back on the commitment which the United States had made and voted for in the partition of Palestine mandated by the United Nations. The indispensability of the United States at the present time to Israel makes the near withdrawal of American support in early 1948 look very foreboding indeed. It was undoubtedly the oil interests and a revived fear of Communism that heavily influenced thinking in Washington. President Truman in his memoirs expresses his annoyance at individuals whom he calls "extreme Zionists." He relates how he told his aides that he did not want "to be approached by any more spokesmen for the extreme Zionist cause." Truman was so upset at developments that he even put off seeing Dr. Chaim Weizmann. When he did finally see him on March 18, 1948, he assured Dr. Weizmann that the position of the United States had not changed in the least.

To the consternation of the world, however, twenty-four hours after Dr. Weizmann visited the White House, U. S. Ambassador Warren Austin announced at the Security Council a complete reversal of the U.S. position. He proposed a temporary trusteeship for Palestine under the Trusteeship Council of the United Nations. Ambassador Austin appears to have panicked at the increasing violence in Palestine and, as a result, utilized a dubiously valid legal argument that the United Nations did not automatically fall heir to the responsibilities either of the League of Nations or of the mandatory power of Great Britain.

It is uncertain whether President Truman even knew about the reversal of the U.S. policy on Palestine at the U.N. In his memoirs he acknowledges that "Some Zionist spokesmen branded this [the trusteeship proposal] as a reversal of American policy." He goes on to state that the trusteeship scheme "was not a rejection of partition, but rather an effort to postpone its effective date until proper conditions for the establishment of self government in the two parts (Jewish and Arab) might be established. . . ." On the very same page, however, President Truman contradicts himself when he states that anybody in the State Department "should have known . . . that the Jews would read this proposal as a complete abandonment of the partition plan on which they so heavily counted and that the Arabs would also believe that, like them, we had come to oppose the solution approved by the General Assembly." Truman concludes that, "in this sense, the trusteeship idea was at odds with my attitude and the policy I had laid down."

Although the trusteeship idea was clearly at odds with what the United States had committed itself to and what both the Jews and the Arabs understood by the decision of the General Assembly, Dean Rusk, then chief of the State Department's U. N. Division, came out vigorously in defense of the trusteeship plan.

Editorial opinion was outraged at the reversal of the Truman Administration. Angry grumblings came from the Zionists and from Palestine. The very concept of a trusteeship evaded and obscured the fundamental question of whether the Arabs would ultimately get control of the entire country or whether a part of it should be reserved for the Jews. The proposed trusteeship raised the most fundamental doubts about the ultimate American position. Some even felt that the entire trusteeship plan was merely an attempt to perpetuate under United Nations auspices the White Paper policy of 1939 and the ban on further Jewish emigration to Palestine.

The U.S.S.R. came out against the inexplicable trusteeship plan proposed at the eleventh hour by the United States. The Jewish community rejected the somewhat bizarre proposal made on May 3, 1948, by Dean Rusk, then Assistant Secretary of State. Rusk proposed an extension of the mandate for ten days after May 15, the date of its expiration. He also proposed an emergency trip to Israel by air of designated Arab and Jewish representatives.

Rusk's ideas, as well as the whole concept of trusteeship, faded away and the state of Israel was formally proclaimed, as scheduled, at midnight on May 14, 1948.

The confusion and chaos in the State and Defense Departments, as revealed in the diaries of James Forrestal, must be said to be frightening to persons who wanted then the establishment of Israel and who now desire the safety and security of that nation.

Perhaps President Truman learned to distrust the State Department on Israel as a result of the proposed trusteeship—an idea which has been attributed only to the State Department. With respect to the recognition of Israel, President Truman kept his own counsel and at 6:00 P.M. on May 14, 1948, issued the following statement:

This government has been informed that a Jewish state has been proclaimed in Palestine and recognition has been requested by the provisional government thereof.

The United States recognizes the provisional government as the *de facto* authority of the new state of Israel.

The State Department continued its vendetta against the new state. They were concededly not supporters of Truman's first ambassador, the Honorable James G. McDonald. They perpetuated the de facto instead of de jure status as long as they could. President Truman noted in his *memoirs* that he "was well aware that some of the State Department experts would want to block recognition of the Jewish state." He added that this would not be so "if these men had faithfully supported my policy."

It is disappointing and distressing to find so little real thought or reflection in all that the United States did in the events that led up to the recognition of Israel. No great debate took place on a national level and few if any congressional hearings were conducted in order to establish precisely what Israel should mean in the foreign policy of the United States. Israel was created in a time of emergency when it was desperately necessary to find a haven for thousands of refugees. Its existence was fought by the State Department for reasons which they never discussed or disclosed. Because of the great ambiguity in American policy no one even proposed that there should be a treaty between the United States and Israel. Despite all of the rhetoric about American-Israeli friendship in the first three decades of the life of Israel, the simple fact is that the United States agreed to the creation of Israel only after great misunderstandings were overcome and after powerful objections by powerful people and corporations in America had been set aside.

9

THE MIRACLE OF ISRAEL'S REBIRTH

On May 14, 1948, the seventh and last British High Commissioner for Palestine, General Sir Alan Cunningham, departed from Jerusalem. It was twenty-six years since Britain had been charged by a mandate of the League of Nations to "ensure the peace and security" of Palestine. The League's mandate also required Great Britain to "facilitate the establishment of a Jewish national home." Despite some moments of compliance, it had not "facilitated" a national home for the Jews. It had, however, facilitated an increase in the number of Arab states from seven to eight and ultimately to eighteen. Britain had been the first nation to endorse the idea of national independence for a Jewish community in Palestine, but even Britain, which had valiantly resisted Hitler, became confused in the implementation of its policy with respect to Palestine.

The 650,000 Jews in Israel on May 14, 1948, knew their destiny. The members of the National Council, the provisional government of Israel, met together at Tel Aviv and heard the prayer "Blessed art Thou, our God, King of the Universe, who has kept us in life and sustained us—and enabled us to reach this day." The representatives of the new state proclaimed to the world:

> Accordingly we, the members of the National Council, representing the Jewish people in Palestine and the Zionist movement of the world, met together in solemn assembly today, the date of the termination of the British mandate for Palestine; by virtue of the national and historic right of the Jewish people and of the resolution of the General Assembly of the United Nations; hereby proclaim the establishment of the Jewish State in Palestine—to be called Israel. . . .

The first sovereign act of the new government of Israel was to annul all laws enacted by the British government in accord with the Palestinian White Paper of 1939, which had restricted the emigration of Jews into Palestine and had forbidden the purchase of land by Jews in all but 5 per cent of its area. In a meeting of the provisional government that lasted thirty-two minutes, a Jewish state was proclaimed for the first time since the victory of the Roman legions in the year A.D. 70.

There is nothing in all of history to compare with this resurrection of a people in a land from which they had been separated for nearly nineteen centuries. Supporting the movement that brought about the birth of Israel in 1948 were the undeniable facts that the land now called Israel had given birth to no other single nation and that the Jewish people had not achieved a collective identity in any other land. The mystery and the miracle of the establishment of Israel are compounded by the fact that Israel, unlike any nation known to history, had not been born of a revolution against an occupying power or by a migration to an unknown land. In addition to these unique features, the people of Israel in 1948 still employed the language and embraced the faith which their ancestors occupying the same land had maintained more than three thousand years before.

Perhaps the most significant change in Jewish history came about because the Jews in Israel, for the first time in many centuries, would have some control over their own destiny. The primordial phenomenon in all of Jewish history had been the passivity of the Jewish people; Jewish history was what Jews had endured, resisted, or survived.

In retrospect, one would have thought that the 650,000 Jews in Palestine in 1948—where they had constituted a majority for more than a century—would have been able to placate gradually those non-Jews who felt cheated by the decree of the United Nations. After all, the U.N. partition of 1947 meant that only one half of one per cent of all Arabs were to be a minority in Israel. The same decree ceded only one sixth of one per cent of all of the territory inhabited by the Arabs to Israel. In view of all of the militant claims to Arab solidarity, one would have hoped that the Palestinians could find a home in any one of the score of Arab states. From the beginning, however, the violence of Arab resistance was incredible. The seven governments of the Arab League were conspiring before the mandate's last official hour to destroy Israel even as it was being born. At the break of dawn on May 14, 1948, Egyptian forces advanced into the Negev. The Arab Legion of Trans-Jordan was deployed along the river, and a Syrian brigade was prepared to attack Jewish farming villages in the northern sections of Israel. The U.N. declaration of November 1947 had promised Israel "security, peace and order," but the U.N. could not prevent Egyptian aircraft from dropping their first bombs on Tel Aviv at dawn on May 15, 1948. Although this attack by an Arab nation was now against a recognized member of the family of nations, since the United States and the Soviet Union had recognized Israel, the United Nations still appeared to be incapable of condemning that aggression, which was in violation of the most important section of the U. N. Charter.

The United Nations, born as an anti-Nazi alliance, gave legitimacy to a Jewish state, but it has never been able to give any assurance of the survival of that state. In open defiance of the U.N. partition and Israel's acceptance by the family of nations as an independent sovereign state on May 14, 1948, the Arab states were in defiance of these decrees from December 2, 1947, to January 7, 1949.

This first War of Independence waged by Israel with virtually no significant assistance from any other nation brought to the people of Israel a unique self-reliance grounded in and justified by the undeniable fact that no nation would risk its manpower or even its arms despite the fact that destruction stared Israel in the face. When one considers the lack of all outside sources, it is astonishing that the Haganah, the amateurish and improvised Jewish armed forces, could have rebuffed so successfully the multiple invasions launched by powerful and well-armed Arab governments. Abba Eban, in his moving book *My Country, the Story of Modern Israel*, states that the war of independence could have gone the other way if the Arab nations had been better organized.

Arab insurgency, after Israel's Independence Day on May 14, demonstrated for the first time that small nations do not abandon their plans when Moscow and Washington stand together against them. Syria, Lebanon, Iraq, Trans-Jordan, and Egypt launched their invasions in direct defiance of a vigorously held American-Soviet position.

A truce negotiated by Count Folke Bernadotte for the U. N. Security Council came into operation on June 11, 1948. At the expiration of this truce one month later, a fierce Egyptian assault commenced. When the Security Council met on July 15, both American and Soviet representatives lashed out at the Arab governments. A resolution was adopted that ordered a cease-fire and threatened the Arab governments with sanctions under the U. N. Charter if they once again defied the United Nations. The Arabs, as much humiliated by the decay of their military resistance as by the strength of international pressure, agreed on July 18 to the truce.

The losses in the War of Independence to the Arab nations were heavy. Israel lost 4,000 soldiers and 2,000 civilians. If a comparable loss had occurred in the United States 1.5 million persons would have been killed.

The memories and the myths of the War of Independence have entered into the psyche of the Israeli people. The victory which they achieved despite almost insurmountable odds contributed to the confidence which Israelis have had since that time in the inherent coherence of a nation deeply divided by cultural and linguistic diversities. There are, nonetheless, Jews in Israel and non-

Jews throughout the world who, even thirty years after the War of Independence, are still startled at the image of a Jewish state being superior in military tactics and strategy. There are also not a few observers who wonder whether the militarism which was indispensable in 1947 and 1948 has engendered attitudes in Israel which may tend to exaggerate the indispensability of military force as a weapon for survival.

It is disappointing to have to note that there exist very few reflections from a Christian viewpoint about the tumultuous events that led to the re-establishment of a Jewish state. Rabbi Abraham Joshua Heschel states in 1969 in his book, *Israel: An Echo of Eternity*, that the return of the Jews to Israel is the action of God, the Lord of history. Rabbi Heschel maintains that the formation of Israel is not only an answer to Auschwitz but also a realization of the Promise. He writes as follows:

> It is dangerous to regard political affairs as religious events; yet since the time of Abraham we were taught that political affairs are to be understood within the orbit of God's concern. We must not expect the history of politics to read like a history of theology. Instances of God's care in history come about in seeming disarray, in scattered fashion—we must seek to comprehend the unity of the seemingly disconnected cords.
>
> To the eyes of the heart, it is clear that returning to the land is an event in accord with the hidden Presence in Jewish history. It is a verification of a biblical promise. It has saved so many lives, it has called for so much dedication and sacrifice, it has revived hope. Returning to the land is an event in which the past endures, in which the future is foreshadowed. . . .

This conclusion by Rabbi Heschel is built upon that profound and persistent yearning for return to the land that has always characterized Judaism.

A Christian will accept Rabbi Heschel's conclusion if he realizes that the Old Testament affirms a lasting union between God and the Jewish people. One of the forceful declarations of the per-

manent nature of this union can be seen in the Book of Hosea.
After this prophet had portrayed Israel as the Lord's unfaithful
wife who had run after false gods, he nonetheless stated:

> *I betroth you to myself forever;*
> *I betroth you in truth and in justice,*
> *In tender love and in mercy.*
> *I betroth you to myself in faithfulness,*
> *And you will know the Lord* (2:19–21).

In view of the undeniably permament alliance between God
and His chosen people, Monsignor John M. Oesterreicher stated
in 1971, in the *Bridge,* an annual volume of Christian-Jewish dialogue, that in his judgment the success of Israel

> is not altogether due to the cunning of her statesmen, the su-
> perior strategy of her generals, the bravery of her soldiers, and
> the steadfastness of her citizens. Rather was it the "out-
> stretched arm" (Exodus 6:6) of the Lord which once more
> rescued His people. . . .
> If God entered history, a Christian cannot but get involved
> in the struggle of men to make the society that they live in
> more human and thus more worthy of His name. Even less
> can he stand aloof as God's chosen people wrestle to lead a
> life of dignity.

Monsignor Oesterreicher, a convert from Judaism, concludes
that "today's Israel is new proof that God stands by His covenant; that the last word lies, not with the inventor of the one
'final solution,' but with Him."
The total centrality to contemporary Judaism of the establishment of Israel is a fact which does not appear to have penetrated very deeply into today's literature on Christian-Jewish relations. Indeed, many Christian writers appear not even to treat the
establishment of Israel as a political phenomenon that is crucial
and central to any meaningful dialogue which might develop between Jews and non-Jews. For the Jew in the modern world
Auschwitz, Belsen, Treblinka are not past events but a searing

challenge to every person alive today. Likewise the establishment of Israel is for the Jew an event that has divided the past from the future because it represents the collective affirmation of the world's Jews that they will no longer tolerate ghettos and pogroms in nations which claim to be Christian.

Modern-day Christians must make their own investigation of these events. To use a Hebrew term, a midrash is required. A midrash is the most intimate dialogue between the despairing human soul and its creator. Christianity after both Auschwitz and the founding of Israel must conduct its own midrash on what Christians must do to eliminate every possibility of another holocaust and to prevent the destruction of Israel. Until or unless Christians conduct an exhaustive midrash on these two agonizing questions they do not have the right to call themselves persons who believe in the God of Abraham, Isaac, and Jacob.

10

THE PALESTINIAN REFUGEES:
THE PROBLEM THAT WON'T GO AWAY

From the very beginning of Jewish return to Palestine the Zionists who settled in the Middle East assumed and asserted that a friendly Arab state contiguous to Israel was desirable and necessary. David Ben-Gurion, in his volume *Rebirth and Destiny of Israel*, records that as early as 1931 he had stated that the Arab "right to live in Palestine, develop it and win national autonomy is as incontrovertible as is ours to independence. The two can be realized. We must in our work in Palestine respect Arab rights." Similarly, Chaim Weizmann told the Fourteenth Zionist Congress that "Palestine must be built up without violating the legitimate interests of the Arabs—not a hair of their heads shall be touched. . . ." Weizmann added that the 600,000 Arabs who lived in Palestine had "exactly the same right to their homes as we have to our national home."

It may be that subsequent Zionists and Israelis failed to implement the clear and unmistakable intention of the Jewish founders of Israel. This point is made in a comprehensive and objective book on the Middle East, *The Arab-Israeli Dilemma*, by Professor Fred J. Khouri. Writing in 1968, this author concluded that "the

Zionists failed to treat the Arabs as equal, to cultivate better relations with them, or to consider objectively and realistically how
the problem of the Arabs in a future state could be justly and pa-
cifically resolved." Khouri conceded that Arabs also made mistakes.
He noted, for example, that in the years between the two world
wars most "Palestinian Arab leaders often took negative and intransigent positions, and, by insisting upon getting everything, they
ended up with practically nothing."

The confrontation between Israel and the Palestinian Arabs had
its genesis in the emigration of perhaps 590,000 Arabs from Israel
in 1947 and 1948. But even the very number of refugees has remained in doubt during the thirty-year debate over this agonizing
problem. The Arabs claimed that the number was almost 800,000.
The United Nations' economic survey placed the number of refugees after partition at 726,000. The Israelis said that the number
was about 550,000.

Terence Prittie, in an essay in the volume *The Palestinians—
People, History, Politics*, issued in 1975 by the American Aca-
demic Association for Peace in the Middle East, argues that a
maximum of 590,000 Arabs could have been displaced. He reasons
that fewer than 1.2 million Arabs resided in all of Palestine before
the War of 1947–48. Of this number, 450,000 to 550,000 lived in
areas not ultimately occupied by Israel. Since 160,000 Arabs remained in or returned to Israel, a maximum of 590,000 of the
750,000 Arabs in Israel at the time of partition could have emigrated.

The entire problem is made much more difficult because the
last census that had been taken in Palestine was under the British
mandate in 1931; the Arab nations refused to cooperate in that
count.

The reasons why at least 500,000 Arabs left Palestine are as
open to question as the actual number who fled. There is objective evidence that Israelis in many instances urged Arab residents
to remain. The British supervisor of police in Haifa dated April
26, 1948, reported:

Every effort is being made by the Jews to persuade the
Arab population to stay and carry on with their normal lives,

to get their shops and businesses open and to be assured that their lives and interests would be safe.

The London *Economist,* on October 2, 1948, reported on the migration in these words:

> The Jewish authorities who were now in complete control . . . urged all Arabs to remain and guaranteed them protection and security. . . . However, of the 62,000 Arabs who lived in Haifa, not more than 5,000–6,000 remain. Various factors influenced their decision to seek safety in flight. There is but little doubt that the most potent of these was the announcement made over the air by the Arab Higher Executive, urging all Arabs in Haifa to quit. The reason given was that upon the final withdrawal of the British (May 15) the combined armies of the Arab states would invade Palestine and drive the Jews into the sea, and it was clearly intimated that those Arabs who remained in Haifa and accepted Jewish protection would be regarded as renegades.

It is also significant that the Israel Proclamation of Independence issued on May 14, 1948, contained this paragraph:

> In the midst of wanton aggression, we call upon the Arab inhabitants of the State of Israel to return to the ways of peace and play their part in the development of the State of Israel with full and equal citizenship and with due representation in all its bodies and institutions.

In the extensive literature concerned with the reasons for the Arab migration there is frequent reference to the massacre of 200 Arabs in the village of DerYasin on April 9, 1948. This tragic incident was brought about by a Jewish terrorist group in retaliation for Arab killings of Jews. The leaders of the Zionist movement vigorously denounced the actions of the terrorists and, because of the massacre, became absolutely determined to break up all secret Jewish terrorist organizations.

Utilizing evidence that suggests an opposite conclusion, Professor Khouri asserts that "Israeli authorities used both military force and psychological warfare to compel as many Arabs as possible to leave their homes. . . ." Israelis were motivated toward this alleged course of action in order to "lessen the danger of Arab espionage and threats to Israeli lines of communication." He also states that the Jews urged the Arabs to leave in order to "provide desperately needed land and buildings for the Jewish immigrants pouring in."

It appears that, whatever the actual truth may be about the ultimate reasons for the vast migration of Arabs, the positions taken by Israelis and Arabs immediately after the event have not been altered in any significant way over the past thirty years. The attitudes of the opposing parties are now the same as they were found to be in 1954 in the report of a special congressional study mission to the Middle East. That document asserts that "the Arabs state without equivocation that the refugees were driven from their homes by the Israelis . . . (and) . . . that Israel's frequent expressions of willingness to negotiate a peace are fraudulent." The report notes that the Israelis, on the other hand, assert that "the refugees left their homes voluntarily or under orders from Arab leaders with the assurance that Israel would be destroyed and all Israeli property confiscated." The congressional study also notes that the Israelis are persuaded "that the Arab politicians are exploiting the refugee question as a means of furthering their own selfish purposes. . . ."

Some months after the establishment of Israel in May 1948 the United Nations' mediator, Count Bernadotte, requested Israel to repatriate some of the refugees. He assured Israel that the refugees seeking repatriation would be carefully screened by U.N. officials to eliminate potential terrorists or security risks. Israeli officials were not prepared to accept this recommendation since, in their judgment, Israel was still in a state of war. Bernadotte reported on this matter to the U.N. as follows:

It is . . . undeniable that no settlement can be just and complete if recognition is not accorded to the rights of the Arab refugee to return to the home from which he has been dislodged by the hazards and strategy of the armed

conflict. . . . The exodus resulted from the panic created by
the fighting in their communities, by rumors concerning real
or alleged acts of terrorism, or expulsion. It would be an
offense against the principles of elemental justice if those innocent victims of the conflict were denied the right to return
to their homes while Jewish immigrants flow into Palestine.

In response to the appeals of Bernadotte, the General Assembly of the United Nations passed unanimously on November 19,
1948, a resolution which established the agency which was to become the United Nations Relief and Works Agency for Palestinian refugees (UNRWA).

On December 11, 1948, the General Assembly established a
conciliation commission with instructions to facilitate the repatriation and economic rehabilitation of the Palestinian refugees. A
key section of that resolution read as follows:

> Resolves that the refugees wishing to return to their homes
> and live in peace with their neighbors should be permitted to
> do so at the earliest practicable date, and that compensation
> should be paid for the property of those choosing not to re-
> turn and for the loss of damage to property which, under the
> principles of international law or equity, should be made by
> the governments or bodies responsible.

Israel's reaction to this and similar recommendations was to insist that the return of the refugees was contingent upon the establishment of formal peace. Israel's fear of a "fifth column" of repa-
triated refugees within its own borders was so strong that on June
16, 1948, Prime Minister Ben-Gurion asserted to his Cabinet that
"No Arab refugee should be admitted back." The resistance of
the Israel government to the return of the refugees was so strong
that on May 29, 1949, President Truman, writing to Ben-Gurion,
expressed his "deep disappointment at the failure" of Israel to act
on the refugee matter. Truman "interpreted Israel's attitude as
dangerous to peace" and urged that "tangible refugee concessions
should be made now as an essential preliminary to any prospect
for a general settlement." Truman went so far as to state that if

Israel did not act on this matter "the United States would reconsider its attitude towards Israel."

Several weeks later Israel, once again pressed by the United States, offered to take 100,000 refugees but only if these persons could be settled in such a way as not to endanger the security of Israel. But this offer, rejected by the Arabs as inadequate and resisted by many Israeli citizens on the grounds of security, never came to fruition.

The stalemate about the repatriation of Arab refugees was made even more complicated by a major exodus of Jews from Iraq and other Arab countries to Israel. This influx, which eventually would number 800,000 Jews, permitted Israeli officials to assert that in any future negotiations on the return of refugees Israel would hold Arab governments responsible for Jewish properties involuntarily abandoned in Arab nations.

By 1953 there were 872,000 Palestinian refugees depending upon assistance from UNRWA. Over half of them resided in Jordan, one fourth in the Gaza Strip, and the balance in Lebanon and Syria. Some commentators urge that Arab nations could have assimilated these people if they had so desired. The problem, however, is not that simple since in young Jordan there was no governmental machinery to care for this mass influx of persons. In Lebanon the government was based upon a delicate Christian-Moslem balance that assumed six Christians for every Moslem. If the Palestinian refugees had been accepted as citizens they would have increased the population of Lebanon by 10 per cent, thus threatening the delicate ethnic balance. Egypt, already suffering from an exploding population and a declining per capita income, could not risk having the rural Palestinian refugees settle in the already overcrowded Nile Valley region.

Despite intense pressure from many sources to allow the Palestinian refugees to repatriate, the very possibility of any substantial resettlement became more remote as attitudes on both sides hardened. Serious border clashes and a mounting arms race in 1955 and thereafter brought about a deterioration in Israel-Arab feelings and relationships. In 1955 the growth of strong anti-Arab feelings among Israelis was signaled by the substantial gains which activist groups like the Herut made in the Knesset elections. Furthermore, the purchase by Egypt of huge amounts of sophisticated modern weaponry from the Soviet bloc intensified Israel's fear and hostility with respect to her Arab neighbors. In addition, "repatriation" became in effect an Arab code word for a migration which would signify the annihilation of Israel.

As each year passed the very concept of repatriation was deemed by Israelis and many others to be unrealistic. It was pointed out, for example, that the Palestinians were the only large group of refugees in all of modern history to be the recipients of long-term care and maintenance carried out by an international agency. Commentators noted that the West German Federal Government was successfully absorbing some nine million people into that nation. Likewise, fifteen million refugees in India and Pakistan had made their peace with the political realities around them and accepted either integration or resettlement.

The 1954 U. S. House of Representatives report, noted above, stated that "the objectives should be for refugees to become citizens of the Arab states and, if necessary, they should be made wards of the Arab governments pending admission to citizenship." The report went on to urge that the "United States should serve notice that it will not support the return of the Arab refugees to their former homes within the boundaries of Israel under existing conditions."

In June 1959, U. N. Secretary General Dag Hammarskjöld, recognizing that repatriation was unrealistic, proposed an expenditure of almost $2 billion to be expended over the following five years in order to create productive jobs for a million refugees in Arab lands. The proposal was unequivocally rejected by the Arab nations because it did not call for repatriation. In the next session of the General Assembly the Arabs persuaded the U.N. to shelve the creative and constructive Hammarskjöld project.

Several offers by the highest Israeli officials for compensation to the refugees were rejected by spokesmen for the Palestinians. In November 1958, for example, Abba Eban stated Israel's willingness to compensate the refugees. At the 1963 session of the U. N. Special Political Committee, Golda Meir expressed the desire of the Israeli government to negotiate directly on the refugee issue with the hope of arriving at a mutually satisfactory settlement. On October 8, 1968, Israel's Foreign Minister, Abba Eban, put forth a nine-point peace proposal at the U. N. General Assembly. He announced that Israel would intensify its family unification program, expedite the processing of hardship cases among refugees who had crossed to the East Bank during the June 1967 war, and charter a five-year plan for the resolution of the refugee problem. The response to this proposal was the oft-heard Arab demand that Israel first withdraw from every inch of land deemed by the Arabs to be their own territory.

An outstanding summary of the total conflict of evidence and the complete clash of absolutes with respect to the refugee matter can be viewed in twenty pages (pages 161–81) of Professor Khouri's volume *The Arab-Israeli Dilemma*. Khouri's analysis is as objective and impartial as one could wish for. He states very firmly that "there is little hope that a final solution of the refugee issue could be arrived at until . . . the Arabs and the Israelis have decided to seek a political solution to all of their major differences." Khouri agrees with Martin Buber and those supporting the liberal Israeli magazine *New Outlook*, who have reasoned for many years that the risks inherent in the repatriation of Arabs are less serious than the risks implicit in allowing the Palestinian refugee question to fester and contaminate the entire relationship between Israel and the Arab governments that surround her.

The emergence of the Palestinian Liberation Organization (PLO), to be outlined in a subsequent chapter, reveals some of the long-range dangers in the thinking of some persons that the passage of years would somehow resolve the refugee question into some form of de facto settlement.

It is distressing to have to note that the involvement of Christian churches in the Palestinian refugee question during the years 1948 to 1968 was minimal at best. In 1968, Dr. David Hunter, Deputy General Secretary of the National Council of Churches, and Dr. A. Dudley Ward, General Secretary of the United Methodist Board of Christian Social Concerns, felt compelled to condemn publicly a report submitted to the NCC on the refugee problem. Dr. Ward said that, in his judgment, "The Churches have failed to deal with the central causes of refugees in the Middle East." He went on to state that if the churches had been energetic and forceful in the past twenty years in support of recognition of Israel and in asking questions about the alliances of nations such as Egypt, the churches would have contributed enormously to the resolution of the refugee problem.

It is neither productive nor constructive to explore the issue of culpability for the growth and persistence of the Palestinian refugee problem. Rabbi Balfour Brickner wrote in 1969:

> The economic and social deprivation which the Arab refugees have suffered is real and tragic. Through no fault of their own these poor people have been squeezed in the pincers of an impersonal international political nutcracker.

There is no doubt that the continued existence of refugee camps constitutes a problem for Israel in global public opinion. Those who criticize Israel for not being more resourceful and determined through the past thirty years with regard to this problem are not necessarily being unjust or excessively harsh with Israel; these critics simply reflect what a strong minority opinion in Israel has affirmed since the very beginning of the refugee problem.

At the same time some people undoubtedly employ the existence of refugee camps as a device to express their misgivings about the very existence of Israel or, even worse, their latent or overt anti-Semitism. Eric Hoffer, the longshoreman-philosopher, pungently observed:

> The Jews are a peculiar people: things permitted to the other nations are forbidden to the Jews . . . other nations drive out thousands, even millions of people and theirs is no refugee problem. . . . Everyone expects the Jews to be the only real Christians in this world.

185070

The Committee on International Relations of the U. S. House of Representatives conducted hearings in the fall of 1975 on "The Palestinian Issue in Middle East Peace Efforts." Dr. Mordechai Abir, professor of Middle Eastern Studies at Hebrew University in Jerusalem, one of the witnesses at those hearings, rejected the idea

of a "mini-state" on the West Bank. At the same time he endorsed "a Palestinian State either in a form of a federation or a
unitary one with Jordan"—assuming that the West Bank can be
properly demilitarized. Professor Abir concluded with these words,
which offer some hope for the settlement of an agonizing situation that constitutes a constant threat to peace in the Middle
East:

> I know that the Israeli people are strong in their desire for
> a lasting peace. I know also that they recognize that the
> Palestinian problem had its roots in the general Arab-Israeli
> conflict, and that this problem can only find a solution
> within the context of an overall Arab acceptance of Israel
> and peaceful sentiment. Within the Israeli body politic, there
> is a broad spectrum of opinion as to what should constitute
> the final shape of an Arab-Israel peace. Recent polls demon-
> strate that the great majority of Israelis are neither extreme
> hawks nor extreme doves. Most Israelis continue to evince a
> spirit of compromise and accommodation which flexibly
> looks towards peace and a solution to the Palestinian prob-
> lem, hopefully in the near future.

The fact that some of the refugee camps in Lebanon and Syria
have become training grounds for the Palestinian Liberation Organization constitutes another reason why Israeli "doves" desire to
have a settlement as quickly as possible. Some 40,000 people died
in the civil war in Lebanon in 1975–76; this massacre is partly attributable to the fact that 196,885 registered "refugees" reside in
camps in Lebanon where the PLO has transformed UNRWA
centers into military bases. The PLO had tried to do this, of
course, unsuccessfully in Jordan until they were expelled in 1970
by King Hussein.

The inevitable question about whether the United States will
continue to contribute to UNRWA offers another inducement to
Israelis to settle as quickly as possible. Until 1975, UNRWA had
spent $1,046,000,000; the United States had contributed approxi-
mately 60 per cent or $619 million of this total. In 1975 the
United States increased its normal contribution from $26.7 mil-

lion to $42.5 million because UNRWA faced a serious deficit due to a diminution in contributions.

The sheer size of the estimated three million Palestinians obviously causes the people of Israel passionately to desire a solution. About half of that number are registered with UNRWA. Palestinians residing in Jordan number 625,857: 292,922 on the West Bank; 333,031 in Gaza; 196,855 in Lebanon; 184,042 in Syria. An estimated 800,000 of the 1,632,000 Palestinians receive rations, but about 40 per cent of the total UNRWA budget goes either for health services or for classroom expenses.

During the 1975 congressional debate about the authorization of some $2.2 billion for economic and military assistance to Israel the idea was expressed that this sum or a substantial part of it should be allocated for the repatriation or resettlement of the refugees. An analogy was made to the 100,000 Turks on the island of Cyprus; it was contended that if the United States would resettle or repatriate these 100,000 people the tension and conflict which they caused by living on the island of Cyprus with some 400,000 Greeks would be abated. The problem is, of course, that the Turks, like the Arabs, would in all probability not accept such a solution. The Turks fear Greek imperial aspirations, and the Arabs fear Israeli expansionism.

Geographically, it would appear to be relatively simple to find ways to resettle the Palestinian Arabs who live in refugee camps. The Arab League states have 5.2 million square miles compared to the tiny 8,000 square miles in Israel. But for emotional, psychological, and historical reasons a rapprochement between the Israelis and the Arabs must in all likelihood precede any satisfactory and permanent resettlement of the Palestinians.

Contrary to many popular impressions, Israel's official recognition of Arab or Palestinian identity has been clearly stated at the highest levels of the Israeli nation over a period of years. On July 21, 1974, the government of Israel called for "negotiations without prior conditions" for peace arrangements with the Arab states, including Jordan. The Israeli statement declared that a peace agreement with Jordan would be founded on the existence of two independent states—"Israel, with United Jerusalem as its capital, and a Jordanian-Palestinian Arab state, east of Israel, within borders to be determined in negotiations between Israel and Jordan."

That position was reaffirmed by Israel's Foreign Minister when he addressed the U. N. General Assembly on September 30, 1975. At that time he stated: "It is self-evident that genuine peace in the Middle East must include a just and constructive solution of the Palestinian Arab problem." He made it clear that the solution must be found "in the context of a peace agreement between Israel and Jordan which constitutes the major part of the area of historic Palestine on both sides of the River Jordan—as well as being the homeland of the great majority of the Palestinian Arabs."

There is no one in Israel or indeed in the entire world who is not apprehensive over the stiffening resistance to the Israeli government on the part of 670,000 Palestinian Arabs who reside in occupied West Jordan. The residual and possibly rising resentment by Israel's own 500,000 Arab citizens must also be disquieting to Israeli authorities.

But the most difficult question for the United States Congress to resolve is whether or not further subsidization of the Palestinian refugees constitutes inadvertent and indirect aid to the PLO, which is overtly and covertly seeking to organize the refugees into an intransigent guerrilla force designed to harass and attack Israel. If Congress concludes that the financial assistance from the U.N. and from the United States to the refugee camps makes the ambitions of the PLO more achievable, a decision will have to be made as to whether such funds contribute to turmoil and a stalemate rather than to peace.

In order to come to a well-informed judgment on this matter, the background of the PLO and Mr. Yasir Arafat must be explored in depth.

11

THE EMERGENCE OF THE PLO
AND MR. YASIR ARAFAT

In January 1964 the Palestine Liberation Organization (PLO) was established at the first Arab summit meeting in Cairo. Although Egypt became at first the main center for the PLO, the new organization rather quickly became the unifying group for the principal terrorist organizations. The activities of the PLO were not by nature or by origin significantly different from the persistent terrorist activities conducted directly by Arab governments against Israel between 1949 and 1964.

In the beginning the PLO made no demands for the establishment of a Palestinian state. To some extent the PLO was the creation of Egyptian President Gamal Abd-al Nasser, who intended to use it as a propaganda and military weapon against Israel. Nasser, then at the height of his power, also intended to use the PLO to bring Jordan under Egyptian domination. With this in view, the Palestinian Army of Liberation was funded by Egyptian money and its manpower was drawn almost completely from the refugee camps.

The establishment of the PLO in Egypt in 1964 inspired similar terrorist organizations in Syria, Lebanon, Iraq, and Jordan. These groups might have been relatively unknown by the entire world even today were it not for their "discovery" by Western television. The taped and filmed essays launched the concept that the Palestinians had been despoiled of their territory and that they were receiving intensive training in the use of weapons in order to regain their "lost homeland." The televised "documentaries" soon produced a star: Yasir Arafat.

But even today few individuals know that, between January 1965 and June 1967, Arafat, with the assistance of the Syrian government, launched 113 sabotage operations against Israel.

In February 1969, Arafat acquired a predominant role for himself and his organization in the Palestinian National Council—the governing board of the PLO.

Despite the splintered nature and the factionalism within the PLO, there can be little doubt that this organization became and remains an organ of the Arab governments and an instrumentality of the Arab League Council. Since at least the Arab summit conference in Rabat in December 1969, the PLO has enjoyed massive financial and military assistance from the Arab governments.

No later than 1970, the PLO set aside all pretense that it was carrying out only a popular struggle for resistance operations against Israel. The truth was that the majority of the Arab population in the areas administered after 1967 by Israel refused to support the terrorist endeavors of the PLO. As a result, the leaders of the Syrian-originated El Fatah, a part of the PLO, decided in 1971 to adopt a policy of launching terrorist attacks against Israeli targets in foreign countries. Thus was Black September created— as a cover for terrorist operations of El Fatah against the Jordanian establishment and in foreign nations.

The terrorist activities of the PLO began on July 23, 1968, with the first hijacking of an El Al airliner. From that date through 1976, Arab terrorists have commandeered or attacked thirty-eight other civilian planes in international traffic. They also killed twenty-six airport passengers at Lod on May 30, 1972, five passengers in Athens on August 5, 1973, and thirty-one in Rome on December 17, 1973. The PLO also claimed responsibility for the mid-air explosion in February 1970 of a Swissair jetliner that killed forty-seven passengers and crew.

The list of outrages goes on and on. Eleven Israeli athletes were slaughtered by the PLO at the 1972 Munich Olympics. In March 1973 seven terrorists stormed a diplomatic reception at the Saudi Embassy in Khartoum and murdered U. S. Ambassador Cleo Noel, his chargé d'affaires, George Moore, and a Belgian diplomat.

The world-wide pattern of terrorism engaged in by the PLO derives directly from the Palestinian National Covenant adopted by the PLO in July 1968 in Cairo. Article IX of that covenant reads as follows:

> Armed struggle is the only way to liberate Palestine and is therefore a strategy and not tactics. The Palestinian Arab people affirms its absolute resolution and abiding determination to pursue the armed struggle and to march forward toward the armed popular revolution, to liberate its homeland and return to it. . . .

Article XXII of the same document foreshadows the condemnation in November 1975 of Zionism by seventy-two nations at the U.N. Article XXII reads:

> Zionism is a political movement organically related to world imperialism and hostile to all movements of liberation and progress in the world. It is a racist and fanatical movement in its formation; aggressive, expansionist and colonialist in its aims and fascist and nazi in its means. Israel is a tool of the Zionism movement and a human and geographical base for world imperialism. It is a concentration and jumping off point for imperialism in the heart of the Arab homeland, to strike at the hopes of the Arab nation for liberation, unity and progress.

On June 8, 1974, the Palestine National Council, meeting in Cairo, adopted a ten-point program which reiterated that the PLO would "struggle by all means, foremost of which is armed

struggle, to liberate Palestinian land. . . ." The 1974 platform of
the PLO rejected any plan "the price of which is recognition,
conciliation, secure borders, renunciation of . . . our people's dep-
rivation of their right to return and their right to determine the
fate of their national soil."

Although the legitimacy of the PLO is open to the most serious
question, a strong and possibly growing political minority in Israel
is prepared to negotiate with the PLO as representative of the
Palestinians in exchange for the recognition of Israel, the renunciation of terrorism, and the acceptance of U.N. Resolutions 242
and 338 as the basis for negotiations.

It is still uncertain, however, whether a political majority within
Israel can be mustered to deal with the PLO. Mrs. Golda Meir,
writing in the New York *Times* on January 14, 1976, expressed
eloquently and persuasively the majority or "hawkish" view in Israel. She raised basic questions about the background of threats
and the intransigence of the PLO.

Mrs. Meir, who was Prime Minister of Israel from February
1969 to June 1974, openly conceded the reality of the Palestinian
claim; she wrote, "Whatever nomenclature is used, both the people involved and the territory on which they live are Palestinian."
But after retracing the activities of the Arabs since she went to
Palestine in 1921, Mrs. Meir noted, with weariness and a trace of
bitterness, that "Israel arose in only one-fifth of the territory originally assigned for the Jewish homeland. . . ." She repeated the
question which she and all Israelis have asked a thousand times:
"Why did the Arabs not set up a Palestinian state in their portion
instead of cannibalizing the country by Jordan's seizure of the
West Bank and Egypt's capture of the Gaza Strip?" She stressed
the question by asking, "Why did the Arabs converge upon us in
June, 1967, when the West Bank, the Golan Heights, the Sinai,
the Gaza Strip and Old Jerusalem were in their hands?"

It is the "Arab denial of Israel's right to exist" that makes it impossible for Israel to "sanction the participation of the Palestinian
Liberation Organization at the Security Council, a participation
in direct violation of Resolutions 242 and 338."

Mrs. Meir's attitude toward the PLO has been criticized as doc-
trinaire and adamant. But it should be pointed out that Mrs.

Meir expressly noted that she does not "disregard whatever national aspirations Palestinian Arabs have developed in recent years." Nonetheless, she is opposed to a "mini-Palestinian state, planted as a time bomb against Israel on the West Bank." But any movement on the part of the PLO toward the renunciation of its position as a "terrorist movement ideologically committed to the liquidation of Jewish national independence" would, in Mrs. Meir's judgment, be sufficient for Israel to collaborate completely. But, she concluded, the PLO has never receded from its fundamental purpose of devising overt schemes for the "immediate or piecemeal extinction" of Israel.

Despite the unyielding opposition of Israel to any recognition of the PLO, this group has attained international recognition, which is probably unprecedented in contemporary history for any ethnic group not representing an actual or potential country. Ever since the PLO was recognized in October 1974 at the Rabat summit as the "sole, legitimate representative" of the Palestinian people, the PLO has scored impressive diplomatic successes. At the U. N. General Assembly the PLO was authorized to take part "in all efforts and international conferences to discuss the Middle East within the framework of the U.N." The PLO also obtained observer status at the U.N.'s Food and Agriculture Organization session in Rome. The PLO has representatives who are accepted as de facto "ambassadors" in some one hundred nations and international organizations.

The PLO describes itself as a movement for national liberation. The emotional appeal of such a description conceals the fact that the PLO, unlike other movements for national liberation, seeks to destroy another state rather than to expel a foreign ruler. The Mau Mau of Kenya, the Haganah in Palestine, and the Congress Party in India all had the common objective of seeking to expel a foreign ruler from their own nation. If the spokesmen for the PLO want the world to accept in any literal sense the concept that it is a national liberation movement, then they are openly conceding the substance of the fear which causes Israel to be so adamant—the fear that the PLO, regardless of whatever "moderate" posture it might assume, desires ultimately and inevitably the expulsion of all of the Jews from Israel on the ground that the land of Israel itself belongs to the Palestinians.

The claim of the PLO to be a national liberation movement is further weakened by the affirmation of the ten points adopted in Cairo in June 1974, one of which is the elimination of Jordan.

The PLO buttresses its self-identification as a national liberation movement by asserting its ambition to create a "secular democratic state" for all Palestinians. It is impossible, however, to imagine a religious Moslem or a Moslem nation advocating or even accepting a "secular democratic state."

The claim of the PLO to be a genuine movement for national liberation is further undermined by its clear connection with Moscow. The establishment of a new Palestinian state would carry with it the possibility and perhaps the certainty that such a nation would be used by the U.S.S.R. to gain additional military and political leverage in the Middle East. The repugnance which Israel has for the PLO can be fully understood if not completely embraced by the fear that a "secular democratic state" contiguous to Israel would almost inevitably constitute a grave military threat by the placement there of SAM missiles and other Soviet weaponry within twenty or so miles of the population centers of Israel.

Israel has pragmatic and legal reasons for not dealing with the PLO. The U.N. Security Council Resolution 242 specifically states that all negotiations shall be conducted among nations and not outside groups. Consequently, Israel is technically correct in asserting that it will negotiate only with Jordan and not with third parties.

One of the central difficulties in the way of Israel's fulfilling its desire to do justice to the Palestinian people is the dispersion of that ethnic group. Seventy per cent of the Palestinians possess the legal nationality of other states. Fifty-three per cent are nationals of Jordan, with about half of that number under Israeli control. An additional 350,000 reside in Gaza, while 800,000 live in Syria, Kuwait, Lebanon, and other nations in the Middle East. It is also significant to note that almost 60 per cent of the Palestinian Arab population today is under the age of twenty, with less than 6 per cent over sixty.

But the diversity and lack of central organization among the Palestinians appear to be more and more irrelevant in view of the fact that they continue to look upon themselves as a nation and that they simply will not fade away.

A visit to a Palestinian school is an ominous reminder that the memory of Palestinian self-identification is being passed on to the next generation. Posters on the wall remind the pupils of the glories of guerrilla warfare, classroom songs concentrate on militant revenge, and textbooks identify Israeli cities with their original Palestinian names.

In Israel the problem of the Palestinians focuses on the options available to the Knesset with respect to the West Bank. The indecision of Israeli leaders concerning the future of the West Bank is made more complex by the belief of Orthodox Jews that the West Bank of the Jordan is a part of the "Greater Israel" spoken of in the Bible. In addition, the right of the Jews to settle on the West Bank was affirmed in the Balfour Declaration. This biblical claim, as ratified by the Balfour Declaration, has rankled in the hearts of some Israelis ever since Jordan formally annexed the West Bank on April 1, 1950. After Israel acquired the West Bank in the 1967 War, a consensus on the occupied area emerged within Israel along the lines of the plan proposed by then Deputy Prime Minister Allon. He urged that political control of the West Bank revert to Jordan but that Israel establish a series of permanent paramilitary settlements along the borders of Israel. Some Orthodox Jews along with not a few Israeli right-wing political leaders, who also tend to be Orthodox in their religion, insisted that Israel retain and settle all of the West Bank as a part of the "Greater Israel" given to Jews in the Bible. The "doves" wanted to return most or even all of the West Bank to Jordan in return for guarantees of peaceful coexistence.

In the ten years since Israel's annexation of the West Bank, some sixty-eight or seventy permanent paramilitary settlements populated by Israelis have been established in that territory. To the Arabs who reside on the West Bank, Israel's intervention is deemed to be a military occupation. Israel refers to the West Bank as an "administered territory"; the term is a euphemism invented by Israel which is without meaning in international law.

The greatest difficulties for both sides have come not from the authorized paramilitary Israeli communities but from groups of religious zealots who have settled in areas of the West Bank contrary to the wishes of the Israeli government. One such settlement in the city of Nablus (an area far from the borders and widely separated from any Israeli community) has been deeply resented by the Palestinians and persistently protested by the Israeli government.

It is obvious that the presence of some seventy Israeli communities on the West Bank constitutes additional difficulties for Israel in handling the PLO's demand for negotiations.

It is easy for Americans and even the most loyal friends of Israel to urge that nation to be "flexible" in its approach to the PLO. Israelis understandably resent the recommendation to be "flexible" since it assumes that there have been concessions or compromises on the part of the PLO. Such concessions simply do not exist. At the same time, Senator Adlai Stevenson, in an on-the-scene report in April 1976, expressed the reality as follows:

> PLO critics who claim that it is unrepresentative of the Palestinians are unable to come up with a substitute. The PLO may be distrusted, disowned and despised, but it is a reality, if for no other reason than that it has no rival organization among Palestinians. As long as this reality persists, it will have to be reckoned with in any future multi-lateral negotiating process.

The Jewish magazine *Moment* for March 1976 published a symposium on the question "Should Israel Talk to the PLO?" The responses cover the spectrum. One opinion offered by Professor Gil Karl AlRoy, a veteran journalist and scholar for some thirty years in the Middle East, concludes that American pressure on Israel to negotiate with the PLO will be seen by the Arabs as a surrender "to the unstoppable Arab tide." Professor AlRoy's major premise that the "real problem for Israel is not with the PLO, but with Washington" may be thought to be extreme. At the same time, he points out very vividly that the United States is almost desperate to placate the oil-rich Arab nations and that in the process the inevitable temptation is to place the future safety and security of Israel in a position secondary to American efforts to prevent that world-wide depression which would come about from another interruption in the delivery of oil from the Middle Eastern states.

The other ten commentators in the symposium in *Moment* rehearse the familiar questions of whether Israel would be committing suicide if it developed a new approach to the Palestinian problem. They all agree that Palestine may have begun years ago as Southern Syria but that today the Palestinians have developed a national consciousness, a common memory, and a sense of shared identity. Arthur Waskow, associated with the Institute for Policy Studies in Washington, D.C., and a member of the executive board of Breira, a project concerned with Diaspora-Israel relations, urges emphatically that insistence by Israel that "no Palestinian state can emerge there is the one policy that means permanent war." He argues that either America or Israel must take the initiative in the present impasse. If Israel allows America to continue to act so that a Palestinian state will emerge, Israel will lose face in world opinion and will be deemed to be a puppet of the United States.

On the other hand, if Israel were to take the initiative by permitting a Palestinian state with stringent limits on arms and demilitarized zones under multilateral control, it could be that world public opinion would be transformed into support of Israel.

Waskow suggests that secret contacts with the PLO be made by the present or prospective Prime Ministers of Israel. He dreams that Rabin, Allon, or Eban could secretly negotiate for the emergence of a free Palestinian state on the West Bank and Gaza "on the sole condition that this state accept its responsibility to live in peace with Israel and negotiate guarantees to that end." He explores the possible consequences of such initiatives and decides that the worst possible effects of such a policy would not be more disadvantageous to Israel than its present policy.

Waskow concludes with these cryptic words: "Much depends on American Jews. If we pushed hard for this initiative, it could happen. If not—continued deadlock, renewed disaster."

The American Jewish community is probably more militant in

its defense of present-day Israeli policy than most Israelis. American Jews understandably suspect that criticism of the "hawkish" attitude of the Israeli government is at least in part a manifestation of anti-Semitic or anti-Israeli sentiments.

It is obvious that the United States Government has been the least critical of all the nations of the earth with regard to Israel's policy vis-à-vis the Palestinians. One of the most direct criticisms of Israel's policy on the Palestinians came in 1976 from then U.N. Ambassador William Scranton, who urged Israel not to establish any additional settlements on the West Bank. In general, however, the United States has reasserted time and time again its abiding loyalty to the state of Israel and has at no time even raised the question of make America's gifts or sales of arms to Israel conditional on a settlement by Israel of the Palestinian question. Such a policy on the part of the United States may well be the next logical or inevitable modification of its policy toward Israel. The adoption of such a policy would be a new and heavy form of pressure on Israel. It would induce and compel Israel to negotiate with the PLO despite the almost universal conviction among Israelis that the PLO is not representative of the Palestinians and that, despite whatever friendship it might express toward Israel, it is or would become the tool of the most anti-Israel sentiments in the Arab world as well as of the most vehemently anti-Zionist sentiments in the Kremlin.

The United States and particularly the United States Congress have fundamental decisions to make with regard to what Israel should do about the demands of the PLO. An incorrect decision could easily bring about a situation in which the safety of Israel would be jeopardized and its future security destroyed.

In 1976, Secretary of State Henry Kissinger enunciated the basic objectives of U.S. policy in the Middle East. He placed the safety and security of Israel as an objective coequal with the maintenance by the United States of a steady and substantial delivery of oil to America by the Arab nations. During the presidential campaign in 1976, Jimmy Carter challenged the underlying concept by which the Secretary of State could consider these two objectives as equal in dignity. Carter contended that the safety and security of Israel must be the primary objective of U.S. policy in the Middle East and that every other policy which the United States desires to maintain in that area of the world must be subordinate to the maintenance of an independent Israel.

The presence and the persistence of the Palestinians may sooner rather than later force the United States into choosing between the two objectives which Secretary Kissinger deemed to be coequal in the Middle East.

The Arabs, the Palestinians, and the PLO, in their desire to erode American loyalty to Israel, have invited the U.S.S.R. to share the dream of the Arab League to expel Israel from the Middle East. The Arabs have also sought to intimidate America by the temporary withholding of oil followed by a quadrupling of its price to America and to Europe. These techniques have not succeeded in undercutting America's commitment to Israel, but a vehement repudiation by the Arab nations of the very concept of Zionism could conceivably erode America's loyalty to Israel. It is appropriate, therefore, to explore the moral, the metaphysical, and the mystical aspects of Zionism.

12

CAN ZIONISM BE THE BASIS
OF A MODERN STATE?

In his autobiography, *Present at the Creation*, Dean Acheson relates that "Zionism was the only topic that Felix [Frankfurter] and I had by mutual consent excluded from our far-ranging daily talks." Acheson conceded that he had learned from Frankfurter "to understand, but not share, the mystical emotion of the Jews to return to Palestine and end the diaspora." Acheson felt that those who had urged Zionism as an American governmental policy had allowed "their emotion to obscure the totality of American interest."

If President Truman's Secretary of State failed to understand Zionism, there is perhaps reason to feel that more misunderstandings than have occurred over the past thirty years might have developed. Nonetheless, the massive global misunderstanding of Zionism since the United Nations General Assembly branded it as racism on November 10, 1975, is a development which can only be described as ominous for the future of Israel.

It seems clear that the Arab nations and the PLO, assisted by the U.S.S.R., having failed to defeat Israel on the battlefields on separate occasions, have transformed their struggle into one that seeks the sanction of world public opinion for the destruction of Israel.

One would have hoped that the PLO could never have gotten seventy-two nations in the General Assembly to condemn Judaism or the existence of Israel. Alleging that Zionism is a form of racism permitted the proponents of this sentiment to deny that they were enemies of Israel or that they were opposed to Judaism as a religion. The adoption of a resolution equating Zionism with racism might have been politically successful for its advocates, but there is some hope that finally the Christian churches have been able to identify as never before with the religious and mystical elements of Zionism.

All of the events leading to the castigation of Zionism at the United Nations by the representatives of some two thirds of humanity deserve the most careful recounting and analysis.

In the proclamation of Israeli independence issued on May 14, 1948, those who subscribed indicated that they represented "the Zionist movement of the world." The declaration of independence traced the origin of Israel directly to the First Zionist Congress convened in 1897.

The relatively sparse number of references to Zionism in the official documents of Israel is probably traceable to the universal agreement among Jews everywhere that the one term used in Jewish literature to describe the last nineteen centuries of Jewish experience before the establishment of Israel was *Galuth* or exile. Throughout the period of that exile, Jewish tradition employed virtually every resource of prayer and ceremony and every opportunity to remind the Jew of his identification with the land of Israel. Every Jewish ritual from the cradle to the grave—at birth, puberty, marriage, and death—expressed ardent hope not only for a spiritual return to Zion but for a political restoration of a Jewish homeland in Israel.

Jewish commentators appear to agree that in Jewish tradition there is no distinction between the aspiration for a spiritual return to Zion and a political restoration of a Jewish state. In the so-called "silent prayer," recited three times each day, Jews have always prayed: "May our eyes behold Thy return to Zion in mercy."

The same prayer beseeches, "Restore our judges as at the beginning and our counselors as in the past."

The prayerful aspiration for the return of the Jewish people to its homeland developed into action on at least a few occasions in the first few centuries of the Christian Era. In the year A.D. 115, some forty-five years after their calamitous defeat by the Romans in the year 70, the Jews fought another war of liberation against the Roman Empire. And in the year 132 a third war was launched against Rome in Palestine. After the war had raged for three years, Roman strength prevailed and Jews were forbidden to enter Jerusalem.

During the centuries that followed, the Jewish dream of liberating Palestine never died and frequently emerged as, for example, in the messianic movement initiated by Shabbatai Zevi (1626–76). The influence of this charismatic individual was so great that people in London wagered that he would be King in Jerusalem within two years. But his subsequent abject surrender to the Turkish Sultan and his final conversion to Islam was a catastrophic blow to Jewish aspirations for a nation of their own. Even the hard skepticism of Spinoza did not prevent him from expressing the conviction that the Jews might one day reconstitute their state.

The aspirations of the Jewish people for a homeland of their own were evidenced through the centuries by the constant Jewish pilgrimages to the Holy Land. These journeys persisted through the Middle Ages, stimulated by the Crusaders, the massacres of Jewish communities in Europe, and the successive expulsions of the Jews from England, France, Spain, and Portugal. In the sixteenth century a community of mystics and intellectuals emerged in Safed in Galilee. From that time forward there were always Jewish communities of significant dimensions in all of the terrain that eventually became known as Palestine.

The unique dual aspiration of the Jewish people for a spiritual return to Zion as well as a political re-establishment of a Jewish commonwealth makes it impossible to impose on them any definition applicable to any other ethnic or religious group. Rabbi Robert Gordis, in his book on American Jewry, puts it this way: "None of the categories variously proposed as definitions of the

Jewish group are satisfactory; neither one 'nation', one 'nationality', one 'religious denomination', nor the meaningless and dangerous term one 'race' does justice to the unique and complex character of Jews in the modern world." Rabbi Gordis has pointed out that in the ancient world "each human group possessed a sense of a common kinship, a special culture and language and a distinctive religion." This was true, he notes, of the Babylonians, the Egyptians, the Phoenicians, the Greeks, and the Romans. But while the ancient culture of these peoples has faded away, the Jews have retained the organic relationship of ethnicity, culture, and religion. These three elements are linked in the Jewish psyche by unbreakable bonds to the land of Israel where all three originated and came to flower. Rabbi Gordis points out that the only term which can describe the Jews is the biblical word *'am* meaning "people." This Hebrew word comes from a Semitic root denoting in all probability "togetherness."

In a mysterious way the "togetherness" of the Jewish people goes back to and depends upon the actual land of Israel. The identification of Jews with the Holy Land does not in any way mean that they have some exclusive claim to its possession. All three of the theistic religions have a genuine concern for and identification with the Holy Land. For Islam the religious significance of the land is secondary, and for Christianity it is historical. For Judaism, however, the land of Israel is crucial and central. The Jewish people have had an unbroken relationship with the land of Israel during thirteen centuries of occupation and more than nineteen centuries of aspiration. But this abiding relationship does not negate in any way the authenticity of the claims of the Arabs who have lived in this land for over a thousand years.

Although the dimensions of Zionism are not always clear even to its most ardent advocates, the nationalistic elements of Zionism are almost self-evident. The children of Israel believe that the Lord chose them to be His people and, as a result, the notion of a distinct peoplehood or nationhood is endemic to the Jewish religion. But conceding the possibility of an undesirable nationalism developing from the implementation of Zionism does not serve as evidence for the proposition that Zionism leads to or constitutes a form of racism. This charge, endorsed by seventy-two nations of the U.N. General Assembly and rejected by only thirty-five (with twenty-seven nations abstaining), is unique in all of the annals and centuries of anti-Semitism.

The two grievances most frequently mentioned by those who claim that Zionism is a form of racism are the Law of Return and the ban on the acquisition by non-Jews of land in Israel that has been bought by the Jewish National Fund. The Law of Return means simply that any Jew from anywhere in the world may come to Israel and be granted automatic citizenship. If non-Jews migrate to Israel they must apply for citizenship, as was required in the celebrated case of Brother Daniel, a man born a Jew who became a Catholic priest.

The contention that this policy is "racist" derives from the feeling that the Law of Return should be extended at least to those Palestinians who once lived in the area which is now Israel. If Israel gives preference to Jews who migrate to that nation such a policy can hardly be called racism; racists believe that race is the primary determinant of human traits and capacities and that racial differences produce an inherent superiority within a particular race. The Law of Return has as its major premise the assumption that Jews of the Diaspora are frequently denied religious freedom and that the only refuge available to them is Israel. The Palestinians, who claim that they have a right to return to land which thirty years ago their ancestors may have owned or occupied, can hardly be deemed to have a moral right equal to that of some 800,000 Jews who were quite literally driven out of Arab lands after the establishment of Israel in 1948. Palestinians who have a legitimate claim to monetary damages can obtain such restitution if repatriation is not feasible. The fact that Arab authorities have made it impossible for the government of Israel to negotiate individually or collectively with dispossessed Palestinians does not raise their provable claim for financial reparation to the same moral level as that of Jews who have been oppressed or persecuted.

It should be noted, moreover, that virtually all of the Jews who have come to Israel have been fleeing from actual, potential, or prospective harassment or worse.

The Law of Return is not grounded on any theory of racism or on any notion that Judaism is superior to other religious faiths. The Law of Return is based on the fundamental notion that Jews are being persecuted or are likely to be persecuted in the Diaspora. There should be one place in the world where they can go and become citizens automatically because they are Jews.

If Israel's practice of being responsive to the exodus is a form of racism, then the very establishment of the state of Israel by the United Nations was itself the result of racism. It may well be that the PLO and others who worked so strenuously to obtain a resolution of the U.N. General Assembly condemning Zionism as a form of racism were utilizing this technique to proclaim to the world that Israel should never have been established. Indeed, the drawing of such an inference from the U.N. resolution is inescapable.

Early in the 1900s the founders of the Zionist movement established a fund to acquire land in Palestine and to establish settlements on it. Regulations were developed which specified that the land could be developed only by Jews. This restriction became more universal in Israel as the nation evolved—with the consequence that the Arab minority, or 11 per cent of Israel's three million citizens, were legally prevented from owning land that had been acquired by the Jewish National Fund. This prohibition was particularly applicable to the kibbutzim, which are situated on the lands acquired by the Jewish National Fund.

Dr. Edmund Hanauer, an American Jewish political scientist and the director of an organization known as Search for Justice and Equality in Palestine, has commented that if Jews or blacks were excluded from owning land in America in a similar way we would call the arrangement anti-Semitic or racist.

There is no analogue to the Israeli situation in America except perhaps the lands which the United States Government has set aside for Indian tribes. No person who is not a descendant of American Indians may purchase this land since it is held in trust for those whose ancestors were wrongfully deprived of it. Those who are anxious to demonstrate that Israel or Zionism is a form of racism might suggest that the Arabs were dispossessed of their lands in the same way that the American Indians were. Clearly, the most feasible settlement of Arab claims should be made, but if the truculence of Arab leaders, sometimes made more difficult by the adamant stand taken by some Israeli officials, makes an immediate settlement impossible, it does not follow that Israel is indulging in a racist policy.

There is no doubt that Zionism as the basis for the establishment of a nation is unique in the annals of mankind. But so is the whole history of the Jewish people. Consequently, it is improper to adopt a procrustean attitude and insist that Israel conform to the usual model of a contemporary state.

Those who seek to downgrade Zionism necessarily operate on the assumption that Israel is the product not of Judaism but only of a political movement called Zionism. But every attempt to dissociate Zionism from Judaism ends up with a caricature of both. From the beginning Judaism was conceived as the interlinking of a people, a Torah, and a land. The Hebrew Scriptures, medieval and modern Jewish literature, the Talmud, and the Jewish liturgy are replete with the idea of possession of or return to Zion. Attempts made in the nineteenth century by early reform Judaism to de-Zionize Judaism, in appreciation for emancipation, were unsuccessful. Zionism and Judaism have always been integral parts of each other. Since the holocaust and the founding of Israel the inseparability of Judaism and Zionism has never been clearer.

In the volume *A Psychohistory of Zionism* by Jay Y. Gonen, published in 1975, the startling point is made that Zionism, conceived by its founders "as the only logical answer to Christian anti-Semitism," had become by the second half of the twentieth century the occasion for the rise of Arab anti-Semitism. Gonen asserts that "psychologically Zionism is the Jewish reassertion of manhood." In Israel, he notes, post-holocaust Jews "proved their overwhelming superiority in both spirit and technology." Nonetheless, he raises the question: "Will the trauma of the holocaust result in a chronic sense of inferiority?" He apparently answers that question in the negative and asserts that "many Jews feel intuitively that Israel is a place where either a regeneration or a final collapse will take place." Gonen feels that "creative Jewish life is likely to take place only in Israel." He hopes for a flourishing Is-

rael interacting with a creative Diaspora but realistically expects
that the "prospects are for a vigorous Israel interacting with an
anemic Diaspora." He concludes, consequently, that "most Jewish
hopes . . . are pinned on the State of Israel."

It is curious that the Arab and other nations in the U. N. General Assembly who desire to degrade and defame Israel should
have chosen the concept of Zionism as their target. Before the organized assault on Zionism began in the U.N. in 1973, the very
word itself was hardly known. The selection of "Zionism" rather
than "Israel" or "Judaism" can have no other explanation than
that the nations who desire to expel Israel from the U.N. or at
least censure Israel within that body did not want to risk the possibility that they would be charged with open anti-Semitism.

The Third World practice of equating Zionism with racism and
colonialism emerged for the first time in the U. N. General Assembly in 1973 when that body voted to declare that there was
"an unholy alliance between South African racism and Zionism."
The first official use in the United Nations of the juxtaposition of
Zionism with racial discrimination appeared in Mexico in July
1975 at the world conference of the International Women's Year.
A resolution adopted on Palestinian and Arab women recommended "the elimination of colonialism, neo-colonialism, fascism,
Zionism, apartheid and foreign occupation, alien domination and
racial discrimination in all its forms. . . ." In the following
month the foreign ministers of non-aligned countries meeting in
Peru utilized in their declaration the same identification of colonialism, racism, and Zionism.

On September 4, 1975, the Third or Social, Humanitarian, and
Cultural Committee of the 30th Session of the U. N. General Assembly opened debate on one of its agenda items—"A Decade for
Action to Combat Racism and Racial Discrimination." The 1973
General Assembly had designated the ten-year period beginning
on December 10, 1973, as the Decade for Action Against Racism.
Those who established this worth-while project never contem-
plated that under its aegis a body of the United Nations would
have a bitter debate between September 15 and October 17,
1975—with the unprecedented result of a condemnation of Zion-

ism as the principal effect of the projected decade-long evaluation of racism.

The complete transcript of the debate on Zionism in the so-called Third Committee of the U. N. General Assembly contains astounding declarations against Israel and Zionism made by Arabs and Third World nations. The unremitting animosity toward Israel is scarcely concealed even though the representatives of many nations spoke diplomatically only about Zionism.

The essential gravamen of the anti-Zionist cause is the allegedly political nature of Zionism and the exclusively theological nature of Judaism. The United Nations debate that led up to the condemnation of Zionism as racism on November 10, 1975, heard dozens of times the contention that all Jews are not Zionists and all Zionists are not Jews.

Ambassador Baroody of Saudi Arabia said, for example, that the "Arab world had no quarrel with Judaism" but rather "with Zionism, a political movement which had originated in Europe and not in the Orient, where the Jews had never been discriminated against and where many persons in the Arab culture happen to be Jews." Ms. Bihi of Somalia asserted that her country and others "were involved in a moral war with the Zionist regime in the Middle East and opposed that regime because Zionism, like apartheid, was used as an instrument for perpetuating oppression and discrimination against one group of people by another, by depriving the Palestinians of their homeland and of their property for believing and professing another religion and for being Arabs." The representative from Iraq, Mr. Zahawie, suggested that Zionism was in fact incompatible with Orthodox Judaism; he claimed that "most Orthodox Jews denounce Zionism as a blasphemy and as an arch-enemy of the Jewish people." To the representative of Iraq, Zionism was not a liberation movement but rather "an act of colonial aggression."

The forty-five African nations were deeply divided in the deliberations about Zionism in the U.N.'s Third Committee. All of the African states (except South Africa, which is never considered as a part of the African bloc) wanted to preserve and enhance the impact of the Decade Against Racism. The African states in the Third Committee reflected the deep division at the meetings in

Kampala when the Organization of African States met there in the summer of 1975. On the final vote in the Third Committee twenty-five of the forty-five African nations or 56 per cent voted in favor of the resolution with two against, fourteen abstaining, and four absent. The several comments by representatives of the African nations suggested on several occasions that they were really not certain about the nature of Zionism and that they wished to disassociate resolutions concerning the Decade Against Racism from the resolution concerning Zionism. But the fact that only two of the forty-five African states ultimately voted against the anti-Zionist resolution indicates the economic and ideological dependence or intimidation of the African states by the Arab bloc.

Ambassador Chaim Herzog of Israel was eloquent in his explanation and defense of Zionism. Similarly eloquent was the representative of the United States along with at least a few highly articulate defenders of Zionism, such as Ambassador Waldron-Ramsey of Barbados. But it is uncertain whether any rational argument based on the historical uniqueness of Zionism could have altered the eventual vote of the Arab, African, and Asian nations whose representatives lashed out at all forms of colonialism and linked Zionism with this despised form of oppression.

But the eloquent remarks of Ambassador Herzog of Israel will remain as solid evidence on which history can judge the justice or injustice of the United Nations' condemnation of Zionism. He noted early in the debate in the Third Committee that the world was witnessing "the first organized attack on an established religion since the Middle Ages." He noted that support for Zionism had been written into the League of Nations mandate and that in 1947 Zionism had been endorsed by the very General Assembly of the United Nations which now sought to undermine the centerpiece of the political architecture of Israel.

The ambassador declared that he was proud to live in a nation that had Arab ministers in the government and Arabs as elected members of the Knesset. Israel, he noted, has Arab officers and men in the armed forces by their own volition and not by compulsion. In addition, he stated, hundreds of thousands of Arabs visit Israel each year and thousands of Arabs from all over the Middle East come to Israel regularly for medical treatment.

Mr. Leonard Garment, speaking for the United States, declared that to "equate Zionism with racism was to distort completely the history of the Zionist movement, born of the centuries of oppression suffered by the Jewish people in the Western world and designed to liberate an oppressed people by returning them to the land of their fathers." Mr. Garment warned the members of the Third Committee that the United Nations "was at the point of officially endorsing anti-Semitism, one of the oldest and most virulent forms of racism known to mankind." He continued by stating that the adoption of the resolution would encourage anti-Semitism and group hostility and "would make it impossible for some countries to cooperate in the elimination of racism and racial discrimination as a part of the work of the Decade [Against Racism]."

Public television in New York filmed the entire debate in the Third Committee of the U.N. It is distressing that the people of the United States saw so little of it. Several networks in Europe showed the whole debate or large parts of it on national television. The complete transcript makes clear to the reader the force and vehemence of the passions underlining the convictions of the speakers. The debate as televised offers an even more dramatic revelation of the profound misunderstandings, unbelievable misapprehensions, and titanic emotions which possessed the minds and hearts of the representatives of seventy-two nations who voted that Zionism cannot form the ideological basis of any nation acceptable to the family of man.

The debate within the Third Committee will be viewed in the future by scholars and historians. The debate in the Plenary Session of the General Assembly is and will be the easily available record for all of mankind to view. It can be described without exaggeration as the most public trial of Jews and Judaism in the history of mankind.

Ambassador Herzog of Israel noted for the representatives of the 140 nations in the U. N. General Assembly that their deliberations on Zionism occurred precisely thirty-seven years after "the night of November 10, 1938, when Hitler's Nazi Storm Troopers launched a coordinated attack on the Jewish community in Germany, burned the synagogues in all these cities and made bonfires in the streets of the holy books and the scrolls of the holy law and the Bible." Ambassador Herzog stated that that occasion, the Kristallnacht, or Crystal Night, "led eventually to the crematoria and the gas chambers . . . to the most terrifying holocaust in the history of man." He pointed out the irony that the United Nations, which began its life as an anti-Nazi alliance, should thirty-eight years later find itself on its way to becoming the world center of anti-Semitism. He recalled that Judaism gave to the world "the Bible, with its Ten Commandments, the great prophets of old, Moses, Isaiah, Amos . . . and the great thinkers of history, Maimonides, Spinoza, Marx, Einstein . . ."

Israel's spokesman at the U.N. pointed out that the term "Zion," referring to Jerusalem, appears 152 times in the Old Testament. During the centuries the term "Zion" expanded to mean for Jewish communities everywhere the whole of Israel. The return of those Jews who so desire to Israel need not in any way collide with the rights of 140 million Arabs settled in twenty states embracing 5.27 million square miles.

Ambassador Herzog concluded by asserting that "Over the centuries it has fallen to the lot of my people to be the testing agent of human decency, the touchstone of civilization, the crucible in which enduring human values are to be tested." He opined that "a nation's level of humanity could invariably be judged by its behavior toward its Jewish population. . . ." He closed with this dramatic challenge:

"The vote of each delegation will record in history its country's stand on anti-Semitic racism and anti-Judaism. You yourself bear the responsibility for your stand before history. . . . We the Jewish people will not forget."

Father Benjamin Nuñez, the ambassador of Costa Rica to the U.N., cited Catholic and Protestant church leaders who had recently met in Memphis and declared in a joint statement that "to compare Zionism with racism is a calumny against the Jews and a return to the old anti-Semitism that was a scourge of mankind for centuries." Father Nuñez asserted that "so long as there exists in the world manifestations and vestiges of anti-Semitism, the Zionist movement has a goal to pursue." If the resolution is adopted, Father Nuñez predicted, it "will serve as a warning to the Jewish people not to intensify their Zionist activities and as a warning to all the free peoples of the world that the Hitlerite and fascist evils have not yet been eradicated from the face of the earth."

In addition, he called the resolution "an unbridled invitation to genocide against the Jewish people." The resolution will, he said, "reopen chapters of history of pain and persecution for that people." Concluding with "a few words to my Jewish brothers," Father Nuñez urged them not to be disheartened since "your long history . . . has permitted you to survive worse resolutions than this, and you will also survive this one."

The statements by national spokesmen in the General Assembly of the U.N. reflected closely what had been enunciated in the Third Committee. The principal exception was the presence in the full General Assembly of U. S. Ambassador Daniel Patrick Moynihan. His angry outbursts cannot be said to be unjustified, although the language and methods of diplomacy were not exactly complied with. Ambassador Moynihan said that "what we have here is a lie, a political lie of a variety well known to the twentieth century and scarcely exceeded in all the annals of untruth and outrage. The lie is that Zionism is a form of racism." Moynihan added that "the damage we now do to the idea of human rights and the language of human rights could well be irreversible."

Before adopting the anti-Zionist resolution the General Assembly defeated by a narrow vote of 67 to 55 an attempt to postpone consideration of the proposed resolution for one or two years.

The final vote on the resolution (72 yes, 35 no, 32 abstaining) demonstrates the immense power of the bloc of Arab countries at the U.N. The total population of these twenty states is 137 million, just 3 per cent of the world's people. The total output of this Arab bloc is about $100 billion a year—not even a tenth of the output of the United States alone. Despite the severe limitations of a very small population and a modest if growing economic output, the Arab bloc swayed a majority of the 142 nations in the General Assembly—104 of which come from the Third World.

Twenty-seven of the thirty-five nations voting against the anti-

Zionist resolution were democracies. Only fourteen of the seventy-two members of the U.N. who voted for the condemnation of Zionism were genuine democracies.

It is baffling to anyone seeking to empathize with Zionism to see that the nations which voted against Zionism included Brazil, Mainland China, Mexico, the Soviet Union, and Portugal. One perhaps can take some consolation in the fact that, although only twenty-nine nations opposed the resolution in the General Assembly's Third Committee, thirty-five nations opposed it in the full Assembly. Consequently, neither the vote on October 17 of the Third Committee nor the vote of November 10 of the full General Assembly reflected the previous automatic majority of 80 per cent or more which the Arab states had always attained up to that moment when they had proposed a resolution that would denigrate Israel.

Asia, with thirty-three states, was more solidified against Zionism than Africa. Of the thirty-three states, twenty-four, or 73 per cent, voted for the resolution, no nation voted against the proposal, and nine nations abstained.

Of the twenty-six Latin American nations in the U.N. only a few voted for the proposition, eight voted against, and twelve did not vote.

All of the twelve East European socialist states voted for the proposition; only Rumania abstained. Of the twenty-three West European nations, four voted in favor of the resolution, eighteen opposed it, and one was absent.

It is indeed disconcerting to note that a total of 86 per cent of the twenty-five African, twenty-four Asian, and eleven socialist nations voted in favor of the resolution that Zionism was a form of racism. There is no denying the fact that the vast majority of mankind voted for the condemnation of Zionism. Mainland China, with one fourth of humanity, voted for the resolution as did India, Pakistan, and Indonesia. Add the population of these vast nations to the peoples of the African and Asian nations which rejected Zionism and one must conclude that well over 60 per cent of humanity voted for the declaration that Zionism was somehow a racist philosophy.

The United States was clearly the staunchest and most powerful friend Israel had in its struggle against the anti-Zionist resolution in the General Assembly. Although the United States lost, it is significant that public opinion in America did not question or quarrel with the vigorous policy pursued by the United States in rejecting all anti-Zionist moves in the U.N. Indeed, it may well be that public opinion favorable to Israel within the United States was deepened rather than diminished by Israel's humiliation at the U.N. A Harris poll released on December 15, 1975, revealed overwhelming disapproval of the U.N. action. A 66 to 12 per cent majority of college-educated persons disapproved of the resolution, as did an even higher 70 to 80 per cent majority of professional people. In fact, nowhere in the country did approval of the resolution reach a mark higher than 14 per cent. The reaction of the public was that the U.N. resolution was aimed more at Jews than at the concept of Zionism. No more than 9 per cent believed that "Zionism is racism." The only qualification that should be put on this poll is that some 42 per cent of the people questioned were either not sure of the issue or simply had not followed the controversy at the U.N.

The anti-Zionist resolution elicited more Christian support for Israel than in all probability any previous event in the history of that nation. Dr. Robert V. Moss, president of the United Church of Christ, issued these moving words:

Since the beginning of the biblical story, the history of humankind, the very souls of whole populations have been corrupted by the evil presence of those who would destroy the Jews. We should not be deceived by the use of the term Zionism. Sponsors of the resolution meant by it Jews and Judaism as well as the State of Israel.

The United Methodist Bishops of America called the anti-Zionist resolution "one-sided . . . indefensible . . . and irresponsible." They said the resolution "solves nothing, adds anguish to Jews . . . endangers support for the United Nations . . . dulls the edge of hopes for combating racism wherever it exists, precisely because definitions of racism and nationalism are now blurred."

Thirteen non-governmental religious organizations accredited to the U.N. jointly expressed fear that the anti-Zionist resolution would hurt chances for peace in the Middle East. The thirteen organizations covered a broad spectrum of religious groups in America.

Jan Cardinal Willebrands, the Vatican's top ecumenical relations official, stated that he was amazed that the resolution made no effort to describe the meaning of Zionism and racism. He said that "with this way of acting, in my opinion, one cannot certainly help either justice or peace, which we all desire, in the Middle East."

John Cardinal Carberry of St. Louis asserted that the U.N. in labeling Zionism as racism has "put itself on record as racist itself."

A significant statement on the anti-Zionist resolution emerged in November 1975 from the Second Annual Christian-Jewish Workshop sponsored by the United States Conference of Catholic Bishops. The sixty participants signed a letter to U. N. Secretary General Kurt Waldheim denouncing the resolution as a "slander against Jews everywhere." The letter continued:

> Zionism is a sacred word and concept in Judaism and as such, it merits the respect and understanding of all Christians aware of their Judaic roots and heritage.

Just prior to the approval of the resolution on November 10, the general secretary of the National Council of Churches, Claire Randall, deplored the resolution, stating that it would "undermine the struggle against racism" and could revive "anti-Semitism in many places in the world."

Similarly, the non-denominational Protestant weekly, the *Christian Century*, deplored the resolution in its November 5, 1975, issue. Its editorial stated:

> Many Jews, as well as Christians, opposed the creation of a state based on the Jewish faith. But that was 30 years ago.

The existence of Israel is no longer debatable. Israel is a reality . . . it [the resolution] is a hostile propagandistic action that has nothing to do with the question of racism.

The World Council of Churches urged the General Assembly to "reconsider and rescind" its endorsement of the resolution equating Zionism with racism. Dr. Philip A. Potter, general secretary of the World Council, asserted that Zionism is "a complex historical process, expressing many different aspirations of the Jewish people over the years and is subject to many understandings and interpretations." None of these, he added, "can properly be used to condemn Zionism as racism." He commented that "Zionism has historically been a movement concerned with the liberation of the Jewish people from oppression, including racial oppression."

America, the national Catholic weekly, edited by Jesuits, editorialized that the anti-Zionist resolution meant that "an essential condition for peace in the Middle East—the recognition of Israel's right to exist—has been denied."

The national board of the Y.W.C.A. lamented that "the ancient and historic longing of the displaced and persecuted people for a homeland has been equated with racism . . . this distortion of Zionist aspirations can only serve to encourage anti-Semitism. . . ."

After all of the sound and fury caused by the anti-Zionist resolution, one goes back and searches for some clue that would yield light as to the ultimate convictions and motivations of those who worked so diligently to bring it about. One can search in the weekly news digest entitled *Swasia*, a publication sympathetic to the Arab-Palestinian cause published by the National Council of Churches, but will find no support for the alleged link of Zionism with racism. The bulletin *Middle East Perspective*, issued by Alfred M. Lilienthal, openly proclaims that Zionism *is* racism but can give only the arguments of automatic citizenship in Israel for Jews, the alleged built-in expansionism necessary if Israel is to accommodate all of the Jews in the Diaspora, and the alleged eviction of Palestinian Arabs by Israel.

Other groups sympathetic to the Arab case, such as the National Association of Arab Americans or the Washington-based Middle East Institute, appear to be very reluctant to defend or even analyze the charge that racism is an inherent part of Zionism.

Unfortunately, there are very few individuals or organizations representing the Arab point of view with which the Congress or the country can interact. As *Time* magazine stated on June 23, 1975, "Arab Americans have long been among the nation's least visible and vocal minorities." Arab Americans in the United States number between 1 and 1.5 million; they are dispersed throughout the nation and divided by their various national and religious origins. It is to be hoped that it need not be stated that criticism of those Arab leaders in the U. N. General Assembly who initiated the anti-Zionist resolution is compatible with the highest admiration and respect which every person, including this writer, should and does have for the venerated traditions of the Arab people and the magnificent contributions which Arab culture has brought to humanity.

The passage by the U. N. General Assembly of the anti-Zionist resolution was a far less drastic development than the Arab nations originally intended. It was clear in early 1975 that they hoped to expel or suspend Israel from the General Assembly just as South Africa was suspended in 1974. Arab governments launched a drive to isolate Israel diplomatically as a third alternative to the warfare which they lost and the negotiations after the October War of 1973 in which they did not want to yield on their traditional positions. Strong assertions by members of the United States Congress to the effect that they would cut off American assistance to the United Nations may have caused several countries to back away from joining in the Arab nations' desire to eliminate Israel from the international body which created that country.

Although one cannot be certain, it seems highly probable that the adamant position of the government and Congress of the United States might well have prevented greater disasters to Israel and to the United Nations than actually occurred in the anti-Zionism resolution of November 10, 1975.

The controversies about Israel's continued participation in UNESCO appear to involve more questions of fact than the anti-Zionist resolution and to that extent did not involve a total confrontation between Israel and the United Nations. Similarly, the difficulties concerning Israel's relationship with the World Health Organization (WHO) and the International Labor Organization (ILO) center not so much on the intrinsic essence of Zionism as on the unyielding position Israel has adopted concerning the participation of the PLO in the affairs of the United Nations.

It is difficult to arrive at a balanced prediction of the long-range effect throughout the world of the anti-Zionist resolution of November 10, 1975. One can fear that its adoption by a world body might well mean a curtailment of the liberties of Jews who reside in the seventy-two countries that voted for the anti-Zionist resolution. On the other hand, the resolution is so vague and ungrounded in fact or reality that there is some possibility or hope that its impact will be minimal and its remembrance brief. In any event, the global dissemination of this frightening resolution should remind Christians that the centuries-long struggle of the Jews for freedom and decency has by no means ended. Christians should remember the searing words of Father Edward Flannery, one of the few world experts on Jewish-Catholic relations, in an article in *The Bridge*, a Jewish-Christian annual, entitled "Anti-Zionism and the Christian Psyche." Father Flannery wrote these sentiments:

. . . it is the Christian above all who is expected to react more strongly to attacks on Jews. It is especially the Christian who is expected to rejoice at the upturn in the fortune of Jews that Zionism, or any other agency, has brought about in our own time. The distance we appear to stand from this horror and rejoicing is the measurement of that estrangement which separates us on the deepest level of our souls.

13

AMERICAN LEGISLATION TO PROTECT ISRAEL FROM THE ARAB ECONOMIC BOYCOTT

Many Americans might not be able to articulate adequately a definition of Zionism, but the American people have never protested the enactment of a law in 1965 designed to shield Israel from an Arab economic boycott against corporations and countries deemed to be contributing in some way to the cause of Zionism.

The language of the Export Administration Act of 1965 is most remarkable. Without mentioning Israel by name, the law sets forth U.S. policy against foreign boycotts as follows:

It is the policy of the United States to oppose restrictive trade practices or boycotts fostered or imposed by foreign countries against other countries friendly to the United States and to encourage and request domestic concerns engaged in . . . export . . . to refuse to take any action . . . which has the effect of furthering or supporting . . . [such] restrictive trade practices or boycotts. . . .

This was the first relatively feeble reaction of the American Congress to the economic boycott against Israel which was initiated in 1946 when the League of Arab States banned the importation of goods from Palestine. This primary boycott was extended in 1951 to encompass foreign countries doing business with Israel.

The Arab boycott has remained essentially unchanged in form since its inception. The central boycott office in Damascus maintains the blacklist, revises boycott regulations as required, and coordinates boycott policy among the twenty nations of the Arab League. The blacklist and boycott rules established in Damascus are not technically binding on any League member; each Arab state may have its own policies and practices. The wealthiest, such as Saudi Arabia, Kuwait, and the United Arab Emirates, employ the most restrictive policies and enforce the boycott most rigorously. The poorer countries of the region, such as Morocco, Sudan, and Algeria, belong to the League but have rarely enforced the secondary boycott established in 1951.

The primary boycott of Israel by the Arab states is, of course, traceable to the conviction of the Arab League that they are at war with Israel. Hence the primary boycott of Israel is similar to economic boycotts imposed in recent years by the United States against such countries as Mainland China, Cuba, Albania, North Korea, and North Vietnam. While such restrictive trade practices clearly are injurious to Israel, primary economic boycotts have traditionally been looked upon as legitimate tools of warfare.

It is the secondary aspects of the boycott which exert a direct influence upon the American economy. Although the counter-boycott measures enacted in the Export Administration Act of 1965 were clearly designed to prevent the Arab nations from coercing American corporations into becoming participants in their economic warfare, both those seeking to enforce and those seeking to evade the strictures of the 1965 measure have sometimes rather curiously attempted to turn this law into one intended to assist corporations and individuals in America.

It was not until the Arab states quadrupled oil prices in late 1973 that the United States abruptly discovered that the Export Administration Act was not really achieving the objectives which had brought about its enactment. To some extent the anti-boycott provisions of the act were not operational because the Arab world was a relatively insignificant market for American goods. Consequently, until 1974 the boycott exerted little provable influence upon the American economy or upon commercial ties with Israel. At the same time it is significant to note that only one or two major American commercial banks had branches or divisions in Israel, although many of them operated in the principal cities of the Arab nations. Although officials of the American banks which have not opened branches in Israel have always denied that the Arab economic boycott had anything to do with their decision, it has never been clear that the absence in Israel of not a few major banking and industrial entities of the United States is traceable exclusively to the prospect of financial gain or loss in Israel.

The situation changed dramatically with the massive accumulation of petrodollars by the oil-producing Arab states. Beginning in 1974, the influx of wealth transformed the Arab economies overnight into a prime market for American goods and services. During 1975, U.S. exports to the Arab states exceeded $5 billion. That figure is certain to increase sharply during the next few years as the investment capital of the Arab states may reach an estimated $500 billion in the early 1980s.

The burgeoning scope of the boycott is well documented in reports submitted by American exporters to the Commerce Department. In 1974 twenty-three firms reported a total of 785 transactions for which boycott compliance or information was requested. During the first nine months of 1975 the number of exporters reporting such requests escalated to 538 and the number of boycott-related transactions to 7,545. During the six-month period ending March 31, 1976, more than 30,000 boycott requests were reported by American firms to the Department of Commerce.

In the vast majority of cases—estimated to be over 90 per cent by a congressional study—American corporations complied with the demands of the Arab boycott officials.

By early 1975 it was very clear that the provisions in the 1965 Export Administration Act were totally inadequate to prevent American corporations from refusing to do business with Israel in order that they might have commercial transactions with the Arab nations. In addition, it was very clear that persons of the Jewish faith employed by American corporations would almost inevitably be discriminated against by U.S.-based companies which accepted the conditions imposed on them in their dealings with Arab nations.

On February 26, 1975, President Ford spoke out against the Arab boycott, stating that discrimination "has no place in the free practice of commerce as it has flourished in this country."

That statement was the first criticism of the Arab boycott ever made by an American President. It marked the beginning of a period of activity in confronting boycott-related issues by both the executive and the legislative branches of the federal government. That activity quickly brought out the fact that the Department of Commerce had until mid-1975 informed American corporations that they were "not legally prohibited from taking action . . . that has the effect of furthering or supporting such restrictive trade practices or boycotts." Such a declaration virtually nullified the strong language of the 1965 Export Administration Act, in which Congress stated that it was the policy of the United States to oppose restrictive trade practices and to refuse to be intimidated by boycotts. Even if this interpretation of the law is plausible, the Commerce Department has been required to acknowledge that it was lax in the enforcement of the Export Administration Act, since until 1975 it had not required companies to report boycott requests—as clearly mandated by law. After the Commerce Department, on October 1, 1975, began requiring the full disclosure by any American corporation of requests received to participate in an economic boycott, this information was kept strictly confidential. After a confrontation with a House committee, the Department of Commerce made the information available to the Congress but not to the country.

The Commerce Department failed in another respect to observe the purpose and spirit of the Export Administration Act. Until December 1, 1975, it circulated to American firms information about trade opportunities which contained boycott provisions. This practice placed a federal agency in the position of being an intermediary for the Arab League. The dissemination of the commercial offerings of the Arab nations has now been terminated by the Commerce Department but it still actively promotes and solicits trade with the Arab states. Intergovernmental commercial commissions have been set up between the United States and four members of the Arab League: Egypt, Jordan, Saudi Arabia, and Tunisia. While the objective of increasing and enhancing American trade relations abroad is laudable, the fact remains that, as long as the Commerce Department continues to serve as a broker between the boycotters and American firms, the Arab boycott will almost certainly continue to flourish in the United States.

The majority view of jurists appears to be that the Secretary of Commerce has the authority to issue regulations under the Export Administration Act which would prohibit compliance with the Arab boycott. Existing American law, moreover, clearly prohibits job discrimination on the basis of religion or national origin. Consequently, any firm agreeing to fire its Jewish or Israeli employees in order to obtain Arab business would be in clear violation of the law. Most boycott demands, however, do not ask for discrimination against individuals; out of 80,000 boycott requests reported by American firms between 1970 and March 1976, only 34 contained provisions which blatantly discriminated against Jews. American companies are usually asked to certify that they will not do business with Israel. In addition, the Arab League seeks to do injury to American corporations which transact business with Israel by requiring those corporations which agree to enter into contracts with Arab nations to boycott American corporations which have commercial relationships with Israel. It can be argued that the Sherman Anti-trust Act forbids the boycott of one American corporation by another corporation solely on the grounds that the first corporation does business with Israel. This is one of the issues involved in a test case brought by the Department of Justice against the Bechtel Company, a West Coast construction firm. The Bechtel Company can argue that the Sherman Anti-trust Act was designed to promote economic competition and that it has no applicability where the motivation to boycott an American company comes not from any aspiration to economic domination but from the political objective of a foreign power.

Clearly the ultimate question involved in America's approach to the Arab economic boycott comes to this: to what extent do America's alliance and friendship with Israel compel the United States to blunt the thrust of the economic warfare against Israel which has been conducted by the Arab nations for more than three decades? Phrased another way, the question comes to this: must American firms participate in the Arab League's campaign to punish Israel economically if these American firms desire to obtain some share of the billions in petrodollars which the Arab nations have to spend?

There is abundant evidence that a federal law banning all American corporations from aiding and abetting the Arab economic warfare against Israel would be accepted by the Arabs and would not be seriously detrimental to American businesses. Arab nations have already accepted substantial cutbacks in official federal promotion of Arab commercial ambitions. After this writer, joined by twenty-four other members of the House, brought suit in a federal court in Washington, D.C., on November 17, 1975, to enjoin the Department of Commerce from circulating Arab offers of business which contained the boycott, the department terminated its activities in this area. Theoretically the Arab nations can go to Europe or Japan for the things they need, but realistically alternative sources for sophisticated radar systems, oil-drilling apparatus, and computers are not easily discovered. In addition, the business community in America would like to have one rule binding on all corporations interested in obtaining business from the newly affluent Arab world. A clear federal statute would offer American corporations the right and the duty to defy the boycott. General Mills and Pillsbury are among a number of major American corporations which have publicly stated their support for antiboycott legislation.

Despite the moral uneasiness which American corporate executives feel in submitting to the Arab economic boycott, the Ford Administration persistently took the unqualified position that legislation to ban compliance with the Arab boycott was both unnecessary and counterproductive. In testimony presented to Congress time and time again by representatives of the Commerce, Treasury, State, and Justice departments, Administration spokesmen asserted that prohibiting compliance with boycott requests would have a grievous impact upon the American economy. It was urged that the Arab boycott was really only a part of the total Arab-Israeli problem and, consequently, could only be solved within the context of an over-all peace settlement in the Middle East. Unilateral legislation, the Ford Administration kept insisting, would serve to antagonize the Arabs and, hence, undercut our diplomatic efforts in that area of the world.

Despite all of the arguments by the Ford Administration and some leaders of American business to the effect that the United States can have both an escalation of commercial transactions with Arab nations and a continued friendship with Israel, the contradictions in such a position are almost self-evident. If the boycott continues to grow in size and effectiveness and if legal steps are not taken to halt its impact, there may well come a time when no company in the United States will do business with Israel for fear that such business would jeopardize the more lucrative markets in the Arab world. In such an eventuality American corporations could still argue that they are not doing injury to Israel, but no rationalization can explain away the fact that American corporations, by submitting to the Arab boycott, are participating in that economic strangulation of Israel which is one of the principal objectives of the foreign policy of the Arab nations.

Even to those who feel that commercial collaboration with the Arab nations is essential to the maintenance of America's capacity to be a mediator in the Middle East, the contradiction between America's firm and unyielding commitment to the safety and security of Israel and her willingness to acquiesce in a massive economic boycott of that nation cannot be denied.

An attempt to evade that contradiction was made, for example, by then Undersecretary of the Department of Commerce, James A. Baker, in testimony before the House Committee on International Relations on December 11, 1975. Baker stated that "compliance with a boycott request by a U.S. firm does not necessarily mean that the firm is, in any real sense, participating in a boycott of Israel." The incoherence in this sentence leads Mr. Baker to the following meaningless conclusion: "For such firms, responses to boycott requests are essentially affirmations of historical experience and existing factual situations."

Mr. Baker appeared to reveal his own priorities when he stated that he did not feel that the appropriate response to the concern over the economic boycott of Israel is "to deny all U.S. concerns access to some of the fastest growing export markets in the world today." Without any evidence whatsoever Mr. Baker alleged that making participation by American corporations in the Arab economic boycott illegal would not eradicate the problem. He noted that the "boycott is imposed worldwide, and no other country has legislated against it." Consequently, he stated, Americans should not be swayed by "emotional considerations in dealing with such a complex issue."

It is uncertain whether Mr. Baker meant to say that America's loyalty to Israel is one of the "emotional considerations" that should be factored out from America's resolution of its guilt concerning its complicity in the use of petrodollars to intensify the economic warfare of the Arab nations against Israel.

Mr. Baker and the Ford Administration persistently denied that they were motivated to oppose all legislation to remove American corporations from compliance with the Arab boycott by the almost fantastic trade possibilities which are now emerging in the Arab world. Mr. Baker reasoned that "the curtailment of commercial relations with the Arab world would dissipate an important source of U.S. political leverage with Arab governments and cripple U.S. efforts to bring about a fair settlement of the conflict in the Middle East and the issues underlying it." To support this dubious contention, Mr. Baker averred that the enactment of a strong anti-boycott law by the Congress would be interpreted by the Arab nations "as a major shift in U.S. foreign policy in the Middle East."

The possibility that the United States would in fact lose some trade advantages by the enactment of a strong anti-boycott law is something that exporters and some public officials do not want to confront. They and all Americans will protest in the strongest language their devotion to the military security and economic stability of Israel, but it is uncertain whether they are prepared to sacrifice in any monetary way for these objectives. The simple fact is that the United States over three decades has been able to maintain its remarkable loyalty and unique allegiance to Israel without being required to sacrifice any significant financial or political advantage. It may be that the Arab economic boycott presents the United States almost for the first time with the question of whether it believes strongly enough in its commitment to Israel to forgo those economic gains which, if accepted, will inevitably mean that more American corporations and banks will refuse to participate in the economic development of Israel.

Understandably, Americans who would gain by commercial transactions with the Arab world seek to play down the harm or even deny that harm is done to Israel. They can note, for example, that in 1975 Israel was the nineteenth largest customer for American exports—even excluding military sales. They can also point to the following statement made in the April 1975 issue of the *Arab Economist* published in Beirut: "An important proviso underlying the entire policy is that blacklisting will not be applied whenever the overall result or results will be more detrimental to Arab economies than to Israel. . . ."

But attempts to minimize the impact of the economic boycott cannot assess the damage done to Israel by the voluntary abstention on the part of American corporations from doing business with Israel, not because of present pressure but simply in order to protect their rights to do business with the Arabs in the future.

The adamant refusal of President Ford to allow any tightening of American law on the Arab boycott virtually paralyzed the Congress' effort to enact any effective legislation. Moral indignation at the tactics of the super-rich Arab nations is pervasive in the Congress and in the country, but it is apparently insufficient to overcome the grasping desires of corporations and banks to secure the lavish profits available to them in Arab lands that are suddenly oil-rich.

Those seeking to have Congress make illegal all capitulation to the Arab boycott have been assisted at least in a minor way by groups of stockholders who have raised the issue of corporate participation in the Arab boycott at the annual meetings of major American corporations. No corporation doing business with the

Arabs has reversed its position as a result of protest by stock-holders, but at least the undeniably moral problem of American corporate enterprise assisting the Arabs' economic warfare against Israel has been raised.

An ecumenical group called the Inter-faith Center on Corporate Responsibility, made up of the major Protestant and Catholic denominations, has sought to use funds invested by Christian churches in American corporate stocks as a way to express Christian concern about aiding the Arab boycott. In 1976 several major Christian denominations notified American corporations in which they owned stock that they would withdraw their investments if the concern submitted to the boycott. The use of church investments to change the policies of those industries which capitulated to the Arab boycott against Israel and to anti-Jewish discrimination is about the only significant recognition by religious bodies in America of the insidiousness of the boycott against Israel and the necessity of withdrawing any participation, however inadvertent or unintended, from such a clearly unethical activity.

One of the most active groups in combating the Arab boycott was the National Ministries Board of the American Baptist Churches. The Baptist group, which owns approximately $30 million in stock, wrote to several corporations and reminded them that "all boycott demands against any country having diplomatic relations with the United States are contrary to the stated policy of our government."

Little if any other activity by religious bodies against the boycott has developed. Even conceding that the legal and international aspects of the boycott are complex and even arcane, the lack of involvement on the part of the Christian churches demonstrates once again that there appears to be a wall of separation between Christians and Jews that allows Christians to be uninformed and thus silent at a moment when the newly rich Arab nations are planning and plotting to bring about by economic means the withering away of the state of Israel. At the same time the United States is the only nation which, having enacted in 1965 a feeble and unenforceable resolution against the Arab boycott, now recognizes that it is inconsistent for America to have authorized some $2 billion for Israel in 1976 while at the same time permitting major U.S. corporations to be involved as accomplices in the conspiracy of the Arab nations to bring about the economic strangulation of the state of Israel.

Such a policy seems to be inconsistent with the commitment made by Secretary of State Henry Kissinger on April 4, 1976. Dr. Kissinger stated:

"The survival and security of Israel are unequivocal and permanent moral commitments of the United States. Israel is a loyal friend and a fellow democracy, whose very existence represents the commitment of all free peoples. . . .

"The United States will help keep Israel strong—to insure that peace is seen clearly to be the only feasible course. We will never abandon Israel—either by failing to provide crucial assistance, or by misconceived or separate negotiations, or by irresolution when challenged to meet our own responsibility to maintain the global balance of power."

During the 1976 campaign, Jimmy Carter promised time and time again that he would sign a bill to mitigate the damage to Israel from the economic boycott waged against that nation by the Arab countries for almost thirty years. The 95th Congress quickly took up the bill which both the House and the Senate had passed in 1976. The Congress made some modifications, mostly weakening, and saw the President sign it into law on June 22, 1977. In his statement on the occasion of his signing Public Law 95-52, President Carter referred to the Arab economic boycott as a "profound moral issue, from which we should not shrink." The President referred to "our special relationship with Israel" and promised that his Administration would "effectively enforce this important legislation."

The 1977 anti-boycott law—written by way of amendments to the Export Administration Act—contained compromises or "loopholes" which could seriously erode the effectiveness of the measure. But the potential for harm to Israel in these provisions cannot be discerned until the regulations implementing these provisions have been adopted and have been in effect for several months or even for a few years. The difficulty in making any assessment of the impact of the new law is further complicated by the continued if diminished confidentiality granted to the applications of American corporations to the Commerce Department for licenses to do business with the Arab nations. Information about these applications must be given to a committee of Congress on request but may not be released by such committee unless it determines that the withholding of it "is contrary to the national interest."

One cannot be certain that the anti-boycott bill which became law on June 22, 1977, will relieve Israel from many of the economic barriers and blockades brought about by an economic war against Israel by virtually all of its neighbors for a generation and a half. But at least the law reaffirms America's commitment to Israel and expresses the desire and determination of the United States to correct its economic policies when they collide with the interests of Israel. Law, however, is a feeble instrument when it must reverse a policy of American industry to do business with the nations of the Middle East even when the conduct of such transactions meant that an American corporation would promise to forgo business with Israel.

If, however, America eroded its commitment to Israel by permitting corporate wealth in the United States to advance the Arabs' economic blacklisting of Israel, America was even more unfaithful to its alliance with Israel by the frightening escalation of military equipment being transferred from American sellers to Arab governments. It is to that ominous threat to the very existence of Israel that we now direct our attention.

14

WILL AMERICA'S SALE OF ARMS TO ARAB NATIONS BRING ABOUT THE DESTRUCTION OF ISRAEL?

The escalation of arms sales to Middle Eastern nations in recent years is staggering. From 1974 to mid-1976 the Arab states bought arms worth $16 billion—$12 billion from Western nations with the balance from the Soviet bloc. Israeli purchases from the West during the same period totaled close to $5 billion.

For more than a generation the United States has been equal or superior to the U.S.S.R. in furnishing arms to the nations of the earth. This role of the allegedly peace-seeking United States is so phenomenal and tragic that the entire list of nations which received almost $30 billion worth of arms in the twenty-four years from 1950 to 1974 should be set forth.

The following chart from the Senate Appropriations Committee reveals that the United States has become the merchant of death.

In fiscal year 1974 the United States reached the peak of its insane distribution of arms. A high point of $10.8 billion in U.S. foreign arms sales was attained in that year. In fiscal year 1975 the total edged down to $9.4 billion and in the following fiscal year decreased to $8.3 billion.

U. S. Military Sales to Foreign Countries, 1950-1974

Following is a list of all nations that have purchased military supplies from the United States between fiscal 1950 and 1974. Top buying nations over the 24-year period were Iran, West Germany, Israel, United Kingdom, Saudi Arabia, Australia and Canada. Figures are in millions.

Nation	1974	1950-1974
Argentina	$ 8.9	$ 149.8
Australia	35.1	1,130.9
Austria	3.1	66.7
Belgium	9.9	147.2
Bolivia	.2	1.2
Brazil	58.7	219.2
Burma	.1	2.6
Canada	93.9	1,126.2
Chile	68.2	127.7
China (Taiwan)	88.3	572.2
Colombia	1.1	21.3
Costa Rica	—	.9
Cuba	—	4.5
Denmark	20.9	145.2
Dominican Republic	.03	2.0
Ecuador	—	4.7
Egypt	—	.4
El Salvador	.4	1.9

Nation	1974	1950-1974
Libya	.02	30.0
Luxembourg	.02	2.8
Malaysia	1.2	49.0
Mali	—	.1
Mexico	.4	13.8
Morocco	8.3	47.9
Nepal	.001	.09
Netherlands	17.6	219.6
New Zealand	4.9	119.5
Nicaragua	.1	3.4
Niger	.008	.008
Nigeria	4.5	7.9
Norway	50.3	288.3
Pakistan	7.9	136.3
Panama	1.9	3.6
Paraguay	.01	.4
Peru	43.6	106.1
Philippines	5.0	13.9

Country		
Ethiopia	.5	1.2
Finland	.01	.08
France	21.1	368.0
Germany	218.6	5,473.5
Ghana	.2	.3
Greece	434.9	764.8
Guatemala	1.0	18.2
Haiti	.3	.5
Honduras	.7	7.3
Iceland	.5	.5
India	.2	62.9
Indochina	—	8.5
Indonesia	.1	1.0
Iran	3,794.4	7,588.6
Iraq	.02	13.2
Ireland	—	.5
Israel	2,117.6[1]	3,675.9
Italy	45.1	712.0
Jamaica	.04	.8
Japan	57.7	424.6
Jordan	50.9	253.9[2]
Kenya	81.4	97.5
Korea	18.2	18.2
Kuwait	9.7	19.6
Lebanon	.6	3.2
Liberia	3.2	—
Portugal	2.5	16.1
Saudi Arabia	587.7	1,286.1
Senegal	—	.006
Singapore	12.1	631.1
South Africa	—	3.1
Spain	147.8	568.4
Sri Lanka	—	.004
Sweden	7.0	49.3
Switzerland	8.4	122.4
Syria	—	.001
Thailand	19.9	65.1
Trinidad/Tobago	—	.09
Tunisia	.7	5.8
Turkey	17.1	243.2
United Kingdom	45.1	1,971.3
Uruguay	1.2	9.4
Venezuela	4.4	179.2
Vietnam (South)	.004	1.2
Yemen	2.6	2.6
Yugoslavia	.004	12.4
Zaire	1.3	20.9
International Organizations	16.8	421.1
Worldwide Total	**$8,262.5**	**$29,290.3**

1 Includes $1.5-billion for which payment was waived in 1974
2 Less than $500
Note: Total may not add due to rounding

SOURCE: Senate Appropriations Committee

In 1975 the Persian Gulf accounted for 50 per cent of the U.S. arms market and sales. Iran, Saudi Arabia, and Kuwait purchased almost $5 billion worth of arms from the United States in 1975. Those three nations had purchased only $128 million worth of arms in fiscal year 1970.

The quality of arms has risen as rapidly as the quantity. The Shah of Iran boasts that his country within the next two decades will be one of the five great world military powers.

It is obvious that the United States does not have an arms sales policy. The lack of a policy has been responsible for the incredible fact that the United States in the three years 1973–75 sold $28.5 billion worth of arms—a sum almost equal to the $29.2 billion worth of arms it sold in all of the prior twenty-four years!

In 1961 the Congress established a policy that military assistance should be given to another nation "solely for internal security, for legitimate self-defense, to permit the recipient country to participate in regional or collective arrangements or measures consistent with the Charter of the United Nations, or otherwise to permit the recipient country to participate in collective measures requested by the United Nations for the purpose of maintaining or restoring international peace and security, or for the purpose of assistant foreign military forces in less developed friendly countries. . . ."

Somewhere in that paragraph officials at the State and Defense departments have found justification for an armada of weapons to be sent to Middle Eastern nations traditionally hostile to Israel. It is difficult indeed to discover the justification for the United States selling some $7.5 billion worth of arms and military construction in fiscal 1976 to Saudi Arabia. External threats against Saudi Arabia are minimal. Unlike Iran, Saudi Arabia cannot claim that it might be assaulted by the U.S.S.R. Nonetheless, the United States is furnishing the entire infrastructure of the Saudi military establishment. By the end of 1976, Saudi Arabia had received 1,000 American tracked vehicles and 1,000 U.S. anti-tank missiles. In addition, the United States has sold to the Saudis over 100 sophisticated combat aircraft, 400 helicopters, 26 naval vessels, and equipment for two complete military harbors.

The assertion by U.S. officials that the acquisition of massive military power is stabilizing for Saudi Arabia can only mean that it is stabilizing for the continued traffic in oil between that nation and the United States. Ironically, it is the American consumer, paying after 1973 the quadrupled price of oil levied by Saudi Arabia, who is ultimately paying the cost of turning that nation into a dangerous arsenal and a powder keg in the Middle East.

Another reason advanced to justify massive arms sales by America in the Middle East is the contention that Soviet influence is thereby diminished in that area of the world. The facts seem to undercut this explanation. Arms sales from the U.S.S.R. have continued to Arab nations—with the possible exception of Egypt—at a rate not less than that maintained prior to the 1973 war.

When all other arguments fail, the defenders of arms sales to Arab nations fall back on the undeniable fact that the Soviet Union, France, and Britain are and will continue to be major arms suppliers and that the United States should not deprive itself of this lucrative market. Such an argument, however, denotes a certain moral bankruptcy and is unworthy of a nation which, almost alone among all of the countries of the earth, has remained faithful in its alliance with Israel.

Massive arms sales by the United States to Arab nations is, in the ultimate analysis, inconsistent with the fact that the United States has given Israel some $2 billion each year since the 1973 war. That amount exceeded the total of U.S. aid in those years to the rest of the world and worked out in each year to nearly $1,000 for every Israeli man, woman, and child. Prescinding from the moral issues involved, the United States cannot pragmatically jeopardize the enormous investment it has made in Israel.

In 1967 the Congress enacted a law on munitions control. It gave the President the power "to control, in furtherance of world peace and the security and foreign policy of the United States, the export and import of arms, ammunition, and implements of war. . . ." The same law forbade all sales of arms abroad without registration and permission from appropriate American officials. Since virtually no presidential action came about as a result of this 1967 law, the Congress itself adopted a provision in 1974 which requires that the Congress be notified in advance of proposed weapons sales of $25 million or more. Congress then has twenty days in which to disapprove the transaction by majority vote of both House and Senate. This law was, however, very feeble since the key question is really not how much the weapons cost but where they are going and for what reasons. In addition, the export of munitions by private corporations would continue to be regulated exclusively by the President and not be subject to congressional control. The law was also defective in that it allowed Congress some participation in the decision to sell arms only at the very last moment after all of the complex and sometimes secret negotiations had been concluded.

The Congress has yet to enact a provision which would require the State and Defense departments to give it a detailed statement on the impact of the proposed sale of arms—just as the government must do when it files the environmental impact statement required before any major federal action affecting the environment can be finalized. Such a requirement is important if America is to avoid conduct which will incite regional arms races in such unstable areas as the Indian subcontinent. Until an arms transfer impact statement is required by the Congress the Pentagon can continue to follow a course of action which, as in the past, has enhanced the power of totalitarian regimes in the Philippines, South Korea, and Chile. Until a rational, long-range plan for the transfer of arms from America to other nations is adopted, the United States will follow a non-policy as it did in furnishing weapons to both sides in the India-Pakistan controversy and in the conflict between Greece and Turkey.

Until the Congress has been granted a clear role of cooperating with the executive branch of government in deciding which arms, if any, shall be exported, the United States will continue to be what it has been over the past decade—the nation that exported more weapons than the rest of the world put together.

The incoherence and irrationality of America's massive shipments of arms to foreign nations will not only hurt Israel but cannot fail to promote war everywhere. Two thirds of U.S. arms sales in 1975 went to developing countries. The total cost of arms shipped abroad is twice the value of all U.S. wheat exports and three times the value of exports of computers. The sale of arms appears to have a life of its own which expands irresistibly; other nations become dependent upon parts for planes and tankers with the result that more and more of their weapons sales come to America.

Such an escalation of the arms industry occurred in France—a nation which recently replaced Britain as the third largest exporter of arms, after the United States and the Soviet Union. The French expanded their arms trade after they retreated from Indochina—just as America exploded its arms exports after the war in Vietnam terminated. The value of French arms exports quadrupled in the 1960s and doubled once again in the recent boom in the years 1972–76. The defense industry in France employs 270,000 people, which is probably more than any other industry in that country.

The process which turned France into a huge munitions factory is already well advanced in the United States. The process is accelerated by economic and political pressures, one of which relates to the balance of payments, since arms exports improve the U.S. trade balance—especially when they are made to oil-exporting countries. The compulsion to sustain markets for arms in the Arab world will deepen if there is any suggestion by the oil-rich nations that a cessation of arms supply will mean an increase in the price of oil or a diminution in the volume of oil available. In short, the involvement of the United States in furnishing arms to the Arab nations may produce a syndrome that could lead to the alteration of America's policy of support for Israel.

The *New Republic* put it well in an editorial on March 20, 1976. Commenting on the isolated political position of Israel and the tidal wave of arms going into the Persian Gulf and Red Sea nations, the editorial noted:

> There is no way that we can guarantee Israel against an attack by its neighbors. The Russian commitment to Syria and the lavish arms shipments from Western states into other parts of the Arab world make the second, and what should be reciprocal, guarantee impossible. The Arabs retain the war option and that by itself makes Syria's peace negotiations

difficult. If we expand the option, we only make the negotiations more difficult, other avenues more tempting. We establish what might be called the necessary conditions for the failure of our own diplomacy.

It is the Pentagon which is inadvertently undermining that diplomacy by its role as middleman in promoting and arranging foreign military sales. With military advisory groups in fifty-four countries, the Pentagon's teams advise these nations on what arms are available and should be bought. Once the foreign nations have made their selections, the Pentagon becomes the contractor and arranges with an American manufacturer to produce and deliver the weapons. This arrangement, obviously very convenient to foreign countries, theoretically allows the Pentagon to restrain a foreign country from buying weapons that it does not need. But the Pentagon is unable or unwilling to exercise such direction, with the result that, as Dr. Fred C. Ikle, director of the Arms Control and Disarmament Agency, put it: "Increasingly we are exporting our newest and most advanced weapons. . . . Uncontrolled arms sales can fuel conflicts and erode the United States influence for peace . . . not just altruism, but our own self-interest tells us we must use restraint."

Although the Pentagon has consistently justified its foreign military sales program on security and foreign policy grounds, it has been alleged that the Pentagon can realize savings by manufacturing larger amounts of high-technology weapons, some of which are to be shipped abroad. But even if some savings could be realized by this technique, such an advantage cannot be compared with the virtual certainty that Middle Eastern nations purchasing arms from America can and perhaps will pursue goals conflicting with those of the United States.

The Congress has now stipulated that a review by the Arms Control and Disarmament Agency is required before any substantial foreign sales transactions can be consummated. In 1976, U.S. military officials proposed a sale of 1,900 sidewinder air-to-air missiles to Saudi Arabia. The Arms Control and Disarmament Agency held that the sale of such a large number is excessive for the defense of Saudi Arabia. Presumably Saudi Arabia needs the missiles to equip the American fighter aircraft that defend the country against neighboring Iraq, which has been armed by the Soviet Union. But the real reason for Saudi Arabia's request may be its growing concern with the fantastic military power of Iran, which has been sold billions of dollars of American arms, including advanced equipment just recently available to U.S. forces.

There is obviously concern that a stockpile of 1,900 air-to-air missiles could be transferred to other Arab states in the event of another war with Israel.

Even if the law provided for more stringent congressional controls over arms sales abroad, it would be difficult for the Congress to interdict the combined pressure and deception of the Pentagon and the munitions manufacturers. A sale of missiles to Kuwait illustrates the ease with which the Pentagon can evade congressional scrutiny of arms transfers. In late 1975 notice of this sale was sent to Capitol Hill on the first day of a ten-day congressional recess. Since existing law gives to the Congress twenty calendar (not working) days in which to disapprove a sale, Congress in this instance had only ten calendar days in which both Houses would have been required to veto the transaction. They did not.

The massive transfer of arms from the United States to dozens of nations is a policy without any solid foundation. One high State Department officer concerned with U.S. policy in the Middle East summed up his feeling this way: "Arms sales are a substitute for policy. They are what we do when we can't think of anything else." Professor Hans Morgenthau, testifying in May 1973 before the Senate Foreign Relations Committee about America's military sales policy, stated: "It is a policy without a rationale at all." When Defense Secretary Elliot Richardson attempted in 1973 to justify arms sales in terms of the balance of payments, Senator Fulbright remarked: "We have noted before that your balance of payments is about the only argument that is valid. All the others have disappeared, so I don't blame you for calling attention to it."

There is abundant evidence to indicate that arms sales are often detrimental to the interests of the United States. Retired Admiral

Eugene LaRocque of the Center for Defense Information stated at a Senate hearing in June 1975:

"Arms sales constitute the first step towards a U.S. commitment to the government of the purchasing country. Sales of U.S. weapons are normally followed by U.S. soldiers, sailors, and airmen, as well as civilian technicians who are required to train the new owners of the equipment."

The economic and political dynamic behind arms sales commits the United States inexorably to selling more and more arms. If, for example, the United States sells supersonic jet fighters to one country, the neighbor of that client state, desiring to maintain the balance of power, requests and receives the same kind of weaponry from the United States. Subsequently other neighbors join the procession, and a regional arms race is on.

This process instills in the American economy an addiction to a consistently high level of arms exports. Trapped by such political and economic forces, American policy soon loses all guiding principles and becomes controlled by the actions and threats of its "customers" for arms. The next step is to rationalize that we have made a "commitment" to our "customers."

All of these rationalizations and fantasies—some of which approach the edge of absurdity—still flow in memoranda from the State Department and the Pentagon. But not a single argument can justify the incredible fact that the United States in the period from 1973 through 1976 sold almost $40 billion worth of arms. Even the National Security Council, which by law is mandated to carry out studies on crucial policies issues, has never systematically examined what will happen in the next five or ten years as a result of the Pentagon's having become the supersalesman for military equipment and materials to countries of all shapes, sizes, ideologies, and degrees of importance.

In the spring of 1976, President Ford vetoed the most comprehensive and far-reaching reform of the policy-making process for United States arms sales ever undertaken. The legislation which he vetoed represented a historic initiative by Congress to increase its oversight with respect to the proliferation of American arms across the world. The Congress desired to reverse a situation which over the past decade has resulted in the United States' exporting as many arms as all other nations combined. The Congress desired to increase its control over government-to-government sales of more than $25 million to all commercial sales. The bill the President vetoed would also have required him to provide Congress with detailed descriptions of proposed arms sales rather than the cryptic information, sometimes classified, now available to the Congress.

The International Security Assistance and Arms Export Control Act of 1976 would also have established an annual ceiling of $9 billion on total arms sales. Although that particular sum could be criticized as somewhat arbitrary, the Congress felt a need to establish some type of over-all limit to the runaway arms sales program.

Since the act had been passed by rather narrow margins in both Houses, the Congress did not even attempt to override the President's veto. History may record that President Ford's veto of this bill furnished an incentive of monumental proportions to the momentum that has been gathering over the past four years in the calamitous sale of arms by the United States to foreign nations. Indeed it may be that President Ford's veto inadvertently set in motion events which will bring about the beginning of the end of Israel as a nation.

On June 23, 1976, in an address to the Foreign Policy Association in New York City, former Governor Jimmy Carter summed up his thoughts on America as "the world's leading arms salesman" in these words:

"I am particularly concerned by our nation's role as the world's leading arms salesman. We sold or gave away billions of dollars of arms last year, mostly to developing nations. For example, we are now beginning to export advanced arms to Kenya and Zaire, thereby both fueling the East-West arms race in Africa even while supplanting our own allies—Britain and France—in their relations with these African states. Sometimes we try to justify this unsavory business on the cynical ground that by rationing out the means of violence we can somehow control the world's violence.

"The fact is that we cannot have it both ways. Can we be both the world's leading champion of peace and the world's leading supplier of the weapons of war? If I become President, I will work with our allies, some of whom are also selling arms, and also seek to

work with the Soviets, to increase the emphasis on peace and to re-
duce the commerce in weapons of war."

It is significant but distressing to note that the political platforms of the Democratic and Republican parties have for twenty
years contained commitments to prevent an arms imbalance in
the Middle East. In 1956 the platform of the Democratic Party
contained these words:

> The Democratic Party will act to redress the dangerous im-
> balance of arms in the area created by the shipment of com-
> munist arms to Egypt, by selling or supplying defensive arms
> to Israel, and will take such steps, including security guaran-
> tees, as may be required to deter aggression and war in the
> area.

The Republican platform asserted that "we are determined that
the integrity of an independent Jewish state shall be maintained"
and at least by clear inference condemned the tidal wave of Soviet
arms which was then beginning to inundate the Middle East.

In 1960 the Democratic platform stated:

> We pledge our best efforts for peace in the Middle East by
> seeking to prevent an arms race while guarding against the
> dangers of a military imbalance resulting from Soviet arms
> shipments.

Similarly the Republican platform pledged continued efforts to
seek "an end to the wasteful and dangerous arms race and to the
threat of an arms imbalance in the area."

The Democratic platform adopted in July 1976 contains the
same condemnation of the promiscuous distribution of arms.
While not speaking specifically of the Arab nations, the Democratic platform contains these words:

> The proliferation in arms, both conventional and nuclear,
> is a principal potential source of conflict in the developing as
> well as the industrialized world. The United States should
> limit significantly conventional arms sales and reduce military
> aid to developing countries, should include conventional arms

transfers on the arms control agenda, and should require country-by-country justification for U.S. arms transfers, whether by sales or aid. Such sales or aid must be justified in terms of foreign policy benefits to the United States and not simply because of their economic value to American weapons producers.

Despite the self-evident wisdom of restraint on the part of America in distributing arms and in defiance of the promises of both political parties and the warnings of experts in arms control, the United States continues to contribute to a global arms race now out of control which commands close to $300 billion in public funds yearly. The disasters which this tragedy brings about are well stated by Ruth Leger Sivard in the volume *World Military and Social Expenditures, 1976:*

> In addition to the growing potential for cataclysmic destruction, the arms build-up represents an immediate and heavy burden on the world economy. It is destructive whether or not the weapons are put to use in war. It contributes to the inflation, retards economic and social development, and diverts resources urgently needed for human well-being. Until it can be put under control it undermines the national and international security which it is intended to protect.

The unsatisfied needs of society stand in bitter contrast to the incredible record of spending for arms and armies. Half the school-age children of the entire world are not yet attending school; one third of the world's adults are illiterate. All governments spend two thirds more for military force than for the health care of four billion people. World military expenditures average $12,330 per soldier while public expenditures for education average only $219 per child of school age.

The United States and the U.S.S.R. account for 60 per cent of the world's military expenditures and for 75 per cent of the world's arms trade. Together these two nations have more military force than all the other nations combined.

In view of this last reality, it is appalling to note that the

United States and the Soviet Union are both in the process of pouring arms into the Middle East. A report to the Congress in June 1976 by the Comptroller General of the United States reported that in 1975 the cumulative undelivered sale orders for military equipment held by the United States totaled about $24 billion. Perhaps about half of that undelivered equipment was destined for the Middle East. The flood tide of American arms to the Arab world will be coupled with the vast amounts of Soviet weapons which have arrived in Egypt, Iraq, Syria, and Libya since the end of the October 1973 war. If America concentrates its sales in Saudi Arabia, Kuwait, and the United Arab Emirates, it can have no assurance that these nations will abide by American law, which forbids the transfer of American-purchased weapons to other nations without the permission of U.S. authorities. During the Yom Kippur War a total of nine Arab states gave their active support to Egypt and Syria. Jordan has in the recent past indicated that it would not remain idle if another conflict arose. Jordan has established a joint military commission with Syria and has stepped up arms purchases. The rupture of relations between Moscow and Cairo in 1974 has apparently not precluded continued shipment by the U.S.S.R. of military equipment to Egypt. The undeniable fact is that the adversaries of Israel are purchasing massive quantities of sophisticated armaments from the Soviet Union as well as from the United States, Great Britain, France, and other Western nations. Conservative estimates have placed the value of the sixty known major arms sales to Arab states from the West and the Soviet Union since 1972 at about $16 billion.

This inundation of weapons into the nations surrounding Israel has terrorized, impoverished, and confused the people of Israel. Israelis operate on the major premise that the Arab states will not negotiate with a weakened Israel. Similarly, Israel will never feel secure enough to make strategic concessions if it believes itself to be threatened. As a result, the people of Israel opt for the status quo and the "hawks" in the government proclaim that they cannot in conscience alter their position as long as the confrontation Arab states and the other members of the Arab League continue to acquire planes, missiles, and tanks from the Soviet Union and the Western nations.

Not a little bitterness is harbored in the soul of most Israelis when they recognize that the United States pressured Israel to withdraw in 1957 without a peace settlement and that the commitments or guarantees given at that time by the United States to Israel were never implemented. The Israelis also recognize that, although more than 90 per cent of all U.S. world-wide military assistance since 1946 has been in the form of outright grants, Israel did not receive any military assistance grant until 1973. The Arab League states, moreover, received from the United States more than $6.4 billion in military and economic aid between 1946 and 1975. During that same period Israel received about one eighth of that sum in economic assistance. Israelis also know that up to June 30, 1975, the United States had contributed $619,264,592 of the $1.1 billion which UNRWA has raised from governments to care for the Arab refugees.

Some Israelis also remember that it was not until 1962 that the United States agreed to sell Israel the first American military equipment received by that nation—the Hawk anti-aircraft missile.

Israel is officially and vehemently opposed at this time to the sale of military equipment by the United States to Egypt or to Jordan; it is opposed in a less adamant way to U.S. participation in the build-up of the military forces of other Arab nations. The anxiety of Israel is understandable, in view of the fact that the strategic line-up, according to figures from the International Institute of Strategic Studies in November 1975, revealed the following:

	Manpower	Planes	Tanks	Artillery
EGYPT	857,500	500	1,975	1,500
SYRIA	280,000	400	1,470	775
IRAQ	385,000	247	1,290	750
JORDAN	110,250	42	440	231
TOTAL ARAB	1,632,750	1,189	5,175	2,256
ISRAEL	606,000	461	4,865	860

In the light of the very substantial military power possessed by Egypt, should the United States sell arms to that nation? That question tormented the Congress during most of 1976. After the Sinai Agreement in late 1974, the Ford Administration announced a proposal to sell six C-130 aircraft to Egypt. High officials in the Pentagon indicated that this proposed sale would represent the first step in a long-range plan to provide the Egyptian army with the most sophisticated weapons in America's arsenal. President Ford stated that the United States had "an implied commitment" to supply arms to Egypt.

The Administration attempted to justify the sale of six aircraft to Egypt by citing the deterioration of the Egyptian armed forces as a result of a halt in Soviet supplies. This contention is open to challenge since the foreign report of the March 24, 1976, issue of the *Economist* of London stated that "reliable military intelligence sources" have reported that "supplies from the Soviet bloc have definitely not dried up, as Egypt has been claiming for months . . . during 1975 and the first few months of this year Egypt received arms worth $1.5 billion from the Russians."

In addition, the International Institute of Strategic Studies in its authoritative analysis, "The Military Balance: 1975–1976," estimated that Egypt's defense expenditures for 1975–76 would total $6.1 billion, far exceeding Israel's expenditure of $3.5 billion for the same period.

Egypt's military strength, furthermore, would be buttressed in the event of another conflict by Saudi Arabia, which has assured Egypt and other confrontation states that they will have access to the Saudis' massive arsenal of sophisticated arms. With a financial guarantee from the oil-rich Arab nations, Egypt, since 1973, has purchased 150 Mirage jets from France, 500 British fighter-bombers, and several hundred tanks, helicopters, missiles, and other equipment. While Israel can obtain its military equipment only from the United States, Egypt, bankrolled by the newly rich nations of the Persian Gulf, has access to all of the world's arms merchants.

The Pentagon continues to insist that having Egypt in the status of a client for our arms gives the United States "leverage." The theory is that, once the United States establishes itself as the principal arms supplier of a nation, it can influence that nation's actions in times of crisis by threatening to terminate further sales or to halt the provision of needed spare parts. The continuing availability of military equipment from Europe, plus the apparent willingness of the Soviet Union to resume arms sales to Egypt, would seem to negate the "leverage" theory.

In 1976, according to the International Institute of Strategic Studies, the Arab countries enjoyed a four-to-one superiority over Israel in combat planes, a three-to-one edge in trained pilots, a three-to-one margin in ships and submarines, and an enormous margin in anti-aircraft missiles. These figures are based on the total military force of the six leading powers—Egypt, Syria, Jordan, Iraq, Libya, and Saudi Arabia.

The proponents of military sales to Egypt argue that the United States should encourage the moderate policies of Egypt's President Sadat and as a part of such encouragement should extend to Egypt the military assistance they request. The United States was generous in extending over $1 billion in economic aid to Egypt during the first calendar year after the Sinai Agreement.

The sale of the six C-130 military transport planes to Egypt is unlikely to alter the balance of power in any significant way. The resistance which the Congress manifested toward that transaction may have induced the Ford Administration to modify its promises to Sadat with the announcement in July 1976 of a $2 billion aid program for Egypt—the largest American development assistance plan to a single nation ever mounted. Egypt's deeply serious economic problems are traceable in large part to the heavy burden of armaments and military forces which it feels are essential to its stability or its position in the Mediterranean world.

The notion that an American undertaking to completely re-equip the Egyptian military machine would cement American-Egyptian relations and make for greater stability in the Middle East is open to the most serious doubt. Theoretically it could develop that in the event of a war between Egypt and Israel the United States would be the principal arms supplier for both sides. It is hard to conceive indeed of simultaneous emergency resupply airlifts to Cairo and to Tel Aviv.

The further involvement of the American government in the

build-up of the Egyptian capacity to make war simply does not contribute to anything constructive in the Middle East. There are many nations in Western Europe that would be happy to sell Egypt all the weapons it desires in return for ample supplies of Arab oil or Arab oil money. It does not seem to make sense to suggest that in the name of even-handedness the United States should furnish weapons for both Israel and Egypt.

The question of selling arms to Jordan, the staunchest Arab friend of the United States, is much more difficult than that of selling arms to Egypt. Jordan is the only country in the area without an air defense system. In requesting U.S. arms Jordan argued that, since weakness is an invitation to aggression, an air defense system would decrease the prospect of war.

The United States during the years 1962–74 provided some military and economic assistance to Jordan. During that period military grants and sales to Jordan totaled $262.7 million. The bulk of that aid has gone to Jordan since 1970, when that nation cut itself off from most of its Arab neighbors and refused to join a militant campaign against Israel in support of the goals and tactics of the PLO.

Since 1970 the United States has been exceptionally close to Jordan diplomatically. It has worked to replace Jordan's military equipment losses in the 1967 war with Israel and in Jordan's brief conflict with Syria in 1970.

Jordan stayed out of the October 1973 war against Israel despite strong pressure from her Arab neighbors (especially Syria). Although there were undoubtedly many reasons for remaining out of the war, King Hussein has repeatedly cited the lack of an effective air defense as the key deterrent to Jordanian involvement.

After the 1973 war, Jordan continuously sought to persuade the United States to provide it with a sophisticated air defense system. Jordan has argued that all of its neighbors, including Israel, Syria, Iran, Iraq, and Saudi Arabia, currently have sophisticated air defense systems and that Jordan is vulnerable to attack without one of its own. Clearly, Jordan felt that the United States owes it something as a reward for staying out of the 1973 war and for standing firm against the PLO.

In February 1975, President Ford approved the sale of some sophisticated equipment for an air defense missile system in Jordan. On March 22, 1975, the Pentagon submitted its report recommending the sale of the Hawk, Vulcan, and Redeye systems to Jordan. President Ford approved the sale on April 15 and communicated his decision to King Hussein before the King visited the United States at the end of April. Up to this point Congress and the American people had not been told of the proposed sale. In early May word of the sale leaked to the press, and Administration spokesmen opined that it would be for a sum somewhat less than $100 million.

Under continuous pressure from the Congress, the Administration finally, on July 10, 1976, submitted two letters of transmittal to the Congress giving notice of the proposed sale of Hawks, Vulcans, and Redeyes to Jordan. The Administration kept secret the details of the proposal, but the New York *Times* reported on July 12 that the sale was slightly in excess of $350 million, including fourteen batteries of Hawk missiles, eight batteries of Vulcans, and some three hundred Redeyes. The Administration was compelled to confirm publicly that these figures were approximately correct.

Jordan insisted that the Hawk air defense missile system was absolutely essential to attack any aircraft flying over Jordanian territory.

Essentially the proposed sale to Jordan would make it far more likely that that country could and would participate in a future war against Israel. The primary excuse or reluctance—the lack of effective air defense—would be solved by the Hawk missiles. Jordan's request for an air defense system tends to confirm the conviction of military theorists that the Arabs hope to launch a new war along three separate fronts, including one through Jordan. With a new air defense system, Jordan would be a far more difficult foe for Israel to defeat than it was in 1967 when Jordan fell quickly before Israeli air power. Since Saudi Arabia is financing the entire transaction by which Jordan would get an air defense system, it seems highly unlikely that Saudi Arabia would attack Jordan or that the Saudis would be unable to control the decisions of Jordan.

It would be the American understanding that the weapons could be used only for the internal security or self-defense of Jordan and that, in addition, Jordan could not turn the weapons over to another country without the permission of the United States. There is, of course, absolutely no way to enforce these provisions, and they have in fact been ignored in the past.

The Ford Administration, in testimony before the Congress, made the following points:

1. Jordan has been a force for peace and moderation in the Middle East and as such it is a nation which the United States has supported and should continue to support.

2. The proposed sale of some $350 million worth of jets did not include any weapons which would tip the balance of military power in the area but would merely give Jordan what every other nation already had.

3. If Jordan didn't get an air defense system from the United States it would certainly get one elsewhere—probably from the Soviet Union through Syria.

4. President Ford had in fact made a commitment to King Hussein to sell him the air defense system and, consequently, any rejection of that arrangement by the Congress would induce Hussein to think that the United States has betrayed and abandoned him.

Countering this argument is the fact that the Hawk missile system is currently possessed by few if any nations outside the NATO alliance. While Jordan claims to feel insecure surrounded by Arab neighbors armed to the teeth, it would seem almost self-evident that Jordan's new weapons are intended to be used only against Israel. Jordan's neighbor, Syria, which agreed to the formation of a joint Syrian-Jordanian military commission following the announcement of the proposed sale from the United States, clearly expects the weapons to be used to defend Syria against Israel in the event of another war. King Hussein admitted as much when he stated that he would use the new American weapons to stop Israel from assaulting Syria on the Jordanian flank.

In view of these facts, the Pentagon-State Department contention that $350 million worth of arms for Jordan would be a "stabilizing influence" approaches the absurd. A State Department witness before a congressional committee inferred that the proposed sale would have less effect than a feather on the delicate strategic balance in the Middle East. This opinion underscores the horrendous fact that a $350 million missile system seems insignificant in the monstrous flood of weapons which have flowed into the volatile Middle East from the U.S.S.R. and the United States.

The sale of arms to Jordan would almost certainly appear to be in direct conflict with the commitments to the safety and security of Israel to which the United States has been faithful for three decades.

If the United States continues to succumb to the pressures of the Arab nations and makes them individually and collectively into an arsenal of unprecedented military power, there will be no option left but for the United States to meet the inevitable requests from Israel for equipment in order that Israel can maintain at least parity among the traditionally hostile nations which surround it. At that point the United States will be under pressure to demand cash from Israel as it does from the Arab nations. Israel will be in no position to offer cash payments nor will it have any sister nations that would even loan substantial sums to Israel. The United States will, therefore, be confronted with the question of whether or not the Congress will appropriate $2 billion or more each year in order to maintain a military strength in Israel sufficient to deter or roll back if necessary the military might which the surrounding Arab nations will have acquired by their purchases from the United States.

If Israel feels that the United States is going to continue its present policy of selling arms indiscriminately to Arab nations and that it cannot rely upon a massive gift of arms each year from the United States, then it has one remaining option and that is to develop nuclear weapons.

Professor Robert Tucker of Johns Hopkins University has written perceptively about this option which Israel could follow if it came to the conclusion that it simply could not otherwise maintain parity or a balance of power with the surrounding nations.

Professor Tucker's article, published in *Commentary* magazine in 1975, was greeted by many persons with the exclamation that Israel would never introduce nuclear weapons into the Middle East. Others pointed out that even if Israel did protect its territorial integrity by threatening to use nuclear weapons, it would bring upon itself a great deal more of the considerable animosity toward tiny Israel that now exists in the family of nations.

But the seminars on defense conducted in the universities in Israel regularly rehearse the very limited available options. The bottom line always comes to this: if America continues to furnish arms to the Arab nations, many of which are already heavily armed by the U.S.S.R., then the safety and security of Israel will be in the gravest jeopardy. No one in Israel has any lasting solution for such a situation. But the development and possession of nuclear weapons would give it some feeling of security against the nations which encircle and threaten it. The possibility of employing nuclear weapons for that purpose should be viewed by Americans with horror but with the realization that the continuation of America's outpouring of arms to Arab nations can have no other consequence but the development by Israel of nuclear warheads for reasons of sheer self-defense.

15

ISRAEL'S CRUEL DILEMMA IN 1977

The virtual repudiation of the interests of Israel by the United Nations and the undercutting of America's commitment to Israel by its furnishing of massive arms to Arab states all converge to highlight the country's dependence on the United States. That dependence was spotlighted and deepened when the United States in effect denied to Israeli forces the triumph which would have been theirs if they had been permitted to complete the near encirclement of the Third Army of Egypt in the October 1973 war. There appears to be no question that America's decision to restrain Israeli military force derived at least in part from the threatened Arab embargo on oil.

It is true, nonetheless, that the restraint upon Israel at its moment of military triumph imposed by both superpowers was in the name of détente. But it seems fair to state that Washington's compelling interest in preventing another war in the Middle East arose from its determination not to permit another oil embargo. The emergence of this motivation ruptured the congruence of interest that up to that time had existed between Israel and the

United States. At least there had not been an open conflict of interest on the part of the United States in its relationships with the coalition of Arab states and Israel. With the embargo on oil and the quadrupling of its price, Washington's interest in the Middle East became much more diverse and complex. Whereas before the October 1973 war the security of Israel was the principal and primordial interest of America, the accommodation of that interest with Arab aspirations became the dominant interest of the United States after the war.

The development by America of a substantial divergence of interest in the Middle East meant that Israel was dependent on America as never before. To be sure, Israel probably would have been dependent upon America in any event, given the newly found oil riches of the Arabs. But the preoccupation of American foreign policy with the continuation of the flow of oil from the Arab states (constituting more than 40 per cent of all the oil the United States consumes) meant a bifurcation of America's priorities in the Middle East.

The step-by-step diplomacy followed by the United States also made Israel more dependent in the sense that it deferred the day when there could be direct negotiations between Israel and the Arab states. The Sinai Agreement between Israel and Egypt brokered by the United States meant that for the foreseeable future the diplomatic realities of the Middle East will include an America that negotiates separately with the parties to the conflict and that these parties must in reality bring their complaints back to the United States.

The fatal flaw in assuming that the Arab states will settle individually if not collectively is the absence of any evidence that the position of the Arab world now is weaker than it was in 1967. Even then, after the crushing defeat of the pan-Arab nations by Israel, there was little evidence of a disposition to compromise or settle. Why should the Arab states after October 1973, buoyed by their best showing in any war against Israel and cognizant of the pressures on Israel by a world trembling in fear of another oil embargo, settle or even compromise their position?

The apparent "peace" between Israel and Egypt as evidenced in the U.N.-patrolled demilitarized zone in the Sinai has been used to suggest that the Arab states will make concessions in the future which they have been unwilling to make in the past. The fallacy in this conclusion is that the trust which some people feel is developing between Israel and Egypt is actually a trust on the part of both of these nations in the military and diplomatic power of the United States. The trust of Egypt (or Syria or Jordan) in the United States will depend upon the capacity of the United States to bring about a change in the viewpoints of the respective adversaries. America, however, has no credible threat of force against the Arabs. Indeed America is increasingly dependent upon the Arab capacity to produce oil and its willingness to sell it to the United States. On the other hand, the United States, consciously or otherwise, can deal with Israel as a client state which is dependent in frightening ways upon the U.S. economy, the American Congress, and even public opinion in America.

This state of things is even more depressing for Israel because no one can predict with any confidence how long it might last. Indeed, for the first time the dependence of Israel on the United States raises some basic questions about whether or not the Zionist dream, which was to create a nation in which Jews would live without fear and in which they could be the masters of their own destiny, has been realized.

Israel's new dependence on the United States—a dependence which presumably will require America to grant Israel some $2 billion each year in military assistance—is compelling everyone to re-examine every strategic, political, and moral argument which has been given over the past thirty years for the seldom-questioned allegiance of America to Israel. Before America began in late 1973 to try to reconcile its divergence of interests in the Middle East it was simple to sum up the reasons why America and Israel were friends and partners in a world where Israel was almost constantly threatened and where the United States was one of the two great superpowers. The protection of Israel was consistent with America's policy of containing Communism. One could say with a rhetorical flourish that America would protect the only "bastion of democracy" in the Middle East. Pre-1973 statements about America's alliance with Israel also usually included some generalities about the necessity of preserving the balance of powers in the Middle East along with some amorphous comments about the unique relationship which had always existed between the David and Goliath of Israel and America. All of those assertions are still true in whole or in part *if* they can be reconciled with America's now urgent interest in the stable maintenance of the flow of oil from Arab countries to our European allies, to Japan, and to the United States. To be sure, that interest has existed during most of the lifetime of Israel. But the Arab world—for reasons which are not entirely clear—did not, prior to 1973, extend the principles behind its thirty-year-old economic boycott of Israel to the nations, including the United States, which for many years have been increasingly dependent on Arab oil. The seemingly abrupt reversal of that position by the Arab nations after the October 1973 war appears to have produced a profound modification of America's policy toward Israel. That policy has, of course, always been ambiguous—perhaps deliberately so. America's commitment to Israel did not mean in 1967 that the American government would bring about the forcible reopening of the Straits of Tiran— even though Israel desired that objective, America's commitment has never been a commitment to defend Israel. In fact, it has not even been a very precise commitment to provide Israel with necessary war matériel. At least the delay for more than a week by the United States Government in 1973 in sending war matériel to Israel would seem to suggest that either the President or the Pentagon or both were not in agreement that America has a commitment to furnish Israel with that military equipment which it might need to defend itself.

In 1977 or shortly thereafter the President of the United States or the Congress or both will in all probability be required to redefine in very specific terms the commitment which the United States has to Israel. If the United States agrees to give some form of guarantee or commitment, such a promise will be credible only to the extent that there is a substantial identification of interests between the United States and Israel. If the American guarantee is to serve as a substitute for the territorial buffers which Israel will be required to relinquish, then the United States commitment will have to be very precise and unmistakable. It will have to leave no doubt that America's concern for the safety and security of Israel will take precedence over America's fear of another oil embargo.

If such a commitment is to be accompanied by the qualification that American military forces will never serve in Israel, there must be a carefully spelled-out agreement of how the United States will reinforce by equipment the efficiency of Israeli forces.

Israel can, of course, seek to protect itself from the debilitating effects of dependence on the United States by developing its own sources of arms. It is doing so, but in the nature of things a small country like Israel cannot be expected, at least in the near future, to manufacture all of the highly advanced weapons it would need to protect itself from a dozen or more belligerent neighboring states, all armed by both the U.S.S.R. and the United States with the most recent sophisticated equipment for air, land, and ocean warfare.

Israel can also, of course, hope that the coalition of Arab states succumbs to the many divisive forces at work within it. But the fact is that the Arab coalition has demonstrated extraordinary staying power. Israel can also hope that the coalition will break up if and when an agreement is made concerning the land annexed by Israel in 1967. This hope is once again, however, unrealistic since Arab hostility is as intense now as it was before Israel conquered the land which the Palestinians insist must be returned.

Israel can, of course, also hope that the United States will quickly discover alternative sources of energy so that its unbelievable dependence on the Arab nations for almost 50 per cent of its energy will diminish or even fade away. But again the facts point the other way: America is becoming more rather than less dependent on Arab oil.

The Israelis have reason to trust the sincere solidarity of American friendship for Israel. The Congress and the country demonstrated that solidarity in the late 1974 enactment of the Jackson-Vanik bill, which extends trade concessions to Russia only if that nation permits the free emigration of Soviet Jews to Israel. At least indirectly the Congress, in passing this unprecedented modification of America's customary commercial relationships with other nations, manifested its desire to share in and implement the Zionist dream that any Jew in the world who so desires can go to a Jewish state where he can exercise to the full his religious freedom. During the years when enactment of such a law was a possibility and in the first two years of its operation some 130,000 Soviet Jews were permitted to emigrate—a phenomenon totally without parallel since the Revolution in Russia in 1917.

The Jackson-Vanik Law may have been indirectly responsible for financial losses to American exporting corporations. Russia's failure to accept the emigration requirement brought about a diminution of détente but few measurable losses to the American economy. But if the United States agrees to guarantee military stability to Israel—with or without the return of the annexed lands—the cost to the American economy could conceivably be disastrous. This assumes that Arab hostility toward Israel remains unabated. It also assumes that the United States would under virtually no circumstances seek by military force to seize the oil wells in Saudi Arabia and elsewhere in the Middle East in the event that the Arab nations close them or cut America off from that volume of oil which is absolutely indispensable for even the most rudimentary functioning of the American economy.

If America came to the point where it must unequivocally choose between the normal flow of oil from the Arab countries and desertion of Israel the argument might well then turn on the question of exactly what the national interest of America in the Middle East is. It has been repeated to the point of tedium that the United States maintains a presence in the Middle East in order to stabilize the balance of power and to prevent war. But if the continued furnishing by the United States of high-technology arms to Israel meant that the United States or Western Europe or both would be cut off from essential sources of energy, could the "national interest" of the United States still reside in the continuing supply of arms to Israel? That question is in all probability the starkest way of representing the moral dilemma which may well confront the United States in the foreseeable future. It is also a way of forcing the Israelis to think about the one option they have if they become convinced that they can no longer rely on the undivided loyalty of the United States. That one option is the development of nuclear arms to be used solely in the defense of the territory and people of Israel.

Few if any people either inside or outside of Israel know whether serious thought or actual effort has been devoted to the development of a nuclear weapon. The persistent rumor that Israel does possess nuclear arms is just as persistently denied—although a bit equivocally—by Israel.

If Israel is seriously thinking of developing a nuclear deterrent it would be primarily because it does not want its own destiny to rest in American hands. On the other hand, American reaction to an Israeli nuclear deterrent would be predictably adverse. Aside from the genuine conviction in America that the proliferation of nuclear weapons is highly undesirable, American officials would undoubtedly be opposed to the possession of such a weapon by Israel because under those circumstances the United States would not necessarily have that power to control events in the Middle East which it now has.

Israelis undoubtedly think also that the development of a nuclear weapon need not necessarily be destabilizing in the Middle East. The theory is that one or more of the Arab nations will eventually develop the nuclear option. The profound tension which now exists between the Arab states and Israel need not become more intense if one or both possess the nuclear weapon—assuming that the distrust between the Soviet Union and China, both nuclear powers, constitutes a comparison.

At least some Israelis feel that a nuclear balance between Israel and the Arab states would have a stabilizing effect. Israel would presumably be much more willing to yield territories while the Arabs would presumably lessen their will to resort to a military resolution of difference. If Israel possessed a nuclear deterrent it might be possible to relinquish the occupied territories without insisting upon concessions which the Arabs almost certainly will not make, at least in the foreseeable future.

One may suppose that Israeli discussion of developing nuclear weapons—and there is little if any evidence that this is a live option in high governmental circles in Israel—presumes that the nuclear force would be for use only on a second-strike basis and con-

sequently that it would be only for deterrence and not for
employment.

There are several sound moral, political, and strategic reasons
why the creation of nuclear weapons in Israel would be a mistake.
Christians and especially Catholics would probably "lecture" Israel on the absolute condemnation of nuclear weapons issued by
the Second Vatican Council in 1965. In the statement on war the
2,200 Catholic bishops participating in Vatican II stated unequivocally that the use of nuclear weapons for offensive or defensive
purposes may never be morally justified. Although Catholic apologists have not repeated that unbending doctrine as often as one
would hope, it can be safely predicted that they would both "discover" and elaborate the doctrine if they had the opportunity to
apply it to Israel.

Israelis in 1977 do not feel that they have been so repudiated by
international society or so surrounded by their enemies that they
must as a last resort turn to nuclear weapons. They still hope that
the U.S.S.R. will soften its animosity toward Israel, that the Arab
nations will loosen the coalition of hate which surrounds Israel,
and that the United States will somehow find a way by which it
can reconcile its basically irreconcilable interests in the Middle
East.

Christians and all non-Jews in America have a profound sensi-
tivity to the awkward and agonizing situation in which Israelis
now find themselves. Americans like to repeat that we have a
moral commitment to Israel which we cannot and will not neglect. At the same time it is inescapable that there are currents of
thought in America which more and more question this unwritten
and imprecise commitment. These persons are not anti-Semitic
nor do they have any bias against the concept of Zionism, but
they are uncertain and confused about America's role in the world
and cannot clearly distinguish between the morass of America's
war in Vietnam and America's commitment to the preservation of
Israel. If they articulated a foreign policy for America based on
the national self-interest of the United States along with some
vague and not too lofty idealism, it is uncertain whether these persons would reason to a bottom line which would reaffirm

America's promise to do what is necessary for the security of Israel. They could argue quite plausibly that after all there are many nations with far more inhabitants than the three million citizens of Israel who deserve the attention and protection of the United States. If it is democracies like our own that U.S. foreign policy seeks to foster and protect, then, these persons would reason, should not the United States give assistance to many other democracies which without American aid might turn into totalitarian regimes? Assistance to these countries, moreover, can be given and their democracies preserved with infinitely less financial commitment than the $2 billion which the United States has granted to Israel in each year since the 1973 war.

Those who question the commitment of the United States to Israel will find that the shibboleths on which American foreign policy relied until the recent past really mean little if anything to a new generation who never had an emotional association with these ideas or to an older generation who feels deceived and betrayed by the implementation of those shibboleths by the "best and the brightest" in America's war in Vietnam. In short, millions of Americans will be searching in the immediate future for a new, persuasive, comprehensive, and universally acceptable set of reasons why the United States should continue, with unwavering loyalty, to grant massive sums of taxpayers' money for military and economic assistance to Israel.

It is the contention of the next section of this book that the discovery of the fundamental moral and spiritual reasons why the United States should continue its alliance with Israel can be found only in a re-examination of the Christian and Moslem viewpoints concerning Judaism. The centuries of persecution of Jews by Christians and the somewhat shorter period of discrimination against Jews by Moslems obviously enters into the present situation. Today Moslem nations manifest attitudes which ultimately may go back to the Koran and Christians display an apathy toward the agonies of Israel that is reminiscent of the ways in which Christians for generations sought to rationalize by theological or utilitarian norms the activities which resulted in ghettos, pogroms, and persecutions for Jews.

16

DOES ARAB HOSTILITY TO ISRAEL DERIVE ULTIMATELY FROM THE MOSLEM RELIGION?

The Israeli Jew who wants an explanation of the depths of Arab hostility toward his nation is reluctant to think that there is something endemic to the Moslem faith that motivates the anti-Semitism or, as the Arabs would insist, the anti-Zionism of the Arab world. His reluctance comes from the fact that relatively large Jewish communities lived for many centuries in peace and harmony in predominantly Moslem nations. Jews may have been looked upon as inferior or second-class citizens in those nations, but they were never persecuted or degraded to the same extent that they were in Christian nations.

Israelis, moreover, find it difficult to think that the Moslem religion is inherently anti-Semitic since such an attitude is unknown in those areas of the world where millions of people follow the Moslem faith and where there are virtually no Jews. One could infer that the anti-Israel obsessions of the Arab nations do not derive from the Moslem faith but rather from the political predicament in which the Arabs envision themselves.

The question of potential or covert anti-Semitism in the Moslem faith, however, is not easy to answer. Some Moslems and even some Israelis, hopeful of resolving the Israeli-Arab impasse by political and diplomatic means, might well insist that Moslem attitudes toward Judaism are irrelevant to the understanding of the thirty-year-old enmity between the Arab nations and Israel. Such a contention may be offered in good faith with a view to minimizing the metaphysical or theological differences between the clashing parties. But it would appear that the amazingly persistent hostility of the Arab nations toward the very existence of Israel cannot be fully understood without some grasp of what Islam has taught about the Jewish faith and the Jewish people.

The statements in the Koran about the Jews are discordant. For some twelve years Muhammad, in his home city of Mecca, proclaimed the doctrine of monotheism without compromise. He preached Allah as the only God and the one all-powerful creator and absolutely just judge. Muhammad, virtually without success in attracting people to his new religion, began to appeal to biblical figures like Moses, Abraham, and Noah. In the year 622 he migrated to Medina, where his preaching was more warmly received by the Arab population. Muhammad's message seemed familiar to the people because of its similarity to the beliefs of the large Jewish community in Medina. Muhammad made an open plea for a community of belief and fellowship with the Jews. He taught that Jews and Moslems should stand together as equals in fighting for a monotheistic faith against the polytheistic unbelievers. He also made Jerusalem the direction toward which Moslem prayer should be directed and mandated fasts similar to those which Jews practiced on great feast days. He also developed a concept similar to the Jewish anticipation of a messiah along the lines of a second prophet like Moses.

Despite the entreaties of Muhammad and the similarities of certain features of his religion with Judaism, the Jews did not accept Islam. One of the many reasons might have been the Jewish feeling at that time that on the basis of their faith and tradition no prophet could be anticipated out of Arabia.

Muhammad felt deeply betrayed by the Jews whom he wanted to be his allies in preaching monotheism. His disappointment appears thereafter in the verses of the Koran. Muhammad wrote that the Jews were the enemy of Allah; the Jews had always been disobedient; they were damned by Allah because of their lies and disobedience, and they would receive the punishment of hell-fire.

Nonetheless, the Jews, like the Christians, occupy a preferred place in Islam because they are the people of the Bible. In its pure and original form the Moslem religion recognizes Moses with his book of revelation, the Torah, and Jesus with the Gospel, which, according to the Moslem faith, proves the Torah. After both of these comes Muhammad with the Koran, which corrects everything which Jews and Christians have corrupted. Consequently, Islam is the religion chosen by Allah in preference to Judaism and Christianity. In a manner somewhat similar to the traditions of those two religions the Moslem faith singles out the Holy Land and Jerusalem as quite literally belonging to Islam. Not too many years after the hegira the followers of Muhammad built on the spot where earlier the Temple of Solomon had stood the Mosque of Omar. This action, among many others, demonstrates that the claim to Jerusalem was not purely spiritual but that Islam considered itself to be the indisputable heir to Jewish tradition. In a sense, Islam created very early in its existence a form of Zionism.

Almost from the very beginning of the Moslem religion, therefore, its adherents looked upon Jews as a people of the past. Moslems considered themselves as the community with the latest prophets and books of revelation and the best or concluding religion.

These beliefs did not bring about a pervasive anti-Semitism in Moslem nations. At least there was no persistent pattern of oppression. This may be explainable by the fact that Jews in Arab nations did not enter politics nor were they outstanding in the theater, the press, or in literature. Consequently the Arabs had no fear of the Jewish presence and were able to remain confident of their own superiority. In a 1972 book entitled *Arab Attitudes to Israel* by Yehoshafat Harkabi, the point is made that "Islamic society was founded on the recognition of religious groups existing side by side, with power and superiority reserved for the Moslem faith." Harkabi asserts that there never was a stereotype of the Jew in the Arab nations as there was in the West and he judges that, "if the Arab-Israel conflict was settled, anti-Semitic manifestations would die out. . . ." He asserts "with the utmost emphasis" that "Arab anti-Semitism is not the cause of the conflict but one of its results; it is not the reason for the hostile Arab attitude towards Israel and the Jews, but a means of deepening, justifying and institutionalizing that hostility" (p. 298).

Although this conclusion cannot be said to be erroneous, it should be noted that discrimination and oppression against Jews was present at virtually every moment during the first thousand years in which millions of Jews lived in Arab nations. Within one century of Muhammad's death, Moslem armies, incited by the Koran, carried out one of the most sweeping and enduring conquests in history. In the vast domain conquered by the Moslems resided approximately 90 per cent of world Jewry. As the Moslem empire was consolidating its grip over this far-flung empire, Moslem jurists developed a jurisprudence for ruling non-Moslems in Arab lands. The legal arrangement, eventually known as the Pact of Omar, decreed that Jews were to be kept in an inferior position to Moslems at all times, that no Jew would bear arms or engage in any occupation which could place him in a position of authority over a Moslem. In addition, Jewish clothing had to be distinctive, all adult Jewish males paid a poll tax and were subject to a discriminatory land tax, the effect of which was to place them in an uncompetitive position in agriculture. Indeed, the special discriminatory taxes levied against non-Moslems over vast areas of the Middle East were so onerous that by the twelfth century virtually all Christians had emigrated from lands conquered by Islam. The Jews remained because they had no land where they could seek refuge from the fiscal burdens of Moslem policies.

Many contemporary commentators, both Jewish and Christian, seeking sincerely not to exaggerate anti-Semitism in Arab lands through the centuries, point to the prominent role Jews played in international commerce in Moslem lands in the Middle Ages as well as to the extraordinary works Jews wrote in the Arab language. As remarkable as is that era of Arab-Jewish symbiosis, it must be pointed out that it endured for a relatively brief span of perhaps three hundred years in the fifteen hundred years of Moslem rule in the Middle East.

Some persons seeking to limit the Arab-Israeli hostility to political factors theorized that there can be no Arab anti-Semitism since both the Arabs and the Jews are Semites. This, however, appears to be only a play on words since the common quality of being Semites has never been a bond between the followers of Moses and the followers of Muhammad. Even after extensive study into the ultimate sources of the profound antagonism of the Arab states to Israel, one must confess that the religious or theological dimensions of that animosity are not always easy to identify. Indeed, Mr. Harkabi, in his probably definitive book, states that Arab anti-Semitism "has been little studied in Israel." He notes that the linguistic difficulty is severe, that those who know Arabic may have felt reluctant to admit the depth of Arab anti-Semitism, and that Israelis, understandably fearing the profundity and gravity of the conflict, prefer to regard it as "superficial and transitory" (p. 225).

The centuries-old negative attitudes of the Arab world toward the Jew were clearly deepened by the expansion of European powers into the Middle East in the nineteenth century. The Western imperialist adventure into Moslem lands challenged the fundamental belief that history was in harmony with the will of Allah. Westernization, with its notions of capitalism and religious tolerance, made Arabs xenophobic. Arab spokesmen sought to return to the basic doctrines of Islam which had been central in Arab history. The fear of the West and the incapacity to deal with non-Moslem people and issues brought about the rapid emergence of an entirely new Arab nationalism. Since Arab history is completely interwoven with Islam it was inevitable that the Arab nationalist movement would rely very heavily on the religious ideas of the Moslem faith. Arab nationalism, strongly Moslem in its orientation, would in all probability have brought about the expulsion of Jews from Moslem lands—even without the interjection of the Zionist issue.

Throughout the Arab world there has been an upsurge of studies by scholars and religionists concerning the relevance and applicability of Islam as a unifying political force or as an instrument for the pursuit of Arab nationalism. This investigation has brought about the resurgence of interest in Muhammad's utter-

ances on the Jews. It is unfortunate indeed for Israel that the Jews
of the world have established this homeland at the moment when
the Arab world finds itself in a state of unrest and disorder. After
centuries of suffering anti-Semitism and extermination, the Jews
sought refuge right at the place and at the time when the Arabs—
also after centuries of degradation—finally came to that moment
when, for the first time in modern history, they are in a position to
try to control their own destiny. It is understandable, if overwhelmingly tragic, that the Jews now become the target of the dis-
content of the Arab world, which itself is seeking both a resolution to the crisis in the credibility of Islam and a place of dignity
in the family of nations. The Arab aspiration for a national liberation movement turns its frustration on Israel and seeks to blame
this country of three million people for all of the disasters that
have come upon a people whose religion and culture for many
centuries played a leading part in human history. The very presence of Israel offends that consciousness of superiority which Moslems draw directly from the Koran. Israel, moreover, is viewed as a
Western or European nation, whose intrusion into the very geographical center of the Arab countries is described emotionally as
a "cancer."

It is paradoxical that at the time when Christians are re-examin-
ing every aspect of their tradition, theology, and liturgy to extir-
pate all semblances of anti-Semitism, the Moslems are re-examin-
ing all of their religious teachings with a view to discovering every
tenet of Islam which may be utilized for anti-Zionist purposes.

The proceedings of the Fourth Conference of the Academy of
Islamic Research, conducted in Cairo in 1968, constitute a
935-page compilation of the statements and discussions of seventy-
seven Moslem scholars. Although this conference of the principal
religious leaders of the Moslem-Arab world was not called for the
purpose of considering the Arab disaster in the 1967 war religiously, one has to conclude that it resulted in a voluminous
vilification of a religion and a people.

A 79-page summary of the proceedings, edited by D. F. Green,
entitled "Arab Theologians on Jews and Israel," published in

1971, reprints the resolutions and recommendations of the conference. These are so implacably hostile to Israel that one hesitates even to reveal them. In the very first recommendation the conference "solemnly declares":

> That the causes for which combat and jihad [holy war] must be taken up as defined in the Holy Koran are all manifest in the Israeli aggression, since the Israelis had launched attacks against the Arab and Moslem territories, violated what is regarded as most sacred in Islam, with regard to both its rights and sanctuaries. . . .
>
> For all these reasons, striving with one's life and wealth against the aggressors has become a binding duty every Moslem has to fulfill in accordance with his means and competence, however remote his homeland might be [from the Moslem territories that were victimized by enemy attacks].

The unqualified finding that all of the conditions for a "holy war" are present in the "Israeli aggression" does not agree with the contention of many serious Arab scholars that the "holy war" can be taken up only as a way of converting non-believers to Islam. To state, furthermore, that every Moslem has a "binding duty" to engage in Arab aggression against the alleged aggression of Israel converts a political conflict into a theological war.

The second recommendation of the conference "calls for strengthening the struggle which is being waged by the Palestinian people, and providing it with all means of escalating the battle to fulfill its objective." The conference goes on to appeal "to all the Islamic governments to cut off all relations whatever with Israel." The final conference report goes even further and states that "cooperation with the enemy in any form is a stab against all Moslems as well as a violation of the teachings of Islam." Moslems everywhere must not overlook "their religious duty of liberating Jerusalem and all of the occupied land. . . ."

The report castigates the friends of Israel and "denounces the support of certain countries for Israel and Israel's aggression, and declares such support . . . a demonstration of enmity towards them [the Arab people] and a total disregard of their sentiments".

It is inappropriate, however, to imply that these religious leaders were manipulating their theological convictions for political purposes. Religious leaders in Islamic culture have traditionally exercised political functions. The Western concept of distinct secular and religious authorities never developed in Moslem nations. That phenomenon makes the recommendations of the Cairo conference even more ominous since there does not appear to be a group of dissenters to raise questions about the notion that the "holy war" must be waged by Moslems against Israel. If the call for a "holy war" is not just the usual rhetoric which has pervaded the Arab world over the past thirty years, it is indeed portentous in view of the fact that Islam claims 19.4 per cent of the world population as its adherents, while the Jewish religion has only 0.5 per cent.

Arab spokesmen have, of course, claimed for many years that they are not anti-Semitic or anti-Jewish but only anti-Zionist. This claim is hard to sustain in view of the presence everywhere in the Arab world of literature containing the worst slanders against Jewry and Judaism. *The Protocols of the Elders of Zion*, the notorious forgery fabricated in tsarist Russia, now has more versions and editions in Arabic than in any other language. Excerpts from the *Protocols* have been found in textbooks used by Arab school children and in reading material given to the armed forces. The claim that the Arab nations are opposed only to Zionism rather than to Judaism breaks down when one sees undeniably anti-Semitic remarks attributed to almost every major leader in the Arab world. In December 1973, for example, King Faisal spoke as follows:

"The Jews are accursed by God through the prophets . . . they have deviated from the teachings of Moses and have attempted to murder Jesus Christ . . . they have no connection or right to have any presence in Jerusalem. . . ."

General Idi Amin, the President of Uganda, was quoted in the New York *Times* of December 13, 1972, as approving of Hitler's murder of six million Jews.

A Catholic magazine in France, *Encounter Today*, editorialized in 1973 about this hate literature with these words:

> This type of propaganda is not new. It has filled pamphlets and school books for years . . . but here the territorial contest is definitely placed on theological ground and hate is openly given a religious basis and justification, feeding the old medieval spirit of holy war with crudely Western anti-Semitic arguments.

It is difficult to believe that the Moslem religion actually authorizes the hatred recommended by the Cairo conference. The basis of the Moslem way of life is the five "pillars"—belief in the creed, prayer five times a day, fasting during Ramadan, alms giving and, if possible, a pilgrimage to Mecca at least once during one's lifetime. On the other hand, the traditional Moslem inseparability of religion from the rest of life makes it possible and inevitable that political leaders can manipulate Moslem views to accommodate their own ideological ambitions. Since the defeat by Israel in 1967 and 1973 of Arab military forces, appeals to pan-Islamic unity contain a theological element and by clear implication a condemnation of Israel.

One can only speculate on the impact which anti-Zionist propaganda from the Arab nations has on the 530 million Moslems in the world. Does it influence the 25 million Moslems in the Soviet Union or the estimated 10 million in western China? Does the anti-Israel obsession of the Arab nations add anti-Semitic accent to the convictions of the 105 million Moslems in Indonesia?

It is very clear that if the Christians in the world knew more about the roots of Arab intolerance toward Zionism they would not have been so startled in November 1975 when seventy-two nations of the U.N. General Assembly branded Zionism as racism.

Although there are many million Arabs who are Christians, the communication and dialogue between Christians and Arabs has been so minimal as to be almost non-existent. Christians, of course, have seldom if ever had much communication with Buddhists, Hindus, or Confucianists. But when three million Jews reside in Israel, driven there at least in part by the hostility of Christians, and when these same individuals have been harassed for three decades by Arabs, both Moslem and Christian, a dialogue between adherents of Christianity and of the Moslem faith would seem to be the minimum that Israelis and all of humanity might expect.

On February 1–5, 1976, the first Islamic-Christian dialogue since before the Crusades was conducted in Libya. The official delegations consisted of fourteen Vatican and sixteen Moslem representatives from ten nations. In addition, some 300 observers and 120 mass media people were present from forty-three nations with Moslem populations.

The conference was sponsored by Colonel Qaddafi. Financed by the government of Libya, it was intended as a pan-Christian and pan-Islamic meeting. The World Council of Churches, invited through the Vatican Secretariat for Non-Christians, declined, reportedly because Libya was subsidizing the meeting.

Serge Cardinal Pignedoli, the president of the Vatican Secretariat, opened the conference by stating that "we begin our dialogue in a spirit of fraternity, not to affront each other, not to judge each other reciprocally and not to minimize our respective faiths. We begin with full respect and with full love one for the other." The Moslem speakers echoed these expressions of good will but regularly added to their remarks strong attacks on the Crusades, Christian missionaries, imperialism, and Zionism.

The entire conference might have passed quietly into history except for a bitter controversy over Recommendation No. 20. This resolution, not subject to any vote on the part of the Christian delegation, read as follows:

> The two sides look upon the heavenly religions with respect and accordingly they distinguish between Judaism and Zionism, the latter being a racial aggressive movement, foreign to Palestine and the Middle Eastern region.

The final declaration was offered to the conference by a Moslem delegate at the closing Friday afternoon session. Neither Cardinal Pignedoli nor other members of the Vatican delegation saw the text in advance. In fact, Cardinal Pignedoli had been asked to visit the palace of Colonel Qaddafi for an audience at the very time that the final anti-Zionist resolution was being presented.

Recommendation No. 21, presented under comparable circumstances, stated the following:

> Adherence to truth, justice and peace, and belief in the rights of peoples for self-determination prompt the two sides to affirm the national rights of the Palestinian people and their right to return to their homeland, and to affirm the Arabism of the City of Jerusalem and the rejection of [its] Judaization, partition and internationalization. . . .

Four days later, following world-wide pressure, Vatican officials issued a statement declaring that Recommendations 20 and 21 of the Libya Declaration were unacceptable. The Vatican Secretariat of State announced: "The Holy See declares that it cannot accept these two articles because their content does not correspond in essential points to the position, known to all, of the Holy See."

It is uncertain whether future Christian-Islamic dialogues will be held or whether Christians might be disinclined to attend such meetings for fear that Moslem groups might exploit these gatherings for anti-Israel purposes.

Efforts by Christians to moderate the anti-Zionist feelings of Moslems will not succeed easily. It may be that European Christians in the second half of the nineteenth century brought some anti-Semitic ideas into the Arab world. It may be that the Arabs learned the alleged distinction between anti-Judaism and anti-Zionism from the West. In any event, Christians in the Arab world now constitute a force seeking to deter Christians outside of the Arab world from recognizing the legitimacy of Israel. Arab Christians were the only organized Christian community in the world to protest the adoption by the Second Vatican Council in 1965 of the "Jewish schema." Furious protests appeared in the Arab press against the declaration issued by all the bishops of the Catholic Church that no individual or collective guilt for the crucifixion of Christ should in any way be imputed to the Jews.

Arab spokesmen and journalists theorized that Israel would be strengthened if the Vatican Council adopted the schema. The suspicion was expressed that the approval of the schema was a step toward Vatican recognition of Israel and the establishment of diplomatic relations with that nation. Although the main Arab argument was that the question was not religious or theological but only political, the Arabs, nonetheless, both Christians and Moslems, offered religious arguments to demonstrate their conviction that guilt for the death of Christ should still be imputed to the Jewish people. Once again Arab spokesmen went to the Koran for arguments to buttress their contention that the Zionist plot had infiltrated the Vatican.

In the ultimate analysis it is really impossible to offer any comprehensive or even comprehensible explanation of the Arab nations' obsessive hatred of Israel. The presence of a tiny nation of three million people amid some twenty nations with well over 100 million people does not present any geographical, political, or religious problem to the Arab world. Indeed, logically and historically the Moslems should be able to coexist in peace with Jews. The parallelism between these two religions is remarkable. Islam accepted from Judaism the doctrine of repentance and atonement —beliefs which are central to both faiths. Like the Jews, the Moslems observe the laws of purity and "cleanliness" derived from the Levitical regulations in the Bible. Arabs practice circumcision, ritual washing and bathing, and have marriage and divorce laws which are practically all derived from their Jewish counterparts— although the attitude of Jews toward women has always been much more advanced than that of the Moslems. In addition, Islam drew ceremonials, rites, and customs from the Jewish reservoir of the Pentateuch, the Talmud, and subsequent traditions.

During the many centuries when Islam was developing its approach to legal-theological problems the process paralleled that of Judaism. The Islamic mullahs or muftis issued decisions and opinions on matters of Islamic law in the same way that rabbis did. This similarity in approach and method, designed to reconcile contradictions and inconsistencies appearing in the Bible or the Koran, led to a parallel intellectual development for Jews and

Arabs when they lived together in geographical and cultural association in Arab nations.

One would have hoped that, despite the aspersions cast on the Jews by Muhammad in the Koran, the adherents of these two faiths could have coexisted at least in tolerance if not in total harmony.

The establishment of Israel terminated whatever rapprochement had been possible for Moslems and Jews. A mass emigration of Jews to Israel from Arab countries began even before 1948—eventually leading to the decimation of Jewish communities which had flowered in Arab nations for many centuries.

With the exception of the Egyptian settlement with Israel in the Sinai, Arab policy continues to echo the "no's" of the Khartoum conference—no negotiations with Israel, no recognition of Israel, no peace with Israel, and no compromise over the rights of the Palestinians.

The Arabs know that they lost their struggle with Israel on the battlefield in the years 1948, 1957, 1967, and 1973. They continue to wage economic warfare through the Arab boycotts and to carry on psychological warfare on the battlefield of public opinion in the U. N. General Assembly.

Will the Moslem nations, as a new war against Israel, intensify their appeal to the Koran and to fundamental Islamic religious principles that in Moslem eyes condemn the Jews?

If it is psychologically impossible for the Jews of Israel to communicate on a theological plane with Moslems, then Christians must make every effort to demonstrate that both Moslems and Christians must have a very special relationship to the first children of Abraham, the Jews. All three religions have a common heritage and believe, unlike all other religions of the earth, that God has given us both creation and revelation. All three religions believe that God sent prophets and communicated with mankind through them and through the sacred books.

Christians must insist, furthermore, that Jews, Moslems, and Christians all worship God through submission, obedience, and prayer. All three religions share from the commandments given to Moses the common command to love our brothers as ourselves.

When one views the common tradition believed in by Jews,

Christians, and Moslems going back to the command of love given by the God of Abraham, Isaac, and Jacob, the scandal of the Christian persecution of Jews and the contemporary "holy war" of Moslems against Jews constitute a scandal that is so staggering as to be almost beyond belief.

Christians would be obligated to atone for their sins against the Jews even if the followers of Muhammad had not turned their most sacred beliefs into instruments by which they could justify their hatred of the Jews. Christians should recognize that if they do nothing the Arab Moslem forces will continue to utilize every weapon available to them to destroy Israel. If, on the other hand, Christians act in an unprecedented and courageous way, it may be that their example as well as the political impact of their actions will be sufficient to cause a relaxation or even a termination of the animosity which the Arab Moslem millions have held for thirty years toward their fellow worshipers of the God of Abraham, the Jews of Israel.

17

CHRISTIAN REACTIONS AFTER THREE DECADES OF ISRAEL'S EXISTENCE

It is very difficult to measure the attitudes of American Christians toward Israel since Israel is unique. One can try to compare these attitudes with Christian concern about apartheid in South Africa, oppression in the "captive nations" of Eastern Europe, or starvation in Pakistan, but the religious-moral-legal problems in Israel are so unparalleled that it is simply not possible to assess the overall Christian attitude toward them. Nonetheless, it is not unfair to Christians in America to state that their attitude toward Israel does not appear to have a theological dimension. At the same time, the very depths of the commitment which America has made to Israel suggest that there exists in the United States a religiously rooted moral consensus that sustains the unwavering promise of America to protect the territorial integrity of Israel. Contemporary public opinion polls demonstrate that virtually every class of Americans supports overwhelmingly this nation's commitment to Israel. Although it is not verifiable from existing polls, it may be that certain groups of largely Protestant fundamentalists are more devoted to Israel because of the literal way in which they accept the words of the Old Testament, in which God promised the land of Israel to His chosen people forever.

In the post-Auschwitz world, Christians have an undeniable duty to extend support to Israel because of the reparation and restitution which humanity and particularly Christians owe to a group six million of whom were slaughtered in nations where Christians simply did not offer that level of resistance which was minimally required.

Although many American Christians might in fact be acting from motives of guilt when they support Israel, it is disappointing and distressing that there are few if any signs of a development in American Christian circles of a theology or moral philosophy with regard to America's obligation toward Israel.

It may be that there is such a moral consensus in the United States because of the goal of human equality that underlies all America's legal institutions. In America the legalization of ghettos or pogroms is now unthinkable—even if arguably this has taken place on a de facto basis with regard to America's black minority. It could be that the moral sentiments underlying the universally accepted concept of equality, human dignity, and due process have furnished up to this time a consensus sufficient for most Americans to join in an almost unquestioned commitment to the preservation of the state of Israel.

The amorphous nature of America's unwritten and almost untested promises to Israel should suggest to Christians and others that it might be dangerous to continue a foreign policy which is so ambiguous that people are afraid to re-examine it or so nebulous that people do not feel that it needs scrutiny.

Secularists in America might well suggest that the United States should treat Israel in the same manner that it treats any of the other 140 nations of the earth. Persons who take this position would understandably resist the addition of any religious element to the policies which America applies to its relationships with other countries. Strict constructionists among this group could argue that America should neither aid nor inhibit religious groups either at home or abroad.

The logic of this position comes out in the conclusion recommended in the Summer, 1976, issue of "The Link," a newsletter published by Americans for Middle East Understanding. In a lead article, Dr. John H. Davis, former commissioner general of UNRWA, writes as follows:

> The most logical thing for the United States to do would be to compromise Israel's existence. But while the United States could survive well without Israel, she cannot survive well at all without both Arab oil and Arab business. But as America enters the year 1976 her commitment to Israel's survival is one that neither the President or Congress is prepared to compromise.

Those who seek to exclude any moral or religious dimension from America's foreign policy must be prepared to accept Dr. Davis' blunt and cruel statement that "the United States could survive well without Israel." They would have to agree when he goes on to state that "America's present Middle East policy . . . conflicts with her basic needs for energy and . . . conceivably could lead to Soviet-American confrontation." The ultimate question comes to this: can the United States fulfill its commitment to Israel if it asserts that its need for energy and its desire for a continuation of détente are placed in jeopardy by its policy of friendship with Israel?

If America's foreign policy is only an amalgam of pragmatic and utilitarian principles based on self-interest, Dr. Davis is logical when he states that "the United States could survive well without Israel." If, on the other hand, America has a special and unique alliance with Israel, then the objectives sought by that alliance must be made paramount to but not necessarily inconsistent with the other objectives of our foreign policy. If our refusal to subordinate the nation's access to oil or its progress in détente to the preservation of Israel requires the acceptance and implementation of moral or even spiritual norms, it would seem that the Christians of America have an urgent and profound duty to evolve those spiritual norms.

Christian bodies in America must develop those norms in connection with the world units to which they adhere. Unfortunately,

the World Council of Churches has a relatively unimpressive record when it comes to its relations with the Jews and Israel. The
predominantly Protestant World Council has devoted an extraordinary amount of time to the eminently worthwhile problem of
liberation politics in the Third World. It has formalized its relations with the Jews through its Committee on the Church and
the Jewish People—a unit which now interacts with international
Jewish committees. The work in 1976 of the new chairman of that
committee, Dr. Krister Stendahl, dean of the Harvard University
Divinity School, is more promising with respect to Israel than almost anything the WCC has done over the past several years.

The WCC's viewpoint toward Israel is unusually ambivalent.
Its declarations have always stressed support for the existence and
security of Israel, but this support, at least according to some
knowledgeable observers, is extended grudgingly, almost as a debt
to be paid for the persecution of the Jews in the Christian West.
The WCC's support for almost every liberation movement in the
Third World is put in very affirmative theological and moral language. But the WCC expresses some admiration for the Palestine
Liberation Organization (PLO) and extends its liberation theology to Israel only with apologies to the Third World.

The struggle which the World Council of Churches has had
with the very concept of the state of Israel has never been resolved. In its First Assembly in 1948, it issued these words:

> We call upon all the churches we represent to denounce
> anti-Semitism, no matter what its origin, as absolutely irrec-
> oncilable with the profession and practice of the Christian
> faith. Anti-Semitism is a sin against God and man. Only as
> we give convincing evidence to our Jewish neighbors that we
> seek for them the common rights and dignities which God
> wills for his children, can we come to such a meeting with
> them as would make it possible to share with them the best
> which God has given us in Christ.

Critics of this statement, both Christian and Jew, have pointed
out that the complete elimination of anti-Semitism is recom-

mended, at least in part, only as a way to create a condition favorable to the acceptance of Christ by Jews.

In 1954 the Second Assembly of the World Council of Churches, meeting at Evanston, Illinois, voted 195 to 150 to strike from a statement any reference to Israel's part in Christian hope. The conflict had not been anticipated nor can the sharply divided vote be necessarily construed as a repudiation by the World Council of Churches of the authenticity of the state of Israel. Political considerations entered into the vote at Evanston. The Middle Eastern bloc, comprising Arab Christians, adopted a point of view almost exclusively political and in opposition to the state of Israel. European theologians sought to eschew the political status of Israel and adopted a wholly theological and biblical stand. Delegates from the English-speaking world were divided, uncertain and confused.

The "Resolution on Anti-Semitism" of the World Council of Churches in New Delhi in 1961 reiterated its previous stands and added the following:

> The assembly renews this plea in view of the fact that situations continue to exist in which Jews are subject to discrimination and even persecution. The assembly urges its member churches to do all in their power to resist every form of anti-Semitism. In Christian teaching, the historic events which led to the crucifixion should not be so represented as to fasten upon the Jewish people of today responsibilities which belong to our corporate humanity, and not to one race or community. Jews were the first to accept Jesus, and Jews are not the only ones who do not recognize him.

As noted previously in this volume, the World Council of Churches, meeting in Nairobi in 1975, reacted with vehemence against the charge that Zionism was a form of racism.

Although there is much to criticize in the Vatican declaration on the Jews, promulgated on October 28, 1965, and the guidelines for its implementation, which were finally issued in January 1975,

Dr. Henry Siegman, the executive vice-president of the Synagogue
Council of America, wrote in *Worldview* magazine in December
1975 as follows:

> The discrepancy between Catholic and Protestant perform-
> ance serves to remind us, first of all, that for all its internal
> weakness and loss of authority, dramatic actions of the Cath-
> olic Church still manage to command the kind of public at-
> tention that eludes the divided and complicated structure
> that is the World Council of Churches.

Dr. Siegman points out, however, that both the Catholic
Church and the World Council of Churches have failed "to as-
similate, morally and theologically, the two seminal events of contemporary Jewry: the holocaust and the establishment of the
State of Israel."

It would appear that the inclusion of either of these events in
the statement of the Vatican Council on the Jews was not a live
option. Rabbi Arthur Gilbert's book, *The Vatican Council and
the Jews*, published in 1968, reviewing all of the agonizing four-
year debate over the statement, does not indicate that serious consideration was given to mentioning the holocaust or Israel.

The Vatican statement on the Jews, *Nostra Aetate*, "marked a
turning point in the history of the Catholic Church and the Jewish people" in the judgment of Dr. Siegman. At the same time,
this writer opines that the declaration, "while celebrated by professional Jewish ecumenists . . . was greeted by the 'Jewish
masses' with skepticism and even resentment." He gives the reason: "In the awesome light of Auschwitz the statement 'absolv-
ing' Jews from the mythic guilt of deicide revealed a meanness of
spirit that constituted its fatal flaw."

One can argue that the Vatican declaration on the Jews was either a monumental step forward or an inadequate statement
which did virtually nothing to undo all of the hideous wrongs
inflicted on the Jews through the centuries by persons who pro-
fessed to be Christian.

The declaration passed in a final vote of 2,221 to 98. The eight
paragraphs of the declaration are reproduced here in their entirety

since this statement, however inadequate, must be the beginning point for Catholics and for all Christians who desire to apply their religious faith and hope not to Judaism as some abstract concept but to a living faith, the predecessor of Christianity, whose adherents now reside in Israel as a result of a world-wide persecution acquiesced in by Christians and Moslems.

TEXT OF VATICAN II STATEMENT ON THE JEWS

AS THIS Sacred Synod probes the mystery of the Church, it remembers the spiritual bond that ties the people of the New Covenant to Abraham's stock.

Thus the Church of Christ acknowledges that, according to God's saving design, the beginnings of her faith and election go back as far as the days of the patriarchs, of Moses, and of the prophets. She affirms that all who believe in Christ—Abraham's sons according to the faith (cf. Gal 3:7)—are included in the call of this patriarch; she also affirms that her salvation is mysteriously prefigured in the exodus of the chosen people from the land of bondage. The Church, therefore, cannot forget that she received the revelation of the Old Testament through the people with whom God, in that loving kindness words cannot express, deigned to conclude the Ancient Covenant. Nor can she forget that she draws sustenance from the root of that well-cultivated olive tree onto which the wild roots of the Gentiles have been grafted (Rom 11:17–24). For the Church believes that by His cross Christ, who is our Peace, reconciled Jews and Gentiles, making the two one in Himself (cf. Eph 2:14–16).

The Church keeps ever before her eyes the words of the Apostle about his kinsmen: "Theirs is the sonship and the glory and the covenants and the law and the worship and the promises; theirs are the patriarchs and from them is the Christ according to the flesh" (Rom 9:4–5), the Son of the Virgin Mary. Furthermore, she recalls that the apostles, the Church's foundation-stones and pillars (cf. Ap 21:14; Gal 2:9), sprang from the Jewish people, as did most of the early disciples who proclaimed Christ's Gospel to the world.

As Holy Scripture testifies, Jerusalem did not recognize the time of her visitation (cf. Lk 19:44), nor did the Jews in large number accept the Gospel; indeed, not a few opposed its dissemination (cf. Rom 11:28). Nevertheless, now as before, God holds them most dear, for the sake of the patriarchs; He has not withdrawn His gifts or calling—such is the witness of the Apostle (Rom 11:28–29). In company with the prophets and the same Apostle, the Church awaits that day, known to God alone, on which all peoples will address the Lord in a single voice and "serve him with one accord" (Soph 3:9; cf. Is 66:23; Ps 66[65]:4; Rom 11:11–32).

Since the spiritual patrimony common to Christians and Jews is so rich, this Sacred Synod wishes to encourage and further their mutual knowledge of, and respect for, one another, a knowledge and respect born principally of biblical and theological studies, but also of fraternal dialogue.

True, the Jewish authorities and those who sided with them pressed for the death of Christ (cf. Jn 19:6); still, what happened in His passion cannot be attributed without distinction to all Jews then alive, nor can it be attributed to the Jews of today. Certainly, the Church is the new people of God; nevertheless, the Jews are not to be presented as rejected or accursed by God, as if this followed from Holy Scripture. May all, then, see to it that nothing is taught, either in catechetical work or in the preaching of the word of God, that does not conform to the truth of the Gospel and the spirit of Christ.

The Church, moreover, rejects any persecution against any man. For this reason and for the sake of her common patrimony with the Jews, she decries hatred, persecutions, displays of anti-Semitism, staged against the Jews at whatever time in history and by whomsoever. She does so, not moved by political reasons, but impelled by the Gospel's pure love.

One thing remains: Christ underwent His passion and death freely and out of infinite love because of the sins of all men so that all may obtain salvation. This the Church has always held and holds now. Sent to preach, the Church is, therefore, bound to proclaim the cross of Christ as the sign of

God's all embracing love and as the fountain from which every grace flows (*Nostra Aetate*, iv).

Both Christians and Jews have severely criticized the final declaration of Vatican II on the Jews. A. Roy Eckardt, a distinguished Protestant scholar on Christian-Jewish relations, states in his 1974 book, *Your People, My People*, that the Vatican's pronouncement on the Jews was a "disaster." He castigates the declaration for not demonstrating "the slightest positive sign of Christian penitence." He deplores the deletion by Pope Paul of the word "deicide" and construes this as a weakening of the council's position because the rejection of the "deicide" charge against the Jews had been included in a draft resolution overwhelmingly approved by the bishops in 1964. Eckardt is also very critical of the placement of the declaration on the Jews in the section on "Non-Christian Religions." He feels that the linking of "the Christian-Jewish relation with other histories is irresponsible and ludicrous." He says that the "absolutely unique relationship of Christians and Jews" was virtually buried within expressions of unity and sympathy for Hindu contemplation, Buddhist realization, and Moslem adoration.

Eckhardt agrees with the judgment of the then Catholic John Cogley who, writing in the New York *Times* on October 16, 1965, expressed the judgment that the Vatican declaration on the Jews had become "a reason for shame and anguish on the part of many Catholics and of suspicion and rancor on the part of many Jews."

Eckhardt is particularly vehement in his criticism of the statement that the council is "not moved by political reasons." To Eckhardt, a professor at Lehigh University and probably the most articulate critic in America of anti-Semitism in the Christian Church, "the stern truth is that political factors played a very large role in the formulation of the conciliar text on Judaism and the Jewish people."

One may question whether Eckhardt's judgments on Vatican II are too harsh. He extends them to all Christians since he states that "Protestant and Orthodox Christians can only find their image in the unhappy events at Rome." But he is correct when he points out that Vatican II did not even allude to the central realities of the Jewish psyche today—(1) the concept that the land of Israel is the incarnation of Jewishness, and (2) the conviction throughout the world that the rhetoric of genocide coming from Cairo, Amman, Damascus, and Baghdad must be taken seriously because this time it will be the "Final Solution." Those fears and feelings, deeply engraved on Jewish consciousness today, do not seem to have any echo in the statement of Vatican II.

It must be pointed out, however, that this first solemn statement on the Jews ever made by an ecumenical council in the history of the Church set forth some principles which, if they were really accepted, not only by Catholics but by all Christians, could transform the negative feelings so many Christians have toward Israel and toward the idea of Jews as a "people" with a unique devotion to the land of their fathers. The Vatican statement speaks of the "spiritual bond" that unites all Christians with Jews. It also makes reference to the fact that the Redeemer, his mother, his apostles, and "most of the early disciples" were Jews.

It dispels and destroys the ambivalence of Christians with regard to the permanence of the mission of Israel. Vatican II declares that now as before God holds Jews "most dear"; God "has not withdrawn His gifts or calling. . . ." Christians and Jews have in common a "spiritual patrimony" which is "so rich, this Sacred Synod wishes to encourage and further their mutual knowledge of, and respect for, one another, a knowledge and respect born principally of biblical and theological studies, but also of fraternal dialogue."

The declaration concludes by affirming that the Church "decries hatred, persecutions, displays of anti-Semitism, staged against the Jews at whatever time in history and by whomsoever."

No full explanation has ever been given for the delay of almost ten years before the issuance of the guidelines for the implementation of *Nostra Aetate*.

The guidelines fail to recognize the central role which the land of Israel occupies in Jewish religious thought. Despite the assertion that the authors desire to understand Jews as they understand themselves, the failure to make any mention of the burning question of Jewish survival in Israel and elsewhere in the post-Auschwitz era raises a basic question of credibility for the guidelines.

Nonetheless, they have a monumental value because they are the first official Catholic document on the highest level of authority to view Judaism not as an anachronistic relic but as a living, vital, and rich contemporary religious movement. At the same time the guidelines fail to comprehend the contemporary Jewish consciousness. Rabbi Marc H. Tanenbaum, the national director for interreligious affairs for the American Jewish Committee, commented on this point in the *Catholic Mind* for May 1975 in these words:

> Any definition of contemporary Jewish religious experience that does not provide for due comprehension and acceptance of the inextricable bonds of God, people, Torah, and promised land risks distortion of the essential nature of Judaism and the Jewish people, and would constitute a regression in Jewish-Christian understanding.

The declaration on the Jews issued by the Second Vatican Council and the guidelines issued a decade later for the implementation of its principles are in many ways historic, unparalleled, and unprecedented in all of Christian history. But their limitations and inadequacies are so severe that one can only hope that they somehow contain the seeds from which a complete understanding on the part of Christians concerning the primal place of Israel in the Jewish psyche may emerge.

The guidelines finally promulgated by the Holy See in 1975 were a bitter disappointment after the issuance in 1969 of a proposed set of truly magnificent guidelines by the Vatican Secretariat on Christian Unity. Likewise, the 1973 Declaration on Christian Relationships with Judaism was more progressive than the subsequent 1975 guidelines. Indeed, the guidelines issued in 1967 by the American Catholic bishops are possibly the best directives yet issued by any group in the world.

It is indeed lamentable that the 1969 proposed Vatican guidelines were withheld from promulgation, presumably because of an alliance of pro-Arab political forces and conservative theologians.

The 1969 document acknowledged that Judaism is a living religion that "endures forever." In addition, it called upon Christians to "ask pardon of their Jewish brothers" for the "persecutions and moral pressures" brought by Christians against Jews. It also affirmed unambiguously that "all intent of proselytizing and conversion is excluded." Finally, it called upon Christians "to understand and respect the religious significance of the link between the people and the land of Israel." Although this recommendation is mild, it does suggest that the document urged Christians to come to terms both spiritually and practically with the momentous and monumental importance of Israel as the dominant existential reality in Jewish self-consciousness today.

One of the finest Catholic statements on the question of the land of Israel was made public in 1969 by Lawrence Cardinal Shehan of Baltimore. After emphasizing the increasing cognizance among Christians of the "permanent election" of the Jewish people, the statement points out that fidelity to the covenant is

> linked to the gift of a land, which in the Jewish soul has endured as the object of an aspiration that Christians should strive to understand. . . . Christians, whatever the difficulties that may be experienced, must . . . respect the religious significance of the link between the people and the land. The existence of the State of Israel should not be separated from this perspective, which does not in itself imply any judgment on historical occurrences or on decisions of a purely political order.

It seems clearer each day that the land of Israel is the supreme testing ground for the Jewish-Christian relationship. It seems clear that a Christian must believe that the covenant between God and His ancient people has not been broken and that it abides; St. Paul wrote to the Romans (11:29) that "the gifts and the call of God are irrevocable." It follows, therefore, that no point of view with respect to the Jewish people or to Israel or to Jewish-Christian relations can escape judgments of a religious and theological nature. The statement on the Jews issued by the Vatican Council in 1965 and the guidelines for this statement issued a decade later affirm the right of Jews to exist as an ethnic group or as a religious community but are silent as to their right to exist as a sovereign nation. Silence does not necessarily deny that right, but it tends to impose on Jews the conception which other men have of Jewish identity. Silence about the authenticity of Israel may reasonably appear to some Jews to be an implicit denial that the emergence of the state of Israel is an essential element of contemporary Judaism.

The shame and scandal of Christianity century after century have been to make demands on Jews to conform to what Christians feel Jews should be. Modern Christians—especially those in America—insist that all Jews individually be guaranteed freedom of religion. Unconsciously, however, Christians yield to Jews only those rights which they would yield to differing Christian denominations.

However unqualified or grandiose a religious freedom for Jews a Christian might conceive, that freedom will not be fulsome or even fair to Jews unless it includes the right of Jews to establish Israel and the duty of Christians to protect the right of Israel as a nation and as the territorial flowering of Judaism.

The late, brilliant Rabbi Abraham J. Heschel wrote that it would be sacrilegious to treat Israel either as a compensation or as an atonement. In his 1969 book *Israel: An Echo of Eternity*, Rabbi Heschel laments the holocaust and, linking it with Israel, states that "the existence of Israel reborn makes life less unendurable. It is a slight hinderer of hindrances to believing in God." He denies, however, the essential link between the holocaust and the state of Israel; he reasons: "There is no answer to Auschwitz . . . to try to answer is to commit a supreme blasphemy." But at the same time "Israel enables us to bear the agony of Auschwitz without radical despair, to sense a ray of God's radiance in the jungles of history."

It is this inseparability of the holocaust and Israel which was missed in the statement made by Vatican II and is overlooked by virtually all Christians in the modern world. Most Christians look upon the nation of Israel as a political entity rather than as a country where the secular and the religious domains are wedded because in Judaism they simply cannot be divorced. Any separation of politics from religion or matter from spirit appears to be fundamentally alien to the Jewish faith. It is because of this monism that Zionism is neither a purely political phenomenon nor a purely religious one.

There is no way to understand Judaism or Israel without an enlightened awareness of the indissolubility of the people, the faith, and the land.

Judaism, consequently, is much more intimately linked to the common peoplehood of Jews and the land of Israel than the Christian faith is associated with Western civilization or Islam with the Arabs. For Israelis, Abraham is not merely a transcendent religious figure, he is also the "father of our people" in the way that George Washington is to Americans.

If we can assume that the most solemn statements issued by the World Council of Churches and the most deliberative pronouncements of the Catholic Church's hierarchy represent the present level of understanding among Christians in the world with respect to Judaism and the land of Israel, we must conclude that Christians generally have a very inadequate and even truncated understanding of Judaism.

If more Christians in America understood the profound intertwining of the religious and political dynamic that brought about Israel, would the foreign policy of the United States be altered to make it consistent with that understanding? No short answer to that question is possible, since very frequently political policies lag far behind the more advanced moral consensus in our nation. But one must say that a widespread understanding of Israel as a nation profoundly linked with both the Christian West and the very essence of Judaism would at least in the long run bring about a better justification for America's friendship with Israel than the tired and tattered contention that Israel is our defense in the Middle East against aggression from the Kremlin or that Israel is the only genuine democracy in that part of the world.

In August 1975 the famous Russian nuclear physicist, Dr. Andre Sakharov, said to me in a conversation of almost two hours that only the Christians of America can save the Jews of Russia. I have wondered since I heard this prediction whether it might be accurately extended to embrace a prediction that only the Christians of America can save the Jews of Israel. The statement sounds pompous and pretentious coming from a Christian, but one must concede that the Christians, if they fully understood their potential and if they so willed, could bring peace to Israel.

It has often been said that anti-Semitism comes about as the result of the de-Christianization of Christians. No Christian who has an even slight understanding of the moral and religious solidarity which exists between Jew and Christian could engage in anti-Semitic conduct. But all of history shows that Christians who are unaware of their roots or who reject the foundations of their faith are quite capable of anti-Semitic conduct, which, in its ultimately hideous form led in our lifetime to the gas ovens and crematoria of the Nazi holocaust.

For centuries Christians believed or felt that the dispersion of the Jewish people was the divine punishment for the crucifixion. That idea, never defensible by theological or historical evidence, persisted through twenty centuries of Christian thought, engaging even the brilliant mind of the Protestant theologian Karl Barth, who wrote this of the Jews:

> According to all of the rules of world history [the Jews] should have disappeared from the international scene after the fall of Jerusalem in the year 70 of our era. Why were they not swallowed up in the sea of other peoples? . . . There is good reason to wonder very seriously whether, after the year 70, one still has a right to talk about a common history of the Jews.

It was because of these and similar statements that Professor Jules Isaac, a Jewish scholar, wrote at the age of eighty-five the searing book *The Teaching of Contempt*. He concluded his short but shattering volume by stating that it is the "mythical and unhappy tradition of the 'deicide people' that does violence to truth, justice, the dignity of Israel . . . and even to her right to live." Although he saw the persistent danger arising as the result

of the "teaching of contempt," Jules Isaac reported that a "purify-
ing stream exists in Christianity and grows stronger every day."
God has given to Christians, he stated, "the power to break at last
with those evil habits of mind and heart and tongue, contracted
over a period of nearly two thousand years of what I have called
the teaching of contempt. . . ."

If American Christians can perceive the vision of Abraham Heschel and follow the mandates of Jules Isaac, they will be able to
add entirely new dimensions to the declarations of Vatican II. If
they do they will be able to give a deeper meaning and a greater
appeal to America's thirty-year-old alliance of friendship with Israel. But unless Christians and others recognize the full meaning
of Israel both for Jews and for Christians, America's bond of
friendship with Israel could wither when the country and the
Congress are pressed by the cost of continuing our commitment
and the lack of any immediate return in wealth or prestige to the
United States.

Albert Camus wrote that "great ideas come into the world as
gently as doves." We can hope that Christians will understand the
vision and dreams of Abraham Heschel and Jules Isaac if they follow Camus's hopeful prediction:

> If we listen closely, we shall hear amid the roar of empires
> and nations, a faint flutter of wings, the gentle stirring of life
> and hope.

18

DEPENDENCE ON ARAB OIL: ANOTHER THREAT TO AMERICA'S COMMITMENT TO ISRAEL

Even if all of the Christians and non-Christians of America agreed with the teachings of Jules Isaac and even if they all agreed to follow scrupulously the directives on Judaism which the Second Vatican Council issued to Catholics, the American Congress and the American people would still be confronted with the undeniable fact that America's increasing dependence on oil from the Arab nations makes it ever more vulnerable to the temptation of preferring a steady flow of oil over the fulfillment of America's commitment to Israel.

The oil crisis which emerged for all of the industrialized nations of the earth after the Arab embargo in late 1973 and 1974 clearly means that the developed and capitalist nations are at the end of a long period of rapid economic growth which was made possible to a considerable extent by the exploitation of the very inexpensive raw materials of the underdeveloped world. The quadrupling of the price of energy by the Organization of Petroleum Exporting Countries (OPEC) signifies a radical shift in economic power between the industrialized nations and those countries which until yesterday were economically primitive.

In view of the obvious temptation for the Arab nations to threaten the United States with a cutoff or sharp diminution of oil if it continues to aid Israel, one would have thought that the United States, conscious of its commitment to Israel, would have looked upon the fourfold increase in Arab oil prices as a warning in disguise, teaching us that we must develop alternative sources of energy. America seems unmindful, however, of its promises to Israel when it allows its dependence on Arab oil to increase sharply. In 1976, Saudi Arabia doubled its oil shipments to the United States—with 1.2 million barrels of oil a day being shipped to American ports. As a result, Saudi Arabia replaced Canada and Venezuela as the main sources of imported oil—a position which those two countries had held since before World War II.

By 1976, America's oil imports had risen from roughly a third to over 40 per cent of its total oil requirements. The share provided by Middle East producers constituted roughly 30 per cent of this 40 per cent.

In 1976, Saudi Arabia alone awarded contracts to U.S. companies for $27 billion worth of goods and services—with implementation of these agreements to be carried out over a five-year period during which Saudi Arabia expects to spend $142 billion in modernizing that nation.

Saudi Arabia and all Middle Eastern oil-exporting countries are in a position to reject all complaints about the soaring price of oil; they simply note the extreme poverty of virtually all peoples in the Middle East and the fact that Western oil companies, at least in Arab eyes, artificially depressed the price of oil for many decades.

It appears, furthermore, that the Arab nations will for the foreseeable future be in a position to dictate the price of oil to all potential buyers. In one single area extending from Kuwait down the coastal region of Saudi Arabia to Qatar—some four hundred miles in length—there is contained 40 per cent of present OPEC production and 40 per cent of the world's known oil reserves.

The susceptibility of the United States to the possibility of a boycott or blackmail by the Arab nations is appalling. Saudi Arabia, with or without other Arab nations, could simply terminate a substantial percentage of all America's energy supplies if the

United States did not terminate all economic or military assistance to Israel. Indeed, in view of the unique economic power possessed by the oil-producing nations in the Middle East, it is surprising that they have not sought to exploit more boldly their petroleum power in their all-out war against Israel. There is little reason to feel that the Arab nations will continue to forgo the opportunity of crippling the economy of America if the United States will not abdicate its friendship with Israel.

The seriousness of this situation is apparently so frightening to contemplate that very few commentators have even explored its potentially devastating effect upon America's commitment to Israel. About the only student of the question to do so is Professor Robert W. Tucker of Johns Hopkins University, whose article in the January 1975 issue of *Commentary* explores the possibility that the United States, to save its own economy and that of Western Europe, would intervene with military power in the Middle East, take over the oil fields, and sell the massive amounts of petroleum produced there daily at a price established by the actual cost of the oil's production. Professor Tucker concedes that the world might well recoil at the possibility of American troops taking over parts of the Persian Gulf. The Russians would presumably send massive forces to expel the U.S. military. At the same time, he theorizes that if the Arabs had another war with Israel and were badly beaten they might well react by imposing an embargo. If one argues that even then it would be unthinkable for America to intervene to protect its vital interests, it must be conceded that America and the world presently live at the mercy of the Arabs and the Russians.

A justification for military intervention advanced by Professor Tucker is the continued dependence of western Europe on the United States for its security. Oil is an essential part of that security, and hence the United States could not fulfill its commitments to NATO if both the United States and western Europe were unable to cope effectively with a cutoff of oil by the Arabs.

Another consideration is the fact that military intervention would improve the position of Israel. Even if such intervention were discontinued in a short time, clearly the Arabs would be more tractable about their oil and would not be so ready to deny it to America again on account of the support which America insists on giving to Israel.

On the other hand, military intervention could do enormous damage to Israel, since it would give credence to the idea that Israel is the justification for Arab intransigence over oil, whereas in reality it is the dream of the Arab nations of becoming economic superpowers which makes them so rapacious.

The acquisitiveness of the Arab nations with regard to their oil would in all probability be the same with or without Israel. Nonetheless, it is undeniable that the oil crisis is one of the most serious causes of the steady erosion of Israel's position in world opinion and in global diplomacy.

Professor Tucker concedes the implausibility of his scenario while emphasizing that America has no evidence to support its blind optimism that somehow the situation will work out so that we can have both an adequate supply of oil from the Middle East and also be faithful to our commitments to Israel.

He admits that his essay operates "very close to worst-case assumptions" while making it clear that there is no reason to expect anything but more outrageous prices and more threats from the Arabs. As he puts it:

> The Arabs now dream of righting a humiliation that for centuries has lain deeply imbedded in their consciousness. Why should men be "reasonable", according to Western lights, when they have come so far and so fast by being unreasonable?

The uncertainties and ambiguities in America's commitment to Israel are once again apparent in the way that the United States has failed to think through the inconsistencies of a policy which permits America to import about one third of its total energy needs from nations which are the sworn enemies of America's friend, Israel. The federal tax structure encouraged U.S. oil companies to deal abroad while the import quotas imposed by American Presidents from 1959 to 1974 made it highly profitable for American oil corporations to develop extensive drilling operations in those nations which have been the enemies of Israel for almost thirty years.

The facility with which America accepted the fourfold increase in the price of oil once again implicitly contradicts America's pledges to Israel. There seems to be no reason why the Carter Administration could not implement existing legislation which would require the submission of secret bids by the OPEC nations individually so that the United States would at least have a chance of buying oil not at the inflated rate billed by the OPEC nations as the "world price" but at a price level which has some correspondence to the cost of the production of the oil.

Those who are less worried about the enormous wealth which is coming to the Arab nations at this time because America spends billions of dollars each year on purchasing Arab oil theorize that the Arab nations might be less hostile to Israel if the standard of living in the Arab nations more closely approximated that of Israel. Unfortunately, no quantifiable evidence is available for such a conclusion, although the development of the Arab nations, like all Third World countries, is a desirable objective.

The stark fact is that Americans simply do not want to admit that their country, by importing almost one third of all of its energy from the Arab nations, is creating the most serious possibility that the United States will at some time have to choose either to restrain its present economic growth or to break its promises to Israel.

Short of military action to seize control of the oil wells in the Middle East, there is, according to all estimates, no means by which the United States can escape dependence on Arab oil in the near future. Despite all measures to conserve energy, America's need grows each day. The development of sources of energy other than petroleum may accelerate, but the United States, nonetheless, will remain heavily dependent upon petroleum for the foreseeable future. In addition, the petroleum-exporting nations are reducing their exports, and this trend can be expected to continue.

A completely logical and totally informed foreign policy for the United States would, therefore, demand that America develop as quickly as possible sources of energy that would make it far less dependent than it now is on oil from Arab nations. It is easy to state as some have that the United States should retaliate in kind if the Arab oil-producing nations boycott it once again. Such retaliation is, however, unlikely to succeed. The Arab nations can obtain from Western Europe most of the economic assistance which they presently receive from the United States. It would seem impossible for the United States to obtain the complete cooperation of all of Western Europe in a boycott against the Arab oil-producing nations. European nations have a far greater degree of dependence on Arab oil than the United States; some nations, such as France, depend upon the Middle East for almost 100 per cent of their energy needs. Consequently, there is no way out for the United States if the Arab nations blackmail it into a choice between continuing the delivery of one third of its energy needs or the repudiation of its commitment to Israel.

Quite apart from executing its anti-Israel policies, Saudi Arabia and other Arab nations have additional reasons for cutting back on their production and sale of oil. The petroleum which these nations have in abundance can be sold much more profitably a few years from now for petrochemical stocks. As a result, the Arab nations can sensibly cut back sharply on their sales of petroleum to the United States for reasons other than their warfare against Israel—even though they could announce this as the reason for the diminution of sales to America. Consequently, the Arab nations could, even without actual blackmail, make the fulfillment of America's promises to Israel much more onerous in the minds of Americans than they actually are.

The immediate development of abundant alternative sources of energy for the United States is essential and indispensable if America is really determined to fulfill its pledges to protect the security and survival of Israel.

19

ISRAEL'S ECONOMIC FUTURE

In assessing America's commitment to Israel, a careful and candid analysis of the economic health and the industrial options available to that tiny nation is essential. This assessment must be tied in with an accurate evaluation of the potential consequences of any political elections which might alter events significantly.

Israel's annual economic growth rate was between 9 and 10 per cent from 1960 through the Yom Kippur War in 1973. Since that conflict Israel has been devastated by a declining growth rate and by runaway inflation, caused and complicated by the fact that it has been required to divert 39 per cent of the annual budget and 33 per cent of the gross national product to defense.

In 1977, Israel improved its economy and its trade deficit by expanding relations with the Common Market nations, thereby acquiring duty-free access to more than 250 million Europeans.

In 1975 and 1976, Israel had a staggering 40 per cent annual rate of inflation—compared to 9 to 11 per cent for the United States and Canada and 24 per cent for Great Britain.

In recent years Israel has suffered an absolute decline in industrial productivity. In 1976 it was approximately 60 per cent lower than in the United States and 40 per cent lower than in Western Europe. To some extent this low rate of productivity is attributable to the enormous defense spending, which in 1973—the year of the Yom Kippur War—was 49 per cent of the total national budget and 19 per cent of all of the economic resources of Israel, including the aid received from the American government and the contributions of world Jewry.

In 1975 the average per capita income in Israel was about $2,700; of that sum more than 50 per cent was taken in taxes. Since it is hardly possible to tax at a higher rate, the annual deficit of Israel reached, in 1975, the astronomical sum of $4 billion—the highest debt proportionately of any nation on the earth.

Since Israel must buy most of its raw materials overseas and must, in addition, import a large part of its military supplies, one of its essential needs is to increase the volume of exportable goods. This objective is made much more difficult because of the substantial number of Israeli adults in the military—a phenomenon which along with other factors contributes to a chronic shortage of workers. In order to correct this situation, Israel regularly seeks to attract as permanent immigrants a large number of Jews of the Diaspora. In a very real sense, the economic future of Israel in the long run, and possibly even in the short run, depends upon the number of Jews who will migrate to settle on a permanent basis in Israel. Aside from the possible influx of a very large number of Soviet Jews, it does not appear that Jews outside of Israel, either individually or collectively, will be moving to Israel in the immediate future. But such a prediction could turn out to be completely erroneous if the anti-Zionist sentiments of the Third World nations emerge at the local level as a new form of anti-Semitism. It is possible, for example, that the repressive government in Brazil, having voted in favor of the U.N. resolution that Zionism is a form of racism, might apply the clear implications of this feeling to the 180,000 Jews who reside in that country. It is similarly possible that the military government in Argentina might allow the continuation of widespread anti-Semitism in that country to reach a point where a significant number of the 500,000 Argentinian Jews would decide that the preservation of their personal and religious freedom required them to go to Israel.

But the future size of the population of Israel will always be difficult to estimate because it is quite possible that a large and even overwhelming number of Jews throughout the world might come to the conviction, independently of the presence or absence of any repression in their country of origin, that they should fulfill the dream of Zionism and live in a nation where geographical, religious, and cultural surroundings make it difficult not to be a Jew. Israel, however, will not have any overwhelming migration unless a sizable number of America's six million Jews reach the conclusion that they should discover their destiny in the land of Israel. No more than 27,000 American citizens, according to one figure, have migrated to Israel for permanent residence in the thirty years of Israel's existence. But if even 1 per cent of America's Jews, or 60,000 persons, per year migrated to Israel, the result in a decade of the addition of 600,000 Americans to the Israeli population would be enormously significant. The exodus to Israel of such a number could in all probability come about by a small religious movement that would arouse the mystical and Zionist aspirations of some of America's young, Jewish adults or possibly middle-aged Jewish couples. While it is true that virtually everyone who has gone to Israel over the past three decades has been seeking to escape repression or even extinction, the maturing of Zionist theology and the sophistication of Israel's self-identification could combine to attract an impressive number of Jewish Americans who were appalled and alienated by a culture with a compulsion to downgrade the religious convictions of all citizens as the ultimate irrelevancies.

Predictions about the future economic health of Israel, complicated by the abiding need for massive military expenditures and made highly speculative by the total uncertainty of the possible influx of Jewish migrants to Israel, become even more unreliable when the political dilemmas surrounding Israel are factored into the equation. It would appear that Israel's position vis-à-vis the Arabs has improved since the signing of the Sinai Agreement. The incredible slaughter in Lebanon, with the subsequent intervention of Syria into that nation, may have seriously undermined the position of the Palestinian Liberation Organization. In a series of events which has confounded even the best-informed experts on the Middle East, the hitherto radical Syria has become a force for stability in the Middle East and has apparently served to tame the Palestinians as a military force. It may be that the flaming rhetoric of the PLO, which demanded the dissolution of the Jewish state and its absorption into a secular state of Jews and Arabs, has now retrenched to the familiar call for a Palestinian state limited to the West Bank and Gaza.

In early 1977, President Sadat of Egypt continued his initiative for peace with the concurrence of President Assad of Syria, who agreed not to oppose Sadat if Egypt would approve Syria's virtual occupation of Lebanon.

In view of the four wars which the Arab nations have waged against Israel, it was understandable that Prime Minister Rabin of Israel spoke only very guardedly about the possibilities of tranquillity and peace in the Middle East. To Rabin, peace means the acceptance by the Arab countries of the existence of Israel as a Jewish state. Such an acceptance would mean not merely a decision to end the state of war but an acceptance of the opening of borders to the movement of people and goods and to the meeting of minds.

Much as Israeli leaders would like to accept the notion that its Arab neighbors are prepared to negotiate at least a treaty of nonbelligerence, events elsewhere in the world persuade them that Arab hostility toward Israel has not ended. On November 25, 1976, the General Assembly of the United Nations, by a vote of 90 to 16, with 30 abstentions, endorsed a proposal calling for the return of all Palestinian refugees to their home and the establishment of a state in Palestine under the control of the PLO. In addition, the General Assembly for the first time endorsed a specific timetable for an Israeli pullback and decreed that the new state must be in place by June 1977. Predictably and understandably, Israel's ambassador, Chaim Herzog, called the resolution a prescription for "national suicide" and charged that the General Assembly had been "hijacked by a group of Arab extremists."

When Israel sees what the PLO is still able to do in its anti-Israel maneuvers at the U.N., Israel tends to conclude that, if in fact the PLO was weakened by its defeats in Syria, that weakening might only have been marginal.

But Israelis increasingly understand that a "decision not to decide" and a posture of not seeking negotiations could conceivably lead to a collision with the Arabs and a major schism with the United States. The then Secretary of State Kissinger put the dilemma this way in a speech in Baltimore in May 1976: "We do not underestimate the dilemmas and risks that Israel faces in a negotiation. But they are dwarfed by a continuation of the status quo."

It would seem that a continuation of the status quo will increase Israel's foreign debt, now nearly five times that of any other country, inhibit Jews of the Diaspora from coming to a troubled and indecisive homeland, give an excuse to the Arabs to acquire more arms, and—perhaps most importantly—raise doubts in the United States Congress about the wisdom of continuing a policy of friendship to a nation which is in deep financial trouble, chronically at war with its neighbors, and increasingly the target of Third World hostility at the United Nations.

Doubts of this nature have really never arisen in the United States Congress. It may be that the consensus that America should aid Israel is so deep in the Congress and in the country that doubts about the wisdom of this alliance could not be created by even the most turbulent internal or external problems that confronted Israel. But the more realistic possibility is that American public opinion, while favorable to Israel, has many "soft shoulders." American public opinion made virtually no protest during the many months of the "reassessment" of U.S. relations to Israel—a policy which brought about the complete embargo of arms to Israel from March 1975 to January 1976. Similarly, little protest was raised when President Ford fought hard in 1976 to cut the so-called "transitional quarter" of aid to Israel. When the U.S. delegation at the United Nations in November 1976 joined in a Security Council "consensus statement" deploring Israeli policy in Jerusalem, on the West Bank, and in the Gaza Strip, few Americans were alarmed. Despite the protestation of the State Department that this vote represented no change in American attitudes toward Israel, the vote was contrary to all previous American positions on this issue.

If most Americans can be indifferent or silent when reversals come to Israel, would it be possible for America's commitment to the security of Israel to be eroded in a "step-by-step approach?" The answer seems to be clearly yes. The way to stop the possibility of such an erosion seems to be a deepening of the fundamental premises and moral assumptions of America's abiding agreement to do all that is necessary to preserve Israel. America's pledge to Israel was summed up by Jimmy Carter, campaigning in New Jersey in October 1976, in these words: "The survival of Israel is not a political issue. It is a moral imperative." As President-elect, Carter restated the issue in these words: "There will be no change in my basic commitment that the issue of the very security and survival of the State of Israel is not negotiable."

It has been the central thesis of this volume that America's commitment to Israel cannot and will not be kept unless Christians, contrite over the unbelievable sins of Christians through the centuries against Jews, recognize that the Christians of this generation—especially in America—are called upon by their religion and by their government to undertake whatever extraordinary remedies might be necessary to protect Israel, a nation made necessary by the holocaust acquiesced in by most of the world's Christians.

20

CHRISTIANS AND
THE SIN OF ANTI-SEMITISM

In the ultimate analysis, all political resolutions of problems confronted by Jews in Israel or throughout the world simply have to
be superficial. Political solutions to the oppression of Soviet Jews
or the aspirations of the Palestinians are desperately needed but
cannot be lasting so long as anti-Semitism or even indifference toward the Jewish people remains in the minds of those who shape
public opinion in the Christian nations. The ultimate cause of the
centuries of agony endured by the Jewish people and the very establishment of Israel can be found only in the attitudes of Christians and their distortion of what Christianity means.

Anti-Semitism in Christian history is one of the great blindnesses
which brought about centuries of horror for those people who in
Christian theology are recognized to have been given a very special place by the God of Abraham, Isaac, and Jacob. The
blindness that brought about anti-Semitism can be compared to
the centuries of confusion among Christians in their attitudes toward the colonialism of the European powers. In retrospect, it is
clear beyond doubt that no highly developed nation can morally

enter uninvited a less developed nation and despoil much of its natural resources. Christian moralists throughout Europe sought to justify colonialism by theorizing that it was a means by which divine providence would bring about the evangelization of the "heathens." The present antipathy of the former colonies of Christian nations toward those countries which exploited them furnishes abundant proof that Christian theologians did not take into account all of the ethical factors that should have been evaluated in an assessment of the morality of European nations "invading" African or other cultures in the name of bringing to these territories culture and Christianity.

A similar but much worse collective confusion has beset Christian theologians through the ages with regard to what Christianity expects in the attitudes of Christians toward Jews. It is probably not too strong to suggest that Christian theology by its negative approach to the Jewish people almost encouraged Christians to have a death wish for the Jews. Father Hans Kung, in his book *The Church*, published in 1967, put it this way:

> But it is important . . . to realize that Nazi anti-Semitism, however much it may have been primarily the work of Godless and criminal men, would have been impossible without the preceding 2,000 years of "Christian" hostility to the Jews, which hampered Christians in offering convinced and energetic resistance to it on a broad front.

There is some evidence that Christians today are finally discovering within themselves the sin of anti-Semitism. But like the person who seeks to give up adultery and have "the end of the affair," the Christian infected with anti-Semitism will discover every rationalization that permits him to continue his inner hostility to Jews—or at least to justify his apathy toward their global problems and the future of Israel. Christians who think at all about anti-Semitism have to conclude that Jacques Maritain was correct in 1939 when he wrote in his volume, *A Christian Looks at the Jewish Question*, that anti-Semitism "seems to be a pathological phenomenon which indicates a deterioration of Christian conscience."

Some Christians, aghast at the anti-Semitism that is so prevalent and pervasive among Christians, have written in a way which suggests that in Christian doctrine itself there are elements of anti-Semitism. For example, Dr. A. Roy Eckardt, distinguished Protestant editor and teacher, wrote in his 1967 volume, *Elder and Younger Brothers*: "All the learned exegesis in the world cannot escape the truth that there are elements not only of anti-Judaism but of anti-Semitism in the New Testament."

Dr. Rosemary Ruether, a Catholic theologian, put it somewhat differently in an article in the *Christian Century* on February 14, 1968:

> Built into the treatment of the Jewish and Christian Bibles as Old and New Testaments respectively is the idea of Judaism as a superseded and obsolete religion, superseded not simply historically but theologically, superseded in terms of the covenant of God with Israel itself.

These scholars and many others have pointed out the profound differences between Judaism and Christianity, but they would appear to distort and even defame Christianity if they mean to leave the impression that well-informed Christians adhere to doctrines which ineluctably lead to anti-Semitism. Despite a hundred generations of anti-Semitic activity indulged in by Christians, it seems overwhelmingly clear that anti-Semitism is an aberration of Christianity and not endemic to that religion. Only by misunderstanding or rejecting the Christian message could a Christian fall to the level of anti-Semitic prejudice. Every Christian would have to accept the profound statement of Leo Tolstoy, the Russian Christian author, when he wrote:

> The Jew is that sacred being who has brought down from Heaven the everlasting fire, and has illumined with it the entire world. He is a religious source, spring and fountain out of which all of the rest of the peoples have drawn their beliefs and their religion.

An acceptance of that concept would surely preclude a Christian from harboring anti-Semitic attitudes.

The irreconcilability of anti-Semitism with a Christian outlook on human existence was set forth dramatically by the fervent French Catholic, Leon Bloy, in these words:

> Suppose that there were people round you continually speaking of your father and mother with the utmost contempt, who had nothing to offer them but insults and offensive sarcasms, how would you feel? Well, this is just what happens to our Lord Jesus Christ. We forget, or rather we do not wish to know, that our Lord made man is a Jew, nature's most perfect Jew, the Lion of Judah, that his mother is a Jewess, the flower of the Jewish race; that the apostles were Jews, as well as all the prophets; and finally that our whole sacred liturgy is drawn from Jewish books. In consequence how may one express the enormity of the outrage and blasphemy of vilifying the Jewish race?

Even if a Christian erroneously attributes to the Jews of Christ's time some culpability for the crucifixion, he is still forbidden by basic Christian teaching to harbor anti-Semitic ideas. In a magnificent short volume entitled *Christianity and Anti-Semitism*, the Russian author Nicolas Berdyaev wrote as follows:

> When Jews are cursed and persecuted because they crucified Christ, the principle of generic vengeance is accepted . . . but this sort of vengeance is unalterably opposed to Christianity, for it contradicts the Christian idea of individual dignity and responsibility. Besides, Christian morality permits no vengeance of any sort, neither that aimed at the individual nor that which spreads and becomes transmitted to all the descendants. Vindictiveness is sinful, and it is right to repent of it. Descent, race, reprisals—all these notions are foreign to pure Christianity; they have been brought into it from outside and derive from the paganism of antiquity.

Berdyaev continues by stating that "anti-Semitism is fatally sure to develop into anti-Christianity; it must reveal its anti-Christian nature."

Father Hans Kung, in his book *The Church*, states that "any kind of anti-Semitism is radically impossible" for the Christian. He continues:

> The Church, being the new people of God, cannot possibly speak or act in any way against the ancient people of God. It is a sure sign that we are opposed to the one true God, if we are opposed to the Jews. Israel remains a living witness of the reality of the living God. The Father of Christ and of the Church remains the God of Israel.

Alongside this unequivocal repudiation of anti-Semitism Father Kung in the same book does not seek to mitigate what Christians have done to Jews in the "centuries-long history of horrors, of suffering and death, culminating in the murder of millions by the Nazis. . . ." He sums up the record of the Church with these words:

> The Church preached love, while it sowed the seeds of murderous hatred; it proclaimed love, while it prepared the way for atrocities and death. And these acts were perpetrated against the compatriots and brothers of him who taught the Church: "What you did to one of the least of these my brethren, you did to me."

While Father Kung asserts that "a new era in relations between Israel and the Church has begun," he recognizes that protests against anti-Semitism in the past were made by Catholic "individuals or outsiders" whereas:

> Official representatives of the Church, and often its higher signatories, withdrew into cautious, politic and opportunistic silence, or spoke only hesitantly and softly, in words which were diplomatically shrouded in qualifications, and failed to display any prophetic power or spirit of commitment; words, in short, which fell short of the Gospel of Jesus Christ.

In a very moving book, *Anti-Semite and Jew*, published in France in 1946, Jean-Paul Sartre makes this intriguing parallel:

> Richard Wright, the Negro writer, said recently: "There is

no Negro problem in the United States, there is only a white problem." In the same way, we must say that anti-Semitism is not a Jewish problem; it is *our* problem.

The situation of the Jew, as Sartre saw it in 1946 in France, may or may not be better today. Sartre describes the permeation of Western culture by anti-Semitism in these chilling phrases:

> Since the Jew is dependent upon opinion for his profession, his rights and his life, his situation is completely unstable. . . . He carefully watches the progress of anti-Semitism; he tries to foresee crises and gauge trends in the same way that the peasant keeps watch on the weather and predicts storm. He ceaselessly calculates the effects that external events will have on his own position. He may accumulate legal guarantees, riches, honors; he is only the more vulnerable on that account, and he knows it. Thus it seems to him at one and the same time that his efforts are always crowned with success—for he knows the astonishing successes of his race—and that a curse has made them empty, for he will never acquire the security enjoyed by the most humble Christian.

The predicament of a person who can never enjoy a freedom from fear and anxiety attainable by "the most humble Christian" is compared by Sartre to the state of the hero in Kafka's novel *The Trial*. Sartre puts it this way:

> Like the hero of that novel, the Jew is engaged in a long trial. He does not know his judges, scarcely even his lawyers; he does not know what he is charged with, yet he knows that he is considered guilty; judgment is continually put off—for a week, two weeks—he takes advantage of these delays to improve his position in a thousand ways, but every precaution taken at random pushes him a little deeper into guilt. . . .

A magnificent expression of a Christian's moral duty to avoid anti-Semitism is found in the writings of Jacques Maritain, who fought anti-Semitism in every form from the Dreyfus affair to

Nazism. Maritain wrote in an essay, "Answer to One Unnamed," printed in the volume *Ransoming the Time* in 1941, as follows:

> I say that in a time wherein anti-Semitic persecutions have assumed an unheard-of proportion, wherein thousands upon thousands of miserable people have been put outside the law, subjected to brutalities and humiliations beyond description, to slow death, to the "spontaneous" violence of the mob or to the horrors of concentration camps . . . in such a time the only realism which matters . . . is not to speak a word, not to write a word which could serve as any excuse whatever for degrading hatred, and thereby to find oneself someday accused of the blood or despair of creatures of God.

Father Kung sums up the hopefully pervasive and passionate conviction of Christians at this time: "Only one thing is of any use now: a radical metanoia, repentance and rethinking; we must start on a new road, no longer leading away from the Jews, but towards them. . . ."

But if the prose of Christians rejecting anti-Semitism is prolific and sometimes "purple," all of the rhetoric and repentance does not seem to reach the question of the intertwining of anti-Semitism with the future of Zionism and the nation of Israel. Those Christians who, like Maritain, are in the forefront of propounding the hideousness of anti-Semitism seldom take the next and inevitable step of asserting that indifference toward Israel as a nation can also be a subtle but insidious form of anti-Semitism. Father Kung seems to be in this category since, after urging Christians to banish every form of anti-Semitism—especially "after the most terrible catastrophe in the history of the Jewish people"—he does not appear to connect the concern which he urges for the Jewish people with the emergence of the state of Israel. He speaks only of the "unexpectedly hopeful new beginning of the State of Israel." He continues with these puzzling words:

> Now after thousands of years this old and yet surprisingly young people has begun its own life as a state again; this is an

event which ranks as the most important in Jewish history since the destruction of Jerusalem and of the temple and one with religious consequences, both positive and negative, which it as yet is too early to assess.

Unfortunately Father Kung does not explain why the rise of Israel was "unexpectedly" hopeful, nor does he intimate anything about what he apparently sees to be some possible "negative" religious consequences of the establishment of Israel.

It is, of course, harsh and sometimes unwarranted to impute anti-Semitism to Christians who are unenthusiastic about the establishment of Israel. But at least some anti-Jewish feeling is not infrequently present among those who fail to empathize with the mission of the state of Israel. Arnold Toynbee, who wrote many times that Israel should never have been permitted to be born, has as a relatively consistent theme in most of his writings an expression of his lack of sympathy with Judaism as a religion. Since Toynbee saw little value in Jewish self-identity, either in religious terms or as a people, he transferred that antipathy to Zionism and to its creation, Israel.

It may be that an unintended anti-Judaism or anti-Semitism will persist in the feelings of those Christians who continue to insist on defining Judaism only in its relationship to Christianity. These persons are not necessarily less than enthusiastic about the establishment of Israel, but they, along with other Christians who look upon Judaism as something superseded or anachronistic, are prone to ask these questions:

1. If a Christian recognizes the establishment of Israel as an imperative of the religious freedom of Jews, does he thereby give recognition and assent to the belief of some but not all Jews that the land of Israel belongs by divine right to the Jewish people?

2. If the viability and the defense of the nation of Israel should become a very heavy burden on those states which have supported Israel, could a Christian be justly accused of being anti-Judaism if he acquiesced in the downgrading or dismemberment of Israel as a nation?

3. Did Zionism flower into the establishment of Israel in 1948 primarily because of the acute plight of hundreds of thousands of Jewish refugees, or would Zionism have eventually flowered into the same reality because of the basic convictions of Jewish teaching that a significant number of the world's Jews should settle around Jerusalem in order to fulfill the promise and pledge of the God of Abraham?

Those who are indifferent to the state of Israel seldom articulate these questions but would assert if challenged that Judaism is only a religion and that Zionism is a political movement created by Jews but not motivated ultimately by Jewish theology. Zionism is, in other words, assumed to be a purely political and secular development that arose because of historical rather than religious reasons. Only ignorance permits Christians to subscribe to such a definition of Judaism since this narrow, sectarian view of the Jewish faith has long since been abandoned by virtually every group within the Jewish community.

It may be that the persistent presence of anti-Zionism in the minds of those who are militant against anti-Semitism cannot be totally comprehended until one has decided upon some ultimate definition of anti-Semitism. Sigmund Freud in *Moses and Monotheism* was perhaps the first to suggest that "hatred for Judaism is at bottom hatred for Christianity." If Freud is correct, then those who are sympathetic to Judaism but indifferent to Zionism may be expressing their ambivalence with respect to certain Christian values by rejecting or at least not accepting Zionism. Freud's theory reasons that the Christian soul, which resents the burden placed upon it by Christian ideals, transfers this resentment not to its true object, Christianity, but to a substitute, the Jewish people. If this theory is credible, it would appear to follow that any Christian who finds his religious faith difficult and burdensome would be inclined to transform his irritation with it into some form of anti-Semitism. It is plausible to see as a result of this theory how a Christian, having eliminated anti-Semitism from his life as a result of his religious convictions, might seek to transfer his dissatisfaction with his Christian faith into some mode of anti-Zionism.

But the foregoing analysis must be accepted most tentatively if at all. As Father Edward H. Flannery stated in a brilliant essay, "Anti-Zionism and the Christian Psyche," in the *Journal of Ecumenical Studies* in 1969: "Anti-Semitic etiology is complex and derives from every level of human experience." Despite this complexity Father Flannery asserts that "one of the chief repositories of an unconscious anti-Semitism is often cloaked in a commitment to anti-Zionism."

The subtle latent or unconscious anti-Zionism among Christians is undoubtedly promoted by the silence of the churches and the theologians. The 1975 Vatican directives on Catholic-Jewish relations, for example, failed to take note of the Jewish people's historic attachment to the land of Israel. A. Roy Eckardt, in his 1974 study, *Your People, My People*, concedes that, on the question of a distinctively religious affirmation supportive of Israel, "current Christian scholarship and reflection are in a condition of massive uncertainty and debate. . . ." Some Christian theologians express discomfort with the notion that Jewish self-understanding might be advanced as capable of authenticating a geopolitical claim. But Father Flannery, writing in 1971 in the *United Synagogue Review*, asks the crucial question: "Is not the refusal to allow a theological consideration of Israel a residue of the deicidal myth, which included the idea that Israel could never return to its homeland or temple . . . ?"

Father Flannery continues with this question:

> Further, if we must believe with Saint Paul that Judaism still has the covenants and promises (Romans 9:4–5) and these originally involved the land, on what ground must the land be excluded from them in post-Biblical times?

Christian theologians recognize the triad of ideas which are inseparable in Judaism: the people, the Torah, and the land. At the same time theologians are reluctant to advance theological justifications for the state of Israel because if these justifications are accepted a double standard comes into effect which places the state of Israel above other national entities while, on the other hand, if the justifications are rejected the secular foundations of the state of Israel might be challenged.

The inability of so many Christians to extinguish their anti-

Zionist feelings in the same way that they have eliminated their anti-Semitic prejudices derives from the uniqueness of anti-Jewish feeling. There is absolutely no historical analogue to anti-Semitism. The practice of sociologists and behaviorists of subsuming anti-Semitism under the category of prejudice may lead us only to superficial resemblances that conceal the incomparability of anti-Semitism with any other phenomenon.

Reinhold Niebuhr pointed out more than once that the persistence and peculiarity of anti-Semitism come from the fact that Jews differ in two decisive ways—religiously and culturally. Because of this the hatred manifest in anti-Semitism is unique in all of human history in its historical permanence and its geopolitical pervasiveness. All other prejudices remain by contrast transitory and localized.

The unique feature of anti-Semitism is that it has metastasized into the entire universe. The contempt for the Jews which persisted through all of the Christian centuries has infected the United Nations, where the international wrath reserved uniquely for the state of Israel finds no parallel or precedent in time or place.

The awful and awesome omnipresence of anti-Zionism confuses and bewilders the Christian who has recognized that anti-Semitism is sinful. It appears that only a very few Christians have yet recognized that the anti-Semitism of the Christian West has become the anti-Zionism of the Third World and the United Nations.

Alice and A. Roy Eckardt, in their 1970 book entitled *Encounter with Israel: A Challenge to Conscience,* described the poisonous effects of anti-Jewish prejudice in these words: "Apart from anti-Semitism there appears no convincing way to account for the ferocity of today's politicidal and genocidal attitude toward Israel within and beyond the Arab world."

Christian anti-Semitism in the Western world may be declining, but anti-Zionist feeling may possibly be increasing. The Eckardts concluded in 1970: "The churches do not act effectively or courageously to oppose today's politicide campaign against Israel because their own repressed enmity toward the Jewish people is too powerful an inhibiting force."

21

CHRISTIANS AND
ISRAEL'S LIMITED OPTIONS

Even Christians who are very well informed about Judaism in the modern world still seem unprepared to deal with Israel as a nation. Father Hans Kung, for example, in his 1976 volume *On Being a Christian*, notes that "Christians had not expected . . . the re-emergence of the State of Israel." Apparently an incomprehension of the meaning of Israel and an inability to deal with it constitute some of the reasons why the Holy See has never extended diplomatic recognition to Israel.

The Christian tradition of looking upon Judaism exclusively as a religion has inhibited or incapacitated most Christians from participating in whatever world-wide debate exists concerning the internal political policies of Israel. Christians would hesitate, for example, to criticize Israel's policies in the Six Day War as Rabbi Joachim Prinz has. Rabbi Prinz, former president of the American Jewish Congress and vice-president of the World Jewish Congress, wrote in the Jewish magazine *Moment* in December 1976 that their victory in the 1967 Six Day War "made the Israelis cocky and overly self-assured." That victory, he continued, "initiated a

new and morally unrestrained atmosphere in Israel. . . ." Rabbi
Prinz made these remarks in connection with his plea that Israel
recognize Diaspora Jewry and accord to it "the right to express its
views on Israeli affairs." He complained of the "preposterous and
appalling" religious scene in Israel and asserted that "world Jewry
cannot be expected to contribute to Israel's economy while being
denied the right to complain about the non-recognition of its
religious diversity."

If the criticism of the Jews of the Diaspora is not particularly
welcome in Israel, Christians around the world understand that
any critical or dissenting views they might have about Israel would
be even less welcome.

Most Christians would be reluctant to offer the criticism advanced by Rabbi Balfour Brickner in his article "Cradle of a Dove
Zionism" in *Worldview* magazine for August 1976. Rabbi Brickner deplored the views of those Israelis who feel that they have
some divine right to create new settlements in towns designated
by the Israeli government as belonging on a permanent basis to
the Arabs. He asserted that American Jewry "does a disservice to
Israel by remaining silent on this issue at this time."

He also expressed his disagreement with the almost universal Israeli view that the United States should not sell six C-140s to
Egypt. In this connection Rabbi Brickner raised fundamental
questions as to whether the goals of Egypt and Jordan are not
different now than they were in 1948 and 1967. He urged that the
"stereotypical answers of the past no longer suffice."

Many American Christians would like to express their views on
the internal politics of Israel, but they are so afraid of revealing an
unconscious anti-Semitism or being thought to do so that they retreat into silence. Their silence is also in some cases the product
of a deep and passionate desire that Israel succeed regardless of
any mistakes its government might make.

American Christians would express the most resolute determination to do everything necessary to prevent another holocaust.
But they would in all probability deny even the possibility that
the nations surrounding Israel or any other international force
could effectuate another mass slaughter of Jews. Christians would

undoubtedly be horrified if they became convinced that the indifference or apathy of Christians toward the state of Israel could inadvertently bring about the downfall of that country.

But the unavoidable and undeniable realities of the modern world unmistakably give to Christians in the industrialized world the power to make Israel into a relatively prosperous country secure from assault by its neighbors or, on the other hand, a land which is subjected to such harassment by its neighbors and intimidation by the family of nations that its viability will be eroded or even eliminated. This dependence of Israel on Christians and on the Western nations is, of course, really no different from the inferior state in which Jews have for centuries found themselves. Ironically, however, it was the very establishment of the state of Israel as a monumental expression of faith that was intended to deliver the Jewish people from all subservience to Christians and to other nations. It was in Israel that the Jewish people did the one thing possible to break the centuries-old bitter connection between hatred of Jews and Jewish powerlessness.

It is disconcerting to say the least for the Jewish people to discover that, after they have been faithful to the ageless yearning to return to the homeland and loyal to the quintessence of Jewish religious ideals and beliefs, the fulfillment of their biblical destiny to live in peace in Israel depends on the attitudes of people in those predominantly Christian nations who to some extent acquiesced in the holocaust and who did all too little to assist Jews in their exodus from Europe and the Arab nations to Israel.

One of the few major statements to have been made by a Christian group was a declaration in 1973 by theologians convened under the auspices of the National Council of Churches of Christ and the National Conference of Catholic Bishops. This statement, which is reproduced in its entirety at the conclusion of this chapter, was the result of some three years of work and study by the foremost Christian scholars in the area of Christian-Jewish relations.

The almost historic declaration notes that "a major source of friction in contemporary Christian-Jewish relations is Christian hostility and indifference to the State of Israel." The statement goes on to note the difficulty which Christians have in establishing the relationship "between the chosen people and the territory comprising the present State of Israel." The Christian theologians concede bluntly: "There is no Christian consensus on these questions." The declaration does, nonetheless, affirm that "there is reason for Christians to rejoice that the Jewish people are no longer required to live in enforced dispersion among the nations, separated from the land of promise."

The only significant Catholic statement which might be stronger than this joint Catholic-Protestant declaration is the affirmation by Jacques Maritain in his book, *A Christian Looks at the Jewish Question.* He states that the land now occupied by the Israelis is "the only territory to which, when we consider the entire spectacle of human history, it is absolutely and divinely certain that a people have an incontestable right."

He continues with these striking words:

> The people of Israel are a unique people in the world because a land, the land of Canaan, was given to them by the true God, the only God above all, creator of the universe and of the human race, and what God has given once is given forever.

If the convictions set forth in the Catholic-Protestant statement reproduced at the end of this chapter or the affirmations of Maritain were widely subscribed to in the Christian communities of Europe, the options available to Israel would be substantially more numerous and more inviting than they are. Israel would have far less reason to fear that European nations and the United States would compromise their loyalty to it in order to acquire an adequate supply of oil from the Arab nations. Similarly, if a complete comprehension of the mission of Israel were present in the Christian countries of the West, Israel would have far less to fear from the economic boycott against it which now, with the enormous wealth of the oil-producing Arab nations, can bring new disasters to the state.

It is impossible to say whether or not the diminution or extinction of anti-Semitic and anti-Zionist sentiments in the Christian West would mean that the non-Christian nations of the earth would be less hateful toward Judaism and Zionism. Anti-Semitism, as the Catholic-Protestant statement noted above put it, is a "difficult virus to counteract." It would seem logical, however, to reason that a lessening of anti-Jewish feeling on the part of the Christian world would almost inevitably bring about a scaling down of the anti-Zionist passions of the Third World.

The absence of clear positions on Israel on the part of American Christians does not negate the presence of strong feeling among Americans for the security of Israel. In a poll conducted by Louis Harris and analyzed in the New York *Times* magazine on April 6, 1975, it was revealed that by a margin of 66 to 24 per cent Americans favor sending Israel what it needs in the way of military hardware. This finding was most remarkable in view of the decisive 65 to 22 per cent majority who opposed at that time America's giving military aid to other nations. In a parallel finding, a 68 to 20 per cent majority rejected the concept that the United States needs Arab oil and consequently must get along with the Arabs "even if that means supporting Israel less."

This same Harris poll found, nonetheless, that "31 per cent of the non-Jewish public in the United States hold attitudes about Jews which can be described as anti-Semitic."

However comforting that Harris poll might be, it should be viewed only in the context of the deep anger of most Americans in 1974 and 1975 against the quadrupling of oil prices by the OPEC and Arab nations.

No poll has ever been conducted or probably could be conducted as to how American Christians, as Christians, feel about Israel. Because of complex circumstances which are unclear, baffling, humiliating, and frightening, American Christianity does not seem to have even approached the question of evolving a Christian-oriented approach to the place which Israel as a nation should have in the mind and heart of a modern Christian.

One would have hoped that the numerous Christian-Jewish dialogues that have occurred during the past decade would have evolved some consensus as to what Christian churches should say about the attitude and relationship which Christians should have toward Israel. It appears, however, that of all of the national

Catholic hierarchies in the world only the U. S. Catholic Conference has issued a statement urging Catholics to recognize and accept the unique place which the modern nation of Israel has in
the theology and faith of contemporary Jews. In a statement in
1975 commemorating the tenth anniversary of the historic declaration by Vatican II on the Jews, the nation's Roman Catholic
bishops mentioned the state of Israel with respect and acceptance
—something which the Second Vatican Council had failed to do.

In all probability, the finest Catholic statement on the nature
of the state of Israel was issued by a French Episcopal Committee
for Relations with Judaism. Published on April 18, 1973, and
reprinted in its entirety in the *Catholic Mind* for September 1973,
this declaration was received with jubilation by the 600,000 Jews
in France but provoked charges of "blasphemy" against the
Roman Catholic bishops of France by the ambassadors of the
Arab nations in Paris. The press across the Arab world charged
the Catholic bishops with interference in politics in favor of Israel. A spokesman for France's hierarchy denied that the document was intended as a recognition of the state of Israel; the pas-
toral statement, he said, merely took note of the fact of the
existence of Israel as a country.

If one had some hopes from the controversy over the statement
that it would at last articulate a Catholic viewpoint on what the
thirty-year-old nation of Israel should mean to Catholics, then one
is destined for severe disappointment. The statement opens its
section on Israel with this tone of hesitation:

> At present it is more difficult than ever to pronounce a se-
> rene theological judgment on the Jewish people's movement
> of return to their "own" land. Confronted with this move-
> ment, we as Christians cannot forget that God once made to
> the Jewish people the gift of a land wherein this people was
> called to reunite. . . .

After two paragraphs in which veiled references are made to the
Arab challenges to Israel the bishops' statement affirms:

> Universal conscience cannot deny to the Jewish people that
> have suffered so many vicissitudes in the course of history,

the right and means of its own political existence among the nations.

The Episcopal Committee statement phrases what it conceives to be the central question about Israel in these words:

An essential question that must be faced by Christians as well as by Jews is that of knowing whether this reassembling of the dispersed Jewish people, which was effected under the constraint of persecutions and through the play of political forces, will or will not finally prove to be, despite all these dramas, one of the ways of God's justice both for the Jewish people and, at the same time, for all of the peoples of the world.

That timorous sentence is hardly a celebration of the birth of Israel. In fact, it seems to pose questions as to the essential wisdom of establishing Israel and about the long-term viability of this nation. It is neither an accolade nor even an affirmation of the righteousness of the cause of Israel. But, incredible as it seems, this is the most affirmative statement made by any authoritative Catholic ecclesiastical group since the establishment of Israel! The statement never mentions Israel, never names Zionism and, for reasons which it does not explain, claims that it is "more difficult than ever" at this time to come to some theological judgment on the return of the Jewish people to Israel.

The statement is so nebulous that it is difficult to understand the repercussions it caused in the Arab world or the jubilation it produced in the Jewish community in France and elsewhere. These reactions would seem to demonstrate that the enemies and friends of Israel recognize the enormous power Christians would have if they were persuaded that they should extend admiration and respect to Israel as the place where Jews both by the mandate of international law and the blessing of the God of Abraham have a right to dwell in peace.

Christians will come to this conclusion when they recognize that they are forever bound to the Jewish people and that finally the Catholic Church in Vatican II came to a historic turning point in its attitude toward Judaism. The 2,200 Catholic bishops at Vatican II broke with the attitude of the entire two thousand years of Catholicism.

Christians will recognize Israel as Jews recognize Israel when Christians fully understand that it was through the people of the covenant that the faith in one God has been inscribed in the history of humanity. According to biblical revelation, it was God himself who constituted the Jewish people, brought them up and sealed them with an eternal alliance, as is stated in Genesis 17:7. St. Paul describes that alliance as "irrevocable" (Romans 11:29).

A Christian, consequently, errs seriously when he looks upon Judaism as a relic of a venerable but completed past. As the French Episcopal Committee statement put it, the vocation of the people of God's covenant "makes the life and prayer of the Jewish people a benediction for all nations of the earth. As a result, the church, far from envisaging the disappearance of the Jewish community, comes to know itself in the search for a living bond with that community."

For its own sake, therefore—if for no other, better reason—the Christian needs to understand Judaism because thereby he comes to know himself more intimately. It is only the growth in Christian knowledge of what Judaism has been and is in the modern world that will bring about that widespread Christian support of Israel as a nation which appears to be indispensable for the security and survival of that beleaguered country.

Catholic and Protestant Christians have worked together in America on moral problems which bewildered the nation and confounded its ethical leaders. Catholics, Protestants, Jews, and humanists worked together to eliminate that racism which existed in basic American immigration law from 1920 to 1965. Similarly, religious groups in America came together in the early 1960s and can rightfully take a part of the credit for the enactment of the Civil Rights Act in 1964 and the Voting Rights Act in 1965. The virtually united opposition to the war in Vietnam of the churches and synagogues in America might well have been the ultimate reason why the Congress and the country terminated its participation in that disaster.

It would be encouraging indeed if one could write a scenario as to how religious leaders in America could evolve a moral and even theological basis for this nation's abiding support for Israel. But in this instance the churches themselves must eradicate from the depths of their souls all of the centuries of anti-Semitism and the decades of anti-Zionism which have caused them to be mute, barren, and paralyzed when they are asked to speak out on the state and the future of the three million Jews in Israel. In Israel's Proclamation of Independence adopted on May 14, 1948, the founding fathers appealed "to the Jewish people all over the world to rally to the side of the Jews of the land of Israel . . . and to stand by them in the great struggle for the realization of the age old dream: the redemption of Israel." That appeal should stir the heart of the Christian as well as that of the Jew since the Christian shares the same Bible, the same faith, and the same heritage as the Jew.

Christian shame and Christian guilt might help to rectify all of the sins and scandals which Christians have inflicted on Jews over the past twenty centuries. But the essence of the Christian religion is precisely that love of God and love of man which is the very centerpiece of Judaism. And it is only that love which can make Christians and Jews aware of their common patrimony and bring about that Jewish-Christian friendship which should be the natural and expected relationship between those who are ultimately the children of the God of Abraham, Isaac, and Jacob.

Father Edward Flannery put it all very well in his beautiful essay, "Anti-Zionism and the Christian Psyche":

We conclude where we began: it is the Christian above all who is expected to react most strongly to attacks on Jews. It is especially the Christian who is expected to rejoice at the upturn of the fortune of Jews that Zionism, or any other agency, has brought about in our own time. The distance we appear to stand from this horror and rejoicing is the measurement of that estrangement which separates us on the deepest level of our souls.

APPENDIX TO CHAPTER 21

A Statement to Our Fellow Christians*

1. The Church of Christ is rooted in the life of the People Israel. We Christians look upon Abraham as our spiritual ancestor and father of our faith. For us the relationship is not one of physical descent but the inheritance of a faith like that of Abraham whose life was based on his trust in the promises made to him by God (Gen. 15:1–6). The ministry of Jesus and the life of the early Christian community were thoroughly rooted in the Judaism of their day, particularly in the teachings of the Pharisees. The Christian Church is still sustained by the living faith of the patriarchs and prophets, kings and priests, scribes and rabbis, and the people whom God chose for his own. Christ is the link (Gal. 3:26–29) enabling the Gentiles to be numbered among Abraham's "offspring" and therefore fellow heirs with the Jews accord-

* This statement was released in the summer of 1973 by a group of Christian theologians who worked for four years on the subject "Israel: the People, the Land, the State." The group was convened and assisted by the Commission on Faith and Order of the National Council of Churches of Christ in collaboration with the Secretariat for Catholic-Jewish Relations of the National Conference of Catholic Bishops. The group studied and discussed papers by Jewish and Moslem scholars, as well as by Christians. The secretary of the Theological Working Party has been from the beginning Sister Ann Patrick Ware. The chairman for the first three years was Professor Littell; he was succeeded in October 1972 by Professor Pawlikowski. Study papers on various aspects of the group's work are available.

ing to God's promise. It is a tragedy of history that Jesus, our bond of unity with the Jews, has all too often become a symbol and source of division and bitterness because of human weakness and pride.

2. Christians can also enrich themselves by a careful study of postbiblical Judaism to the present day. Such enrichment is especially imperative in light of the far-reaching value crisis that now affects the entire Western world. If religion is to play its rightful role in the value reconstruction that is now beginning, its approach will have to be ecumenical. And in the West this means, first of all, the recognition that two religious traditions, not a single Judaeo-Christian tradition, have shaped our culture; and secondly, the genuine and open sharing of insights and differences between Jews and Christians, each realizing that one's understanding of the spiritual nature of the human person remains incomplete without the other.

3. The singular grace of Jesus Christ does not abrogate the covenantal relationship of God with Israel (Rom. 11:1–2). In Christ the Church shares in Israel's election without superseding it. By baptism and faith the Christian, as the Roman liturgy says, passes over to the sonship of Abraham and shares in the dignity of Israel. The survival of the Jewish people, despite the barbaric persecutions and the cruel circumstances under which they were forced to live, is a sign of God's continuing fidelity to the people dear to him. For our spiritual legacy and for all that the Jews have done for the whole human race we Christians are grateful to God and to the people whom God has chosen as a special instrument of his kindness.

4. The new ecumenical atmosphere in theological research and the tragic reality of the Holocaust together with the present Middle East conflict urge us to reconsider the relationship of Christians to Jews. We Christians have readily acknowledged that God made a covenant with the Jews in the past, promising his paternal care for his chosen people in return for their fidelity. Unfortunately many Christians have assumed that the validity of Judaism

ended with the beginning of Christianity, the rejection of Jesus as Messiah marking the dissolution of the covenant. This assumption conflicts sharply with Paul's declaration that God did not annul his promise to the chosen people since God never takes back his gifts or revokes his call (Rom. 11:28–29). The Apostle dismissed as altogether untenable the notion that God had rejected his people. There is thus strong Scriptural support for the position that God's covenant love for the Jewish people remains firm. The continuity of contemporary Judaism with ancient Israel demonstrates the abiding validity of Jewish worship and life as authentic forms of service to the true God.

5. The fierce persecution of Jews by Christians through the centuries should be seen as a fratricidal strife as well as a vast human tragedy. In many instances Christian preachers and writers disseminated slanderous stories about the Jews. From the apostolic age the Church accepted uncritically the condemnation of the Pharisees as hypocrites even though the Synoptic Gospels picture Jesus as generally agreeing with what many Pharisees in fact stood for. Whole generations of Christians looked with contempt upon this people who were condemned to remain wanderers on the earth on the charge, in fact false, of having killed Christ. Anti-Jewish polemics became a perennial feature of Christendom and reflected gross ignorance of Jewish history and religion. This sin has infected the non-Christian world as well.

6. A major source of friction in contemporary Christian-Jewish relations is Christian hostility and indifference to the State of Israel. In dialogue among Christians on the Middle East question there exists a startling variety of opinions, some of which exacerbate already existing Christian-Jewish misunderstandings. We urge the churches therefore to give their prayerful attention to such central questions as the legitimacy of the Jewish state, the rights of the Palestinians, and the problem of the refugees—Jewish as well as Arab. Only a conscience seeking to be well-informed and free of prejudice can help to bring about peace with justice in the Middle East.

7. The validity of the State of Israel rests on moral and juridical grounds. It was established in response to a resolution of the U. N. General Assembly, after termination of the British Mandate. However, involved in the potentially explosive political conflict in the Middle East is a theological question that demands careful scrutiny. What is the relationship between "the people" and "the land"? What is the relation between the chosen people and the territory comprising the present State of Israel? There is no Christian consensus on these questions. Genesis explicitly affirms a connection between the people and the land (Gen. 15:18), and even within the New Testament certain passages imply such a connection. Therefore, Christians who see Israel as something more than a political state are not wrongly theologizing politics by understanding the existence of the Jewish state in theological terms. They are merely recognizing that modern Israel is the homeland of a people whose political identity is sustained by the faith that God has blessed them with a covenant. There is reason for Christians to rejoice that the Jewish people are no longer required to live in enforced dispersion among the nations, separated from the land of promise.

8. We have traditionally viewed the Jews as a people having a universal dimension. God wanted them to set up a special society dedicated to the fulfillment of the messianic aspirations for righteousness and freedom. Even when dispersed they became a summons to the human conscience to safeguard and protect the rights of all people. Here in the United States the Jewish contribution to the advancement of human rights remains outstanding. Now the question arises: Is the Jewish people so universalistic as to exclude the possibility of their having a state of their own? It does seem to many observers that the localizing of Jewish activities gives a greater opportunity to fulfill their universal vocation than would an unfocused global presence.

9. As a political state, Israel is open to all the temptations of power. The charge is sometimes made that Israel is belligerently expansionistic as a result of its military triumphs in the Six-Day

War. Visitors to Israel, however, can easily discover that the over-riding concern of the majority of Israelis is peace, not more terri-tory. Israel's anxiety about national defense reflects the age-old human yearning for security, the anxiety of a people whose history has been a saga of frightful persecution, climaxed by the Holo-caust of six million men, women and children. Against such a tor-mented background, is it surprising that the Jewish people should want to defend themselves? It would be quite unrealistic and unjust to expect Israel to become a sort of heavenly society of which more is expected than of other nations. This does not mean that Christians must endorse every policy decision by the Israeli government. Most Jews, both within Israel and without, do not do so. Rather, Christians must refrain from the type of criticism that would use the failure of Israel to live up to the highest moral standards as an excuse to deny its right to exist. Such a view would be a double standard, one not applied to any other nation on earth.

10. As Christians we urge all nations in the world (our own na-tion, Israel, and the Arab states included) to recognize that there is no way to secure lasting peace based on the balance of military power and the use of fear as a deterrent. Rather, the only road leading to peace is trust in and understanding of neighbors and partners. We urge the Church to attend to its role as agent of rec-onciliation.

11. At present antisemitism is unfashionable and seems to have gone underground in the United States, though some recent stud-ies show it is on the rise. But even an underground antisemitism surfaces from time to time in various forms and disguises. New Left literature has excoriated the Jews not as Jews but as Zionists. Some Christian publications in the United States and Canada have even resorted to more subtle forms of antisemitism, exploit-ing the claim that Israel is "judaizing" Jerusalem and its environs and driving Arabs from their homes in the Holy City. An-tisemitism, however, is a difficult virus to counteract. It has a per-vasiveness that infects our whole civilization and manifests itself

in education, housing, job opportunities and social life. Fortunately some Christian churches are working hard to excise from their liturgy and education any antisemitic references.

12. Those who refuse to learn from history must relive the errors and evils of the past. In times of civil disorders, agitators have arisen and will continue to appear in our society attempting to make the Jews the scapegoats for the evils of an era. If problems like inflation and unemployment continue to escalate, if a depression should set in, we can be fairly sure that the radical Right and/or the radical Left will make Jews out to be the culprits.

13. The pressure of our violent times urges us as Christians to live up to our calling as ministers of reconciliation, ready and willing to stifle rumors about the Jews and to build up an atmosphere of brotherly understanding in Christian-Jewish relations. We strongly commend Jewish-Christian dialogue as a favored instrument by which we may explore the richness of Judaism and the Jewish roots of our Christian faith.

14. The pain of the past has taught us that antisemitism is a Pandora's box from which spring not only atrocities against Jews but also contempt for Christ. Whatever the antisemite inflicts on the Jews he inflicts on Christ who is "bone of their bone and flesh of their flesh." In the words of St. Paul, "They are Israelites and to them belong the sonship, the glory, the covenants, the giving of the law, the worship and the promises; to them belong the patriarchs, and of their race according to the flesh is the Christ" (Rom. 9:4–5).

Signers of the statement, who were also members of the study group (with church and institutional affiliations given for identification):

Dr. Markus Barth
University of Basel
Basel, Switzerland
(Reformed Church, formerly United Presbyterian)

Dr. Roland de Corneille, National Director
League for Human Rights
Toronto, Canada
(Anglican)

Dr. A. Roy Eckardt
Lehigh University
Bethlehem, Pennsylvania
(United Methodist)

The Rev. Edward H. Flannery
Secretariat for Catholic-Jewish Relations
Washington, D.C.
(Roman Catholic)

Dr. Robert T. Handy
Union Theological Seminary
New York City
(American Baptist)

Dr. Walter J. Harrelson, Dean
Vanderbilt Divinity School
Nashville, Tennessee
(American Baptist/Disciples of Christ)

The Rev. William H. Harter
Margaretville-New Kingston Parish
Margaretville, New York
(United Presbyterian)

Dr. Franklin H. Littell
Temple University
Philadelphia, Pennsylvania
(United Methodist)

Sister Rose Thering, O.P.
Institute of Judaeo-Christian Studies
Seton Hall University
South Orange, New Jersey
(Roman Catholic)

Dr. John T. Townsend
Philadelphia Divinity School
Philadelphia, Pennsylvania
(Episcopal)

Msgr. John M. Oesterreicher, Director
Institute of Judaeo-Christian Studies
Seton Hall University
South Orange, New Jersey
(Roman Catholic)

Dr. Bernhard E. Olson
National Director of Interreligious Affairs
National Conference of Christians and Jews
New York City
(United Methodist)

The Rev. John T. Pawlikowski, O.S.M.
Catholic Theological Union
Chicago, Illinois
(Roman Catholic)

Rt. Rev. Leo Rudloff, O.S.B., Abbot
Benedictine Priory
Weston, Vermont
(Roman Catholic)

Dr. J. Coert Rylaarsdam
Marquette University
Milwaukee, Wisconsin
(Reformed Church in America)

The Rev. John B. Sheerin, C.S.P.
The New Catholic World
New York City
(Roman Catholic)

The Rev. Theodore Stylianopoulos
Holy Cross Greek Orthodox Seminary
Brookline, Massachusetts
(Greek Orthodox)

Dr. Hans Eberhard von Waldow
Pittsburgh Theological Seminary
Pittsburgh, Pennsylvania
(Lutheran Church in America)